Steve Carlton
and the 1972 Phillies

Steve Carlton and the 1972 Phillies

BRUCE MORGAN

McFarland & Company, Inc., Publishers
Jefferson, North Carolina, and London

All photographs are from the National Baseball Hall of Fame Library, Cooperstown, New York.

LIBRARY OF CONGRESS CATALOGUING-IN-PUBLICATION DATA

Morgan, Bruce.
    Steve Carlton and the 1972 Phillies / Bruce Morgan.
      p.   cm.
    Includes bibliographical references and index.

    ISBN 978-0-7864-6836-2
    softcover : acid free paper ∞

    1. Carlton, Steve, 1944–   2. Baseball players — United States — Biography.   3. Philadelphia Phillies (Baseball team) — History — 20th century. I. Title.
GV865.C317M67 2012
796.357092 — dc23
[B]   2012010689

BRITISH LIBRARY CATALOGUING DATA ARE AVAILABLE

© 2012 Bruce Morgan. All rights reserved

No part of this book may be reproduced or transmitted in any form or by any means, electronic or mechanical, including photocopying or recording, or by any information storage and retrieval system, without permission in writing from the publisher.

On the cover: Philadelphia pitcher Steve Carlton, 1972

Front cover design by Rob Cheney (http://robcheney.com/)

Manufactured in the United States of America

McFarland & Company, Inc., Publishers
  Box 611, Jefferson, North Carolina 28640
    www.mcfarlandpub.com

Table of Contents

Preface	1
1 ♦ Jaw Dropping Numbers	3
2 ♦ The Trade	13
3 ♦ Hope Springs Eternal	20
4 ♦ Lefty's Striking Start	26
5 ♦ Catching the Fever	44
6 ♦ Tailspin Takes Over	51
7 ♦ Carlton Slumps	62
8 ♦ Desperate Times	71
9 ♦ Protecting His Teammates	86
10 ♦ Finishing What He Started	103
11 ♦ The New Manager	112
12 ♦ The Streak Marches On	134
13 ♦ Lum Breaks It Up	154
14 ♦ A Wise Encounter	169
Conclusion: How Does '72 Rank?	177
Chapter Notes	183
Bibliography	197
Index	215

Preface

Mike Schmidt and Steve Carlton were as much apart of my childhood as Big Wheel and fighting with my brothers. Michael Jack and Lefty were my heroes. Even now, years later, I can still see Schmidt hitting four home runs at Chicago's Wrigley Field and Carlton baffling the Pittsburgh Pirates' Dave Parker with all those sliders in the dirt. And when Schmidt jumped into Tug McGraw's arms following the final out of the 1980 World Series, I jumped for joy while watching the game in the basement of my parents' home.

So after working for more than 20 years as a sports reporter and preparing for the challenge of writing a book, it was logical for me to go in the direction of my childhood heroes. To the best of my knowledge, nothing had been written about Carlton's unbelievable 1972 season, when he won 27 games for a last-place Phillies team that notched just 59 total victories. I was both surprised and grateful for a potential idea. That idea led me to doing roughly 50 interviews over a two-year period, and it was a heck of a journey.

At times, it was fascinating as Carlton's friends, former teammates and opponents gave me a glimpse of one of baseball's all-time legends. At other times, it was exhausting as I tried to pore over countless newspaper and magazine articles at the Lancaster Public Library and the Chester County Library System, attempting to get my hands on anything I could that would enhance my project. Among the many things I learned was that Lefty was as serious and intense as they come on game days and between the white lines. But off the field, with his teammates at least, he was friendly, fun and supportive to the utmost degree. I actually had the opportunity to meet Carlton at an autograph show. Given his feelings toward the media — and that I was writing this book — I figured it best to remain anonymous. But he was nothing short of engaging and amicable as he greeted fans, which isn't necessarily the case with all Hall of Famers.

Throughout the course of this project, I met a lot of wonderful people

I never dreamed of interviewing. Understandably, with Carlton being a very private individual, my impression was that many tried to stay as close to the vest as they could (so as not to hurt their friendship with Carlton) while being as gracious with me as they could. Nobody was more helpful than Phillies announcer Chris Wheeler. He was there from the start of Carlton's career in Phillies pinstripes and has an incredible memory even 40 years after Lefty's magical 1972 season. In my discussions with Wheeler, he found that balance between speaking positively and yet being forthcoming. I approached him not once, not twice, but four times, and on each occasion, he patiently answered all my questions. That included one Saturday night that he gave me his full attention, even with a close college football game involving his beloved Penn State Nittany Lions playing Temple on the TV monitors overhead in the pressbox at Citizens Bank Park. Long-time Philadelphia Phillies public relations man Larry Shenk, Reading Phillies Director of PR/Media Relations Tommy Viola and Jason Guarente of the Lancaster Barnstormers also receive my heartfelt thanks for helping me get in touch with people and patiently dealing with my emails and phone calls. While I owe a debt of gratitude to Wheeler, Shenk and Viola, I also could not have done this book without the help of my friend, Ed Gruver, at Lancaster Newspapers. Having already written a number of fine books, including one on Sandy Koufax, Ed took me under his wing while answering my many questions, lending me direction, and offering me tips and suggestions.

As Ed would attest — and as I have learned — you cannot write a book without the support of family and friends, and I certainly had that. Many thanks go out to my friends in the newsroom, including (alphabetically) Andy Fasnacht, Stan Hall, Todd Ruth, Steve Seeber, Karen Shuey, Jessica Spangler, Chris Torres, and Preston Whitcraft. Thanks to Sandy Vigilante for making a road trip to acquire a permission signature for me, to my bosses at the *Lititz Record Express* and Lancaster Newspapers for keeping me on the payroll in tough economic times, and to countless others for their words of encouragement. Then there are my families, both on the Morgan and Tindall sides, to whom I express my deepest appreciation. My parents, Fred and Shirley Morgan, took me to my first Phillies game in 1974, when Carlton pitched against the Cincinnati Reds, and they have always been there for me. My brothers Steve, Brian, and Patrick, with whom I had sibling scraps in my childhood, are now my close allies. My father and all my brothers are proud Marines, and my mother is a Marine's wife. They are all true heroes. Most of all, thanks to my wife, Leslie, and children, Brooks and Kendall, for their undying love and support. They have put up with me through this whole process, and I cannot thank them enough.

♦ 1 ♦

JAW DROPPING NUMBERS

One by one, a steady flow of autograph seekers stopped by Bull's Barbecue stand to see Greg Luzinski at Citizens Bank Park in Philadelphia. Young and old alike, they snapped pictures, talked baseball, and held out hats, photos, baseballs, and T-shirts for a signature. This is the same Luzinski who slugged 223 home runs with the Phillies from 1972 to 1980 and remains a link to the Phillies' first World Series championship in 1980, so he remains a fan favorite in Philadelphia. On this particular day, the "Fightin' Phils" were playing the St. Louis Cardinals and their star slugger Albert Pujols. So it seemed fitting that "the Bull" would be talking about another great link to the Phillies' past that started his career with the Cardinals before being traded to the Phillies in 1972. His name just happened to be Steve Carlton.

Widely known by his nickname "Lefty," Carlton cemented his status as a Hall of Fame pitcher in Phillies pinstripes, winning 241 games and racking up 3,031 strikeouts during his 15-year career in the City of Brotherly Love. It was the 1972 season, however, that started it all for Carlton. One year after winning 20 games for the St. Louis Cardinals, Lefty was shipped to the Phillies for Rick Wise and reeled off a 27–10 record. Not only did he win the first of his four Cy Young awards that year, as a unanimous selection no less, but Carlton also became the first pitcher to win the award with a last-place team. Lefty, who also pitched for the San Francisco Giants, Chicago White Sox, Cleveland Indians, and Minnesota Twins at the end of his 24-year major league career, shattered the major league record formerly held by Frank "Noodles" Hahn for most wins pitching for a last-place team. Hahn was 22–19 for the Cincinnati Reds in 1901. Overall, Lefty was one of three National League pitchers to earn 20 or more wins during the 1972 season, with Chicago Cubs ace Fergie Jenkins (20–12, 3.20 ERA) and New York Mets stud Tom Seaver (21–12, 2.92 ERA) also reaching that mark. No one, however, topped the monumental numbers that Carlton compiled. While Lefty racked up 120 points in bringing home the Cy Young Award, Pittsburgh Pirates ace Steve Blass was a distant second with 35 points.

"He cost me the Cy Young," laughed Blass, who finished 19–8, with a 2.49 ERA in 33 games for the National League East champion Bucs in 1972. "That was before they had agents. I never even knew I finished second until a year later. I wish I had known in negotiating. I had a good year. But 27 wins out of [Philadelphia's] 59 [total wins]? That was the ratio. That's not even close. Everybody was second. He was dominant. When you do that with a ballclub that wins 59 games, it's not too good. It's 10 good. That is beyond good ... just remarkably consistent with a ballclub that probably didn't get him a lot of runs. If you lose 59, you've got various aspects that weren't working. But Carlton was."[1]

Without much working for the Phillies in 1972, the team finished an eye-popping 37½ games behind the National League Eastern Division champion Pittsburgh Pirates, compiling an abysmal 59–97 record, their sixth poorest in franchise history. Remarkably, Carlton earned 45.8 percent of Philadelphia's wins. That shattered the former record, which was held by the New York Americans' Jack Chesbro, whose 41 victories in 1904 represented 44.6 percent of his team's wins. To put into perspective just how miraculous and rare Carlton's season was in 1972, compare it to other benchmark achievements since 1900. According to an article by Allen Lewis in a January 1973, issue of *Baseball Digest*, pitchers winning 25 or more games for a second-division team has occurred fewer times than a batter hitting .400 or driving in at least 165 runs or piling up 400 or more total bases or winning the Triple Crown. It's been done fewer times than a pitcher registering ten or more shutouts or posting an ERA of 1.75 or lower, or racking up 30 or more wins. Those feats are considered some of the most difficult to achieve in baseball, and yet according to Lewis, each one has been accomplished 13 or more times in modern times. Winning 25 or more games for a second-division team had only been done 11 times.

Even pitchers reeling off at least 15 wins in a row had been done with more frequency. Incidentally, Lefty put together a 15-game winning streak of his own in 1972. From June 7 to August 17, a span that also included three no-decisions, Carlton won 15 consecutive decisions. That shattered the Phillies' team record of 12 set by Charlie Ferguson in 1886 and it easily obliterated the modern-day record of nine previously held by Grover Alexander (1911–17; 30), Ken Heintzelman (1947–52), and Robin Roberts (1948–61). That streak highlighted Carlton's 27–10 season, a performance that no other pitcher had previously achieved for a team that did not finish in fifth place or better.

Yet, as Cincinnati Reds Hall of Fame broadcaster Marty Brennaman has noted, few talk about that incredible 1972 season that Carlton put together for the Phillies. Nowadays, even as the pendulum has swung back to the pitchers following the steroid era, it is hardly ever mentioned. Even in the "Year of the Pitcher in 2010," when major league pitchers threw six no-hitters, Lefty's feat seemed to go unremembered. "He was pitching for a bad team that was probably susceptible to kicking the ball around, so that makes his feat of 27 wins even more impressive," Brennaman said. "The offense was probably not real good. I mean ... God, we may never see that again. We haven't since '72. And we may never see it again. It's one of those amazing seasons and people never talk about it, and every time I look back and see something that reminds me of what he did that year, for this team, it's stupid."[2]

Remarkably, Lefty won those 27 games in a shortened season, as the first-ever players' strike in major league baseball history cost Philadelphia six games from its schedule. In the process, Carlton tied the National League record for most wins by a left-hander, joining Los Angeles Dodgers legend Sandy Koufax, who won 27 in 1966. Lefty and Koufax trail only Hall of Famers Hal Newhouser and Lefty Grove for most wins in a season by a left-hander. Newhouser, a seven-time All-Star with the Detroit Tigers, won 29 games in 1944, while Grove, a six-time All-Star with the Philadelphia Athletics and Boston Red Sox, earned 28 wins in 1930 and 31 in 1931 while capturing American League Most Valuable Player honors.

Bill Conlin of the *Philadelphia Daily News* may have nailed it perfectly when he wrote during the 1972 season that Carlton pitching for the Phillies was like a Pulitzer Prize winner writing for *Jack and Jill*. Carlton's performance "was incredible, not only because of the shortened season, but because we weren't a real good team," Philadelphia's fiery shortstop Larry Bowa remarked. "We were a very young team, but it seemed like because of our youthfulness and everything, the nights that he pitched, we elevated our game. And I think in the back of our minds, we also knew that if we could get two runs or three runs, we'd have a good chance of winning. Whereas in that particular year, anybody else who pitched, we weren't that good on the mound. In fact, there are not too many phases of the game we were good at. When Steve pitched, it seemed like we took it to another level. I don't know if it was out of fear or what."[3]

Supported by an offense that ranked 11th out of 12 NL teams with just 503 total runs, Lefty won nine games in which the Phillies scored two or fewer runs. He won four more with just three runs of support, and he fashioned an 8–4 record in one-run games. Often times, the Phillies only needed to score one run for him, as he reeled off a string of 30 straight scoreless innings in 1972. Amazingly, during a second stretch that season, Lefty also put together a streak of 26 consecutive innings without allowing a run. While winning 27 of his 37 decisions, Lefty fashioned a winning percentage of .730, making the Phillies the best team in baseball when he pitched. When anyone else took the hill for the team, they went 32–87 for a winning percentage of .269, which was the worst in baseball.

"Impossible," Hall of Fame catcher Johnny Bench said of Lefty's '72 season. "That's how dominant he was and I owned him. I mean, it didn't matter. I said this about Seaver and I said this about so many of the great pitchers — they threw it, you hit it, it was OK because they were going to get you out the next time and everything else. But it boggled my mind that a team could lose that many games and have one guy, every time he went out there so dominant that they won. He was a great competitor, never had a pitch count, and he was probably the first guy to start doing training. He trained his body, he trained his arm, worked on health and the stamina and that part of it, and it was just brilliant. And it was just his presence that demanded the people behind him play."[4]

When the dust settled, Carlton led the league with 41 starts, 346 and 1/3 innings pitched, 27 wins, 30 complete games, 310 strikeouts, a sizzling 1.98 earned run average. His eight shutouts were second only to Los Angeles ace Don Sutton, who finished with nine. Lefty became only the ninth pitcher since 1900 to strike out more than 300 batters in a season, and he was only the second National League hurler to top that figure. "The thing about it is, it's not just great. It's incomprehensible how that could have been possible," ESPN.com senior baseball writer Jayson Stark said. "People talk this year (in 2010) about Felix Hernandez and how when you pitch for a team that bad, it's almost impossible to win [Hernandez was 13–12 with a 2.27 ERA for the 101-loss Seattle Mariners]. How did that guy ever win 27 games with that team, when all their other pitchers combined won 32 games? It defies what you think is possible in sports. That would be the way I'd describe it."[5] To a man, teammates and opponents alike talked about how competitive Lefty was when he climbed to the top of the mound. "Steve was a great competitor and knew what he wanted to do when he went on the mound," Luzinski said. "He was himself, he was totally in control of what he was trying to throw, the type of pitch he was trying to throw to each hitter, and he knew the hitters. Like I said, he was just a deep competitor."[6]

Lefty had three or four pitches that he threw for strikes, including a curveball and a fastball in the low to mid–90s. But his "bread and butter" was a devastating slider, which in 1972 helped him break Jim Bunning's single-season record for most strikeouts by a Phillies pitcher. Carlton's 310 Ks that year were 42 more than Bunning's 268 in 1967. Carlton's strikeout total also ranked second on the all-time list by a left-hander, behind only Sandy Koufax, who whiffed 365 in 1965. "He had one of the toughest sliders to pick up and he had good control of it," Luzinski said. "His fastball was no slouch obviously, but his slider was devastating when he had his good one. It would go down obviously into right-handers and down and away to left-handers. But it was no joy, I'm sure, facing him left-handed. He had great stuff. He stayed inside himself and he had the rhythm and mechanics to hit spots and throw that great slider in tight situations when you expect fastballs. You can find guys that throw hard and they get knocked all over the park. But he had a great mix of pitches and he had a lot of faith to throw that slider for strikes, and within the strike zone to [eventually] fall out of the strike zone in all counts."[7]

Overall, Carlton either tied or shattered nine Phillies team records in 1972. He broke the mark for most wins by a lefty, formerly held by Eppa Rixey, who finished with 22 victories in 1916. It was also the most victories in the National League since Phillies legend Robin Roberts went 28–7 in 1952. Rixey also had to say good-bye to his former record of 25 complete games in a single season. Plus, Lefty's .730 winning percentage blew away Curt Simmons' .680 in 1950, and he also erased Simmons' previous club record of six shutouts in a season. But Carlton was not done there, as he eclipsed Chris Short's mark for innings in a season (297 in 1965) and starts in a season (40 in 1965). Finally, besides breaking Jim Bunning's team mark for strikeouts in a season and Charlie Ferguson's record for most consecutive wins, Lefty also tied Short's record for strikeouts by a left-hander in a nine-inning game when he struck out 14 in a start against the San Francisco Giants on April 25, 1972.

Meanwhile, as Lefty was mowing down the competition, Dan Baker was just getting settled in as the Phillies' first-year public address announcer at recently opened Veterans Stadium. Just one year removed from announcing auto dare devil shows in New England, Baker had a front-row seat for one of the best single-season pitching performances in baseball history. The fact that Baker's first year in Philadelphia coincided with Lefty's debut season for the Phillies remains a great honor for the legendary announcer. "I would've been grateful to announce players that weren't well known," said Baker, who became the major leagues' longest-tenured PA announcer following Bob Sheppard's retirement from the Yankees in 2009. "The fact that I had a chance to announce a future Hall of Famer was a great honor. I was not unaware that we were seeing something special. That doesn't make me an expert. All of us who were at the games knew that something special was unfolding."[8] Baker, in fact, was there for all five of Lefty's 20-win seasons in Phillies pinstripes. After Carlton won 23 games in 1982, Philadelphia went 28 years before finding another 20-game winner, as Roy Halladay finally broke the drought by going 21–10 for the team in 2010. Prior to Halladay, John Denny came closest with 19 in 1983, followed by Shane Rawley with 17 in 1987, Curt Schilling with 17 in 1997, and Jon Lieber with 17 in 2005.

Bob Boone was behind the plate for many of Carlton's starts. He made his major league debut with the Phillies on September 10, 1972, with Lefty well on his way to that magical 27-win season. But with the roster featuring John Bateman, a 31-year-old catcher acquired for Tim McCarver from the Montreal Expos in June of that year, Boone wasn't in the lineup when Carlton pitched that year. "I came up in '72 and I caught every game except when Carlton pitched," Boone remarked. "I was not allowed to catch when he pitched, probably because he was having a great year."[9] But Boone did catch Carlton in spring training in '72. And he was behind the plate with Carlton until the Phillies signed McCarver as a free agent on July 1, 1975. So he had a good vantage point for what made Lefty a Hall of Famer. "He was the best pitcher in baseball [in '72]," Boone said. "I had just started catching. That was my first year catching all the time. The difference between him and everybody else I'd ever caught was huge. It was like driving a Volkswagen to getting into a top Mercedes. I would assume it's something that jockeys experience when they ride great horses."[10]

According to a *SPORT* magazine article by Joe Flower in 1983, Carlton tried a slider in 1969 when he posted a 17–11 record with the Redbirds. Carlton struggled with it in 1970 en route to a 10–19 finish, but he won 20 games for the first time in '71 and then rolled to his 27-win season in '72 with a rejuvenated slider. By throwing eight shutouts in 1972, Lefty became the Phillies' first pitcher with that many whitewashings in a season since Grover Cleveland Alexander registered 16 in 1916.

Tim "Rock" Raines, a seven-time All-Star during a 23-year big league career, said that Carlton was one of the few lefties who gave both left-handed and right-handed hitters a problem at the plate. "His slider was so hard and bit so hard, and he had such a good fastball, I mean it looked like a fastball coming in here and it was hard to differentiate the fastball or a slider," Raines said. "When you can't do that, you've got trouble as a hitter. I was always a fastball hitter, regardless of how hard guys threw. If it was straight, I could hit it. I didn't hit too many breaking balls, but I didn't really swing at too many. Carlton had such a good breaking ball, and it was hard to see it. His slider was so good, it looked like a fastball until you swung at it and saw it [drop off the table]."[11]

Tommy Herr, a switch-hitting second baseman who faced Carlton while playing for the St. Louis Cardinals from 1979 to 1988, noted that Carlton threw his fastball and slider out of the same arm slot and at the same arm speed. "Many hitters were fooled by the pitch because it gave the appearance leaving his hand that it was a fastball," said Herr, a National League All-Star in 1985 when he had 110 RBIs. "It was never a day at the beach when you faced him. I was the kind of hitter that he wasn't afraid of challenging because I wasn't a home run threat. I always felt like if I could lay off the slider and get into fastball counts, I'd get fastballs to hit, which is how things turned out. But I was a guy that against him, the way I tried to approach it was I tried to stay up the middle or the other way, and when I saw something in, I would take it because usually he threw his slider in and his fastball away. But what made him so great was he got hitters to chase the slider, and no matter how much you tried to discipline yourself not to, his deception was so good that he still got hitters to chase it."[12]

To go along with that slider, Carlton also brought intense focus and concentration to the mound with every start. Lefty was known to pitch with cotton in his ears to block out noise from the fans, enabling him to focus solely on the catcher's glove. In '72, Lefty defeated every team in the National League, while the New York Mets were the only team that beat him more than once.

"He was so focused compared to any athlete I've ever known," Phillies long-time public relations director Larry Shenk said.[13] If Carlton was anything, he was totally unflappable on the mound. In 1972, he not only struck out 310 batters, but walked just 87. Raines remembers an incident in the early 1980s which tells the story of Lefty's concentration. Raines had not yet faced Carlton in his career when the Phillies came to Palm Beach, Florida, for a spring training game. But as "Rock" came to learn, Lefty's intensity was the same whether he was pitching a spring training game, any of 741 regular season games in his 24-year big league career, or the decisive Game Six of the 1980 World Series.

"I had never seen him before up close and personal," Raines said. "I was with the Expos and they came to Palm Beach, and I remember him being so focused on what he was doing — and this was spring training. The catcher threw the ball back to him and he didn't see it and it hit him right in the jaw. And he didn't move. He looked down, got the ball, got back on the mound and said, 'Let's go.' I mean, I had never seen that before."[14] If that throw had hit any other pitcher in the face, it might have forced him from the game — or at least brought out the trainer. But the big left-hander remained focused on the task at hand, even in a meaningless exhibition game. "It wasn't like a

Phillies Hall of Famer Steve Carlton follows through while recording one of his 4,136 career strikeouts. In 1972, Lefty became only the ninth pitcher since 1900 to strike out more than 300 batters in one season.

little lob," Raines said. "I mean, the catcher threw it back to him, and 'pop,' and ... he picked up the ball and said, 'Let's go.' When I saw that, I was like, 'Wow. I don't want to hit today. Do I have to hit off him?' This dude, you can't even faze this guy. The catcher can't faze him, nobody can faze him, let alone a hitter. He just took a ball off his jaw and he didn't even budge. I just remember him being a competitor too, man. He got on the mound and he was going to battle you for nine innings if he could. I guess as he got older, it was a little different, but I'm sure before, he was out there for the duration. He's one of the few lefties that gave right-handers a problem. I don't think too many lefties felt comfortable against him either. But right-handers didn't feel too comfortable. And when you have a pitcher that, regardless of what side of the plate you hit on and you have trouble, that's dirty. That is real dirty."[15]

It wasn't only on the mound, however, that Lefty had tremendous focus and mental discipline. Carlton also had 346 hits in his major league career, so he helped his own cause in many starts. And Jerry Martin, a Phillies teammate with Lefty from 1974 to 1978, saw a similar incident with Carlton on the base paths. "He was so focused, and I saw one time he was running down to first base and the throw got away and the ball hit him in the head, and he acted like it didn't

Steve Carlton's final stop on a brilliant 24-year major league career came when he signed as a free agent with the Minnesota Twins on January 29, 1988. Prior to that, after being released by Phillies in June 1986, Lefty also pitched with the San Francisco Giants, Chicago White Sox and Cleveland Indians.

even touch him," Martin recalled. "He acted like it didn't even bother him. The ball hit him in the head, I know it."[16]

Herr said that Carlton's level of concentration was simply different than that of other guys. "From being an opponent of his all those years when I was with the Cardinals playing against the Phillies, there was always something special about him," said Herr, who also was a teammate of Carlton's in Minnesota in 1988. "Nothing could fluster him out there. He was really unflappable during the game. His approach was basically to always pitch to his strengths. He never really deviated from one game to the next when you faced him. He felt confident in what he wanted to do and he just stuck with that. He'd throw sliders down and in to right-handers and try to get you to chase, and fastballs away. Basically, that's how he came after you."[17]

After years of bringing his A-game to the ballpark start after start, it was obviously difficult for Carlton to finally call it quits. The Phillies released the legend on June 24, 1986, but it took Lefty less than two weeks to find a new employer, as he signed with the San Francisco Giants in early July. Unfortunately, Carlton lasted only two months in the Bay City, but he was quickly picked up by the White Sox and finished the 1986 season on Chicago's South Side. From there, Lefty signed as a free agent with the Cleveland Indians in April of 1987, but went only 5–9 with the Tribe in 23 games before being traded to the Twins in July. He then re-signed with the Twins in the off-season, but was released in April of 1988, and that closed the door on his Hall of Fame career. When the dust finally settled, however, Lefty had accumulated 329 career wins, which still ranks 11th all-time among pitchers.

"I always thought he was a perfect example that when it's time to say [good-bye], he's saying [hello]," *Philadelphia Inquirer* columnist Bill Lyon said. "It was a less than heroic ending. He was just hanging on there, shopping around. He certainly still deserved to be in the Hall of Fame and whatnot, but it's incredibly difficult for most of these guys to let go. It's the hardest thing they do because in every sport, you're brought up to say, 'You never, ever give up. Never, ever surrender.' And then there comes a time where those same people are saying, 'OK, it's time now. Last call.' And then they overstay. I don't know that that ever works out. The second act is never as good as the first."[18] The first act, of course, included an incredible career in Phillies' pinstripes, and in 1972, Carlton gave the Phillies all they had hoped for and more when they got him from the Cards for Rick Wise.

◆ 2 ◆

THE TRADE

On February 25, 1972, Rick Wise was at his apartment in Clearwater Beach, Florida, during spring training when he heard a knock on the door. Little did he know that his life was going to change dramatically. On the other side of the door was Eddie Ferenz. The Phillies' traveling secretary had come to deliver Wise the news that he had just been traded to the St. Louis Cardinals for Steve Carlton. Since the time that Wise had been signed by Philadelphia in 1963 as an amateur free agent, the Phillies were the only team he knew. Similarly Carlton had spent all nine years of his professional life with the Redbirds.

And if Carlton was experiencing any of the same emotions that Wise was, there was certainly a bit of disappointment. Just a few months earlier, Wise had finished off the 1971 season with his best numbers since joining the Phillies as a regular in 1966. Besides achieving a personal high in wins with his 17–14 record, and a 2.88 ERA, Wise also posted personal bests with 37 starts, 17 complete games, 272 innings pitched, 155 strikeouts, and four shutouts. One of those shutouts just happened to be a no-hit gem on June 23 in a 4–0 victory over the

A youthful-looking Steve Carlton is shown here in his early years with the St. Louis Cardinals. Lefty went to the World Series with the Redbirds in 1967 and 1968 before being traded to the Phillies for Rick Wise in February of 1972.

Cincinnati Reds. Wise also hit two home runs in that game, then hit two more in a game against the San Francisco Giants on August 28, and finished the season with six round-trippers. Although Carlton was not the ace of the St. Louis staff, he was part of a fierce 1–2 punch at the top of the Cardinals' rotation with eventual Hall of Famer Bob Gibson. Lefty won 20 games for the first time in 1971, going 20–9 in 36 starts with 18 complete games, 273 innings pitched, 172 strikeouts and a 3.56 ERA. At that time, Carlton also held the modern major league record for strikeouts in one game with 19 K's in a losing cause against the New York Mets on September 15, 1969.

"I was the ace of the staff," Wise said, "and I worked seven years with that club to get to that position. I had gone to spring training and was ready to help the Phillies do the best they can the next year. Overall, we had a terrible year in '71. We lost 95 games, I believe. But I had worked hard to finally become the ace of the staff with my All-Star year there, with my six home runs, my no-hitter, my 32 consecutive batters retired during the course of a game in September in a 12-inning game against the Cubs. So I had established myself as the ace and sure, it was disappointing. I had just bought a home and was prepared to be with the Phillies for a long time I thought."[1]

Needless to say, the trade came as a shock to both Wise and Carlton. "I don't know if it was a shocker for the baseball world. It was a shock to me and it was a shock, I guess, to Steve," Wise said. "Although I've told this many, many times—it wasn't about Steve and me. It was about negotiating with our respective teams trying to get what we considered were fair contracts for the types of year we had. And we got to loggerheads with our respective clubs, and as a result, that set up the motion, the seeds for our being traded. Simple as that."[2]

According to reports, Carlton earned $45,000 in '71, while Wise was taking home $32,500. Both were said to be asking for $65,000, and Wise remarked at the time that the Phils had offered only a $10,000 raise. In 1970, Carlton was a holdout in the spring and missed the majority of spring training. He "was having difficulties with [Cardinals owner] Auggie Busch also," Wise said. "He was having problems there. That's the thing—it really was about contracts with the respective clubs. Me with the Phillies and him with the Cardinals. And I remember a quote, if I'm not mistaken, Auggie Busch was saying something [like] 'I won't give him one red cent more.' And I had worked very hard to get the position I was in with the Phillies and I was only making $25,000 after seven years in the big leagues. And John Quinn was offering me a $10,000 raise after winning 17 games and representing the club on the All-Star team, 17 complete games, 272 innings, and all of this sort of stuff. But you have to understand, that was typical of those days. As far as contract negotiations, there weren't agents or anything. John Quinn had low-balled me for years when I was putting up double-digit wins, holding out for $2,500, this kind of stuff, which in this day and age is just ludicrous. People can't comprehend that nowadays. But back then, that was reality and you fought and scratched for every nickel and dime you could get, and I thought I was finally in the position that I could deal from strength because I was only making $25,000 after seven years in the big leagues."[3]

Chris Wheeler, who joined the Phillies in 1971 as assistant director of publicity and public relations, added: "That's the way it was in the old days. They just made a trade like that. They didn't have to worry about agents, they didn't have to worry about his contract, and they didn't have to worry about free agency. They just made deals. So they made that deal."[4] This was the first of two times in his career that Wise would be traded for an eventual Hall of Fame pitcher. On March 30, 1978, the right-hander was shipped, along with Ted Cox, Bo Diaz, and Mike Paxton, from the Boston Red Sox to the Cleveland Indians in exchange for Dennis Eckersley and Fred Kendall. Fortunately for Wise, the Cardinals' complex was close enough to Clearwater that he didn't have to find another apartment. "St. Pete was only 20 miles away, so I was able to maintain the apartment and commute to St. Petersburg to spring training with the Cardinals," Wise said. "That was just luck."[5]

According to Rich Westcott's book, *The Fightin' Phils — Oddities, Insights, and Untold Stories*, Cardinals general manager Bing Devine suggested to Quinn that they trade Wise for Carlton. At that point, Quinn called farm director Paul Owens to ask him for his thoughts, and Owens reportedly said, "Run as fast as you can to the nearest phone." That is also very similar to how Larry Shenk remembers the trade playing out as well. "Paul Owens and John Quinn went to dinner at the restaurant that the Quinns always went to dinner, The Garden Seat in Clearwater, Florida," Shenk said. "[According to] what Paul Owens told me, Quinn said he got a call from the Cardinals earlier that day that Gussie Busch was pissed off at Steve Carlton and he wanted to trade him, and would he trade him for Rick Wise? And Paul Owens said, 'What are you waiting for?'"[6]

Wheeler added, "If you were a baseball person like Paul Owens was, he would have looked at that and said, 'Wow, he's got more talent than Rick Wise.' Just pure ability, pure arm, just as a talent and potential down the road, he's got a chance to be better. And I think basically it was because there was a little salary problem. Bing Devine didn't want to pay Lefty, John Quinn didn't want to pay Wise, and they made the deal. I don't know that [Owens] did that, but I wouldn't doubt that Paul Owens would've said, 'Yeah, go get him.'"[7]

As a reflection of how the times have changed, Shenk said that there were only three or four reporters that needed to be informed about the big trade. That was only a fraction of the throng of media that covers the Phillies in the 2000s. "In those days, I don't think there was a press conference or not because we didn't have facilities at Jack Russell Stadium and there wasn't much of a media," Shenk said. "There were probably four writers there, no TVs at that time of spring training. Maybe we did it at the hotel, I don't recall."[8]

Wise went on to win 32 games in two seasons with the Redbirds in 1972, and '73, while Carlton was on the winning end 27 times alone in 1972 and pitched at the top of the Phils' rotation for more than a decade. Wise, though, might have taken objection to the comments made after the trade by Marvin Miller, the chief counsel to the Major League Baseball Players Association. Miller told reporters that the trade was punitive to Lefty and that it embodied an inequitable situation. The trade was also very unpopular in Philadelphia when it was first made.

And Carlton and Wise were not the only ones surprised by the news. At one time, everyone in the organization — from the players and the coaches and the manager to the front office personnel — stayed at the team hotel. In 1972, the players did not live there anymore, but the front office still did. That, of course, was before the days of cell phones. So while it might have been Eddie Ferenz who went to find Wise at his apartment, Shenk set out to try to locate Wheeler after getting word from Quinn early in the morning that the trade was completed. "To find somebody in those days, you called the hotel or sent somebody out to find them," Shenk said.[9]

Wheeler, as it turns out, was at the coffee shop having breakfast at the Jack Tar Hotel, which is now the Scientologist Headquarters. It was controversial "because Rick Wise was the only thing we had in 1971," Shenk said. "We were in Clearwater in spring training, Chris Wheeler was my assistant at the time, and I got a call from Mr. Quinn saying that they made the trade, and I couldn't believe it myself. So I had to find 'Wheels.' I went down to the coffee shop and said, 'Wheels, we've got a trade that we've got to announce. We've got to go to the ballpark.' He asked, 'Who did we get?' I said, 'Steve Carlton.' [He said], 'Steve Carlton? For what?' [I told him], 'Rick Wise.' [He said], 'Steve Carlton for Rick Wise? I can't believe it.'"[10]

Reflecting, Wheeler said, "When we got [Carlton] from St. Louis, I was thinking we got a heck of a pitcher. But Rick Wise had an unbelievable '71, so it wasn't a popular trade because Rick Wise had pitched a no-hitter, he had six home runs that year — the day he pitched the no-hitter, he had two home runs — so Rick Wise was big in town. Anyway, it's like a lot of things, maybe you don't know the player on the other team all that well. When that trade was made, I remember it was my first year in '71, and Larry and I are sitting in the Jack Tar Hotel. That was our headquarters in Clearwater. And he said, 'What do you think of this? We just traded Rick Wise for Steve Carlton.' And I said, 'I think it's going to be really unpopular. But we got a great pitcher,' because [Carlton] had struck out 19 in that game where [Ron] Swoboda hit the two home runs off him, so you knew he was an unbelievable talent. So now he comes over in ('72) and he pitches pretty well. But we had such a bad team. Wasn't he 5–6 at one point and then won 15 in a row? So he was just average and then he just took off, and we won only 59 games that year, and he won 27 and he was just dominating. We had a bad team and yet when he would pitch, it was almost like they thought, 'We're going to win tonight.' And I can't tell you how, but they would win. It was almost like he willed it through that personality of his. He was that good."[11]

The Cardinals' players, meanwhile, had to be wondering what direction they were going in after they traded both Carlton and Jerry Reuss less than two months apart from each other. Reuss went to the Houston Astros on April 15 in a deal for Lance Clemons and Scipio Spinks. During the 1971 season, Lefty and Reuss combined to win 34 games for the Redbirds. "It was not long after [dealing Carlton] that we also traded Jerry Reuss in that same spring and that's two pretty huge left-handed starters to rid yourself of," Cardinals star Joe Torre said. "I think there was a little disgruntlement (by Reuss). There may have been some unhappiness and Jerry also was outspoken. However, Jerry was more from the St. Louis area, so it was a little bigger blow for him, I think, than for Lefty."[12]

It was certainly a blow for Torre and the Cardinals' players to see Lefty move on to another city. Besides the friendship that Torre had with Carlton, he knew that the Cardinals were giving up a very talented pitcher. "We knew we got a good pitcher [in Wise]. We knew we were giving up a real good pitcher [in Carlton]," Torre said. "But I was one of the player reps, so we knew that we were going to have hell to pay when you go back and tell Gussie Busch that you're going out on strike, and he's been probably better to his players than any owner had been up to that point. We were all rooming by ourselves and if he could have put four in a room, he would have probably at the time ... Gussie Busch wasn't going to be told what to do, and if I'm not mistaken, Rick Wise was making as much as Steve Carlton wanted to make. But it was just a principal thing with Gussie Busch that he was the owner of the club and nobody was going to dictate policy to him, and he traded him."[13]

Wise and Carlton were considered by baseball experts to be mirror images of one another. Lefty had just turned 27 years old in December of 1971, while

Wise would celebrate his 27th birthday just nine months later. Carlton owned 77 big-league wins at that point in his career and Wise had authored 75 wins. At 6-foot-5 and 210 pounds, Carlton had a size advantage on Wise (6-foot-2, 195), and his fastball was known as one of the best in baseball. But as Phillies beat writer Bruce Keidan wrote in the *Philadelphia Inquirer* in February of 1972, Wise had the edge in off-speed pitches with a "wicked curve ball and slider," noting that he wasn't afraid to throw either pitch on a 3–2 count. Although Lefty would become known for his devastating slider over his Hall of Fame career, he wasn't at that point yet. He began to throw the slider in 1969 and went on to win 17 games with the Cardinals while dropping his ERA from 2.99 the previous season to 2.17. But he struggled in 1970 en route to a 10–19 finish with a 3.73 ERA, and by throwing the slider incorrectly, Lefty hurt his arm. From there, Carlton eliminated the slider from his arsenal in 1971. But then after tweaking the way he threw it, he picked it up again in 1972.

Keidan also wrote that Wise had a big edge in control and that his ratio of walks to innings pitched was "consistently among the National League's lowest." In 1971, Wise had a ratio of just 2.3 walks per nine innings, giving up 70 free passes in 270 frames. Carlton, meanwhile, was building a reputation as a strikeout pitcher, with 805 strikeouts in five full seasons with the Redbirds, including 210 during the 1969 season, with 19 alone in a 4–3 nine-inning loss to the New York Mets. But he struggled with wildness in the early part of his career. Prior to coming to the Phillies, his ratio of walks to innings pitched was 3.2 per nine. In 1971 Lefty pitched only one more inning than Wise, but allowed 26 more walks. "When he was a young left-hander, he was kinda wild, but he'd have big strikeout games," Chris Wheeler said. "He was kinda like Nolan Ryan when they were young. Big strikeout games, walk games. That's one of the reasons maybe why the Cardinals traded him too, because they weren't sure that he was ever going to be great like that, or they would have never traded him."[14]

In 1972, however, Lefty's command began to improve. In fact, while pitching 73 more innings than he did in 1971, he yielded 11 fewer bases on balls. His ratio of walks to innings pitched was lowered to 2.3 per nine. Credit Paul Owens for seeing the potential that Lefty had. ESPN, the Comcast Network, and the Major League Baseball Network were not yet in existence, so games were not shown on television every night like they are in today's market. But Owens had done his homework. "I don't know if Owens ever saw him pitch," Larry Shenk said. "But you had to see him pitch for the Cardinals because they were in the post-season and we weren't ... You had scouts everywhere watching, but not to the degree we have today either."[15]

2 ♦ The Trade

Years later, many people consider it one of the best trades — if not THE best — in Phillies history. The Phils' franchise is well known for the blunder in which it traded Larry Bowa and eventual Hall of Fame second baseman Ryne Sandberg to the Cubs on January 27, 1982, for Ivan DeJesus. Philadelphia also has the dubious distinction of trading an eventual Hall of Fame pitcher in Fergie Jenkins, sending him, John Herrnstein and Adolfo Phillips to the Cubs on April 21, 1966, for Bob Buhl and Larry Jackson. But trading for a pitcher who eventually earned legendary status was one of Philadelphia's brighter moments. "I don't know that there's been many better than that," Shenk said. He "wound up being a Hall of Famer and there was nobody else in that category."[16]

Scott Palmer, the Phillies' director of public affairs, believes that the Carlton-for-Wise deal might not only be one of the Phillies' top-ever trades, but also one of the most one-sided trades in baseball history. "I can't think of one [better in Phillies' history]," said Palmer, who arrived in Philadelphia in 1981 as a television reporter with Channel 6. "I remember bad trades ... I'm from Chicago and I remember the Cubs trading Lou Brock for Ernie Broglio. That was one that St. Louis made out on pretty good. That's the only other trade that I can think of in baseball that comes close."[17]

♦ 3 ♦

HOPE SPRINGS ETERNAL

Carlton's mission in 1972 was to help the Phillies end a streak of four straight losing seasons. Prior to Lefty arriving in Philadelphia, the team was tied for seventh in the 10-team NL standings in 1968 with a 76–86 record, 21 games behind the Cardinals. In 1969, they were fifth in the NL East with a 63–99 record, followed by another fifth-place finish in 1970 at 73–88, and then a last-place finish in 1971 with a 67–95 record, leaving them 30 games behind the first-place Pittsburgh Pirates. In fact, since their NL pennant-winning season in 1950, the Phillies had finished as high as third place only two times. Paul Owens, the Phillies' director of farm personnel, acknowledged that he was feeling the heat regarding his job going into the 1972 season. General manager John Quinn and field manager Frank Lucchesi were no doubt feeling the pressure for their ball club to show solid improvement as well.

As a player, Lucchesi hit for little power during a career spent mostly in the mid- and lower minors. At the age of 23, he began managing in the low minors, and then joined the Phillies' farm system in 1956 and went on to win two championships at the Triple-A level. In 1969, Lucchesi led the Eugene Emeralds to the regular-season division title, which punched his ticket to Philadelphia as the Phillies' manager starting in 1970. Lucchesi succeeded George Myatt, who finished the 1969 season with a 19–35 record. Before Myatt was Bob Skinner, who finished the 1968 season and started the '69 campaign with little success. Overall, the Phillies had endured back-to-back losing seasons when Lucchesi took over in the dugout. It did not get any better under the new skipper, as the team lost 43 games more than they won in Lucchesi's first two seasons at the helm. Through 1970–71, Lucchesi led the club to a combined record of 140–183.

The brass, however, surely liked the fact that nine infielders and outfielders were already in camp when pitchers and catchers reported on Saturday,

February 26, hoping the extra work would lead to a fast start once the season got underway. Hope always springs eternal with the start of each new season, and it was no different in the Phillies' camp. Philadelphia believed that it had a lot of young, talented players and that it was assembling the pieces to a contending team. In fact, Owens indicated that he thought the Phillies could make a run at second place in the National League East standings.

"When you go to spring training, everybody feels like, 'Hey, we're going to win the World Series.' I mean, that's the way it is," said third baseman Don Money.[1] The 26-year-old was later traded at the end of the 1972 season to the Milwaukee Brewers, where he was one of the older players on the squad. "The same thing happened in Milwaukee when I went over there," he said. "We had a very young club again. We didn't say, 'Ha, we're all young, we're going to end up in fourth place out of four teams or whatever it is.' It's just, 'Hey, if he has a good year' (you never know). A guy has never won more than eight and you expect him to win 20? A guy never hit .300 and you expect him to hit .300 or more? Well, of course. You're always looking for the good things."[2]

Still, even if people were asking too much of the '72 Phillies, no one would have seen a 97-loss season in their future. "I don't think anybody expected us not to win 60 games," Money said. "You just fall in ruts. That's the way it is. Even in today's game, you'll see some good clubs [and say], 'Man, they lost 16 out of 18 or something like that, how do they do that?' And it happens. You get a great pitched game and you get no runs. The next night, you go out and score nine runs and you get beat 10–9 or something. That's just the way it was. Nobody foresaw that leaving spring training. We just felt that we were going to go out there and do the best we can and see what happens. But it didn't work out too good that year."[3]

What a lot of people foresaw in the spring of 1972 was reason for optimism with a projected outfield consisting of 21-year-old Greg Luzinski, 24-year-old Willie Montanez, and 21-year-old rookie Mike Anderson, all young and promising. Luzinski had just 36 big league games under his belt going into the '72 season, but he had murdered minor league pitching with three straight seasons of 31 homers or more, including 120 RBIs with Double-A Reading in 1970 and 114 RBIs with Triple-A Eugene in 1971, so he was expected to put up power numbers in the middle of Philadelphia's lineup. Montanez was coming off a runner-up finish in the 1971 Rookie of the Year voting following, a season in which he led the Phils with 78 runs, 99 RBIs, and 13 game-winning RBIs. He arrived in Clearwater in '71 with only an outside chance of claiming a spot with the big league club, but after coming north with the Phillies, he proved the decision-makers right by clubbing two home runs in a game three different times and finishing with 30 long balls, which set a Philadelphia rookie home run record. That shattered the mark previously held by Richie Allen, with 29 in 1964. Finally, many believed that Anderson was a can't-miss .300 hitter based on what he had accomplished in the minor leagues from 1969 to 1971. The Phillies' No. 1 choice in the 1969 free agent draft, Anderson hit .364 for Pulaski at the Rookie level, and then batted .313 with 22 homers and 67 RBIs in 1970 at Single-A Peninsula in the Carolina League in 1970. Anderson bypassed the Double-A level in 1971, but hardly missed a beat at Triple-A Eugene, where he was named the Pacific Coast League (PCL) Rookie of the Year and an All-Star outfielder while hitting .334 with 36 round-trippers, 100 RBIs and 111 runs.

In the infield, the Phillies brought back 26-year-old shortstop Larry Bowa, who was establishing himself as a sure-handed fielder with good speed at the top of the lineup in his first two seasons, and Money, whom the Phillies were hoping would revert back to his form in 1970. That season, Money batted .295 with 66 RBIs before suffering through a sub-par year in 1971, hitting .223 with just seven home runs and 38 RBIs. The Phillies also had a platoon at second base with 28-year-olds Denny Doyle and Terry Harmon, who were both solid with the glove. Doyle hit just .231 during a 1971 season in which he battled injuries, but he was expected to improve if he could stay healthy.

"I think the reason they were optimistic is we were starting to build young people," Bowa said. "And they knew we were going to probably get beat up a little bit, but they also knew that we were gaining experience. We went through some tough times from '72 to '74 and you could see everything coming together. But it was a good core group of guys that you really don't see that much anymore because of free agencies, and they make trades now. They trade their minor league players for bigger players."[4] Bowa said that fans knew who they were in Philadelphia before they even reached the big-league level because they followed them through the farm system. The Bowas and the Doyles and the Luzinskis had good seasons playing for Spartanburg (SC) in Single-A, Reading (PA) in Double-A, and Eugene (OR) in Triple-A. In fact, Bowa, Doyle, Barry Lersch, and Bill Champion — teammates on the Phillies' 1972 team — were all part of the 1966 Spartanburg club that won 25 successive games. "We won every year we played in the minor leagues, so it was just a matter of us feeling comfortable and it takes a little while when you get to the big leagues," Bowa remarked. "You're sort of in awe when you first get there and then you say, 'Hey, I can play up here.' And then eventually through experience and hard work, you start putting together a pretty good ball club."[5]

Solid veterans like 33-year-old first baseman Deron Johnson, whom the Phillies purchased from the Atlanta Braves in December of 1968, and 30-year-old catcher Tim McCarver, traded to the Phillies by the Cardinals in October of 1969, complemented the younger players. Plus, the Phillies believed that they had more depth in their system than in recent years. Byron Browne, Roger Freed, Oscar Gamble, Joe Lis, and Ron Stone — all of whom were no older than 26 — were waiting in the wings if anyone stumbled in the outfield, and 26-year-old Tommy Hutton, whom Philadelphia picked up in the off-season from the Dodgers for Larry Hisle, was versatile enough not only to back up Johnson at first base, but also to play in the outfield.

Additionally, John Vukovich could help out in the infield. Bruce Keidan wrote that although Vukovich "played third base like Brooks Robinson, he swung the bat more like 'Our Miss Brooks'" and that "he got to first base as often as the guys in the dandruff-shampoo commercials." He showed his glovework while filling in for Money at third in '71, and he started hitting the ball better in the spring of '72 while seeking to win playing time at second base. "Everybody is optimistic in the spring," Hutton said. "I was just happy to have been traded from the Dodgers to the Phillies and start over fresh with a new organization and a chance to be in the major leagues full time. The bottom line is we had a lot of mediocre talent."[6]

Owens believed that the Phillies' 1972 squad had a lot in common with the 1949 team. That 1949 squad also had a good mix of talented young players and veterans, including Richie Ashburn, Andy Seminick, Granny Hamner, and Del Ennis. It, of course, went on to win the National League pennant in 1950, and Owens believed that the 1972 Phillies were on the cusp of doing similar things. One thing that Owens believed the 1972 team lacked in comparison to its predecessors was a Hamner-type leader. But "the Pope" thought that Bowa, who like Hamner played shortstop, could develop into that leader for the Phillies. "It just takes time for that to happen," Larry Shenk said.[7]

The pitching staff, however, was a question mark. Carlton, of course, was the ace at the top of the rotation. But with Wise's trade to the Cardinals, the Phillies had an overabundance of left-handers vying for spots in the rotation. Including Woodie Fryman and Chris Short, the Phillies potentially had three lefties in their four-man rotation. Short, the last Philadelphia pitcher to reach the 20-win plateau when he posted a 20–10 mark in 1966, arrived in spring training looking like a different pitcher. Besides adding a screwball to his repertoire and growing his hair longer, Short also shaved about ten pounds from his frame. It was believed that Short's trimmer frame would help him with the back problems that he had been experiencing in recent seasons.

Philadelphia was supposed to be reaping the benefits of having young arms such as right-handers Pat Bayless and Lowell Palmer, in addition to lefty Bill Laxton, in the starting rotation by 1972. Carlton was quoted in the spring as saying that the Phillies were just one starting pitcher away from being a contender, but unfortunately, it was not going to be one of those three. Bayless won the organization's Bob Carpenter Award for attitude, hustle, desire and advancement potential in 1971, but he never panned out. Neither did Palmer nor Laxton for various reasons. Plus, signs were pointing toward the Phillies not receiving much help from veteran right-handed reliever Bill Wilson, who suffered a herniated disc in the spring and opened the season on the 30-day disabled list.

Throughout spring training, the Phillies explored opportunities to trade for a right-handed starting pitcher. Lefty Joe Hoerner, who was Philadelphia's top relief specialist coming off a '71 season in which he had four wins, nine saves, and a 1.97 ERA, was a valuable chip for the Phils. Philadelphia was willing to trade Hoerner because he was 35 years old. But the fact that he was still pitching at that age (Hoerner was the oldest player on the Phillies' roster in '72) was a testament to how much he loved the game. He had passed out while throwing an overhand fastball with Davenport (Iowa) in the Three-I League in 1958, the result of a heart problem, which affected his circulation. According to an article written by Bruce Keidan, doctors suggested that Hoerner quit the game for the sake of his health, but instead, he changed his motion to a sidearm delivery, which alleviated the pressure on his heart and made his fastball appear to "explode from his left hip." But Hoerner acknowledged to reporters that if he were to be traded, he would pitch anywhere. There were, in fact, reports that he had been traded to the Houston Astros in the off-season. Two young hard-throwing right-handers — Tom Griffin of the Astros and Gary Gentry of the New York Mets — were high on Quinn's list to obtain, but nothing panned out and Hoerner remained a member of the Phillies when they reported to Clearwater.

Philadelphia was also apparently close to a deal that would have sent Short and Ron Stone, an infielder/outfielder, to the Chicago Cubs in late March for right-handed starting pitcher Milt Pappas. The Cubs already had Steve Hamilton as a left-handed short relief man, so they weren't really considering Hoerner. Chicago, however, thought that Short could be a valuable addition as a left-handed long or middle relief man or as a spot starter. That trade opportunity went up in smoke, though, as Short had a disastrous three-inning spring training outing against the Cincinnati Reds on March 29, surrendering six runs on three homers, two walks, six hits, and a balk.

Bill Champion also made a strong case that spring to go into the starting rotation, delivering back-to-back impressive performances on the hill, including five innings of solid work in a 1–0 shutout of the Kansas City Royals for the Phils' first Grapefruit League shutout. Other candidates for the rotation were righty Dick Selma, whom the Phillies were hoping was back to good health after making just 17 appearances out of the bullpen in '71 because of an arm injury, and righty Barry Lersch. Selma, who was just 0–2 in 24 and 2/3 innings in 1971, was delayed getting to spring training due to complications from minor surgery that February. Once he did arrive from home in Fresno, California, however, Selma described his arm woes as a thing of the past and indicated that he was ready to throw at least 200 innings in '72. Although Lersch was a dismal 5–14 in 1971, the Phillies thought that he was better than his record showed. With Lersch still only 27 years old, Bruce Keidan wrote that no one knew if his future would be as a starting pitcher or as a long or middle relief man.

Ultimately, the Phillies broke camp and headed north, with the brass opting for Selma, Woodie Fryman, and Champion to follow Lefty in the rotation. Lersch would be the fifth starter when the Phillies needed him. After failing to acquire a right-handed starter through a trade, the Phillies were hoping that Champion, who pitched well in spring training, could be that person. Fryman, a tobacco farmer from Kentucky whom Philadelphia acquired from the Pirates with Money in 1967, made it hard for the Phillies to keep him out of the rotation because of how he pitched when healthy. He had recorded back-to-back 12-win seasons with the team in 1968 and '69, and a 10-win season in 1971 when Philadelphia used him as a starter and reliever. Fryman was rebounding from an elbow injury, but the Phillies were looking to get a boost from him as the third starter. Young Ken Reynolds was a dark horse starting the year in the bullpen, while rookie Wayne Twitchell and Bucky Brandon also earned relief roles.

Bruce Keidan, the Phillies beat writer for the *Philadelphia Inquirer*, predicted in the paper's season preview section that the team would avoid another last-place finish that season. But by the same token, he did not exactly list them as the contender that Owens thought they could be. The Pirates, Cubs, and Cardinals were still the teams to beat in the National League East. But Keidan's prognostication for the Phils — if their pitching improved, if Money, Short, and Selma all made decent comebacks, and if they received solid play from rookies Luzinski and Anderson — was a fourth-place finish, just ahead of the Mets and Expos.

♦ 4 ♦

LEFTY'S STRIKING START

The start of Carlton's career in Phillies' pinstripes was delayed due to the first-ever players' strike in major league history. The agreement between the club owners and the Major League Baseball Players Association (MLBPA) over the players' pension plan expired on March 31. A couple of weeks earlier, the Phillies followed in the footsteps of the Cincinnati Reds, Chicago White Sox, New York Mets, and Pittsburgh Pirates in giving a 28–0 unanimous vote authorizing a strike by the Players Association. The session was limited only to players with a minimum of 60 days on a major league roster. But as Bruce Keidan explained in an *Inquirer* article, those votes at that point were a formality and not an official declaration to walk the picket line.

The deadline arrived, however, and player representatives from the 24 major league teams decided by a 47–0 margin, with just one abstention, to go out on strike. Several Phillies players were quoted in the papers as saying that they were surprised the impasse went as far as it did. Some suggested that if another vote had been taken by the rank-and-file, that the outcome would have been a lot closer, or that it could have gone the other way. But on Friday, April 1, the Phillies' players and coaches and manager Frank Lucchesi met behind closed doors at the Fort Harrison Hotel in Clearwater and unanimously backed a strike that the 47 player representatives were voting on in Dallas, Texas, that same day. The Phils' spring training home, Jack Russell Stadium, was opened to a couple of hundred fans in the stands awaiting a contest between the Phillies and the Pittsburgh Pirates. But neither team stepped between the white lines, and it was no April Fool's Day joke. There would be no game and no TV debut for the 1972 Phillies on this day, and at 12:01 A.M. on Saturday, the first-ever players' strike in Major League Baseball history, a work stoppage that many players thought would never happen, was officially underway.

Asked if it was a scary time for the players, who were going out on strike for the first time ever, Chris Wheeler said, "It probably wasn't because you figured everything was going to be all right. You didn't know what it was like to experience them later on and how scary they really became. I think it was kinda like a novelty to them at that time. The union was so new. I don't remember it being scary, to be honest. Plus, they didn't make the money they make now. They didn't want to be unemployed, but it wasn't like they were losing those enormous checks that they started losing later on when there were lockouts and strikes. Then it became a lot of pressure on them because of the money they were losing. At that time, I don't know, it was almost like they got a little vacation early in the year, and you weren't playing in the freezing cold weather. Someone could contradict me on this, but I don't remember it having the urgency, or as you say, the trepidation that they maybe had later on where you're really worried."[1]

The exhibition slates for all 24 big league clubs were wiped out on both Saturday and Sunday, April 2 and 3. Although some players decided to stay in the warmth of the Florida and Arizona climates while trying to find their own place to work out and stay in baseball shape, the majority of them headed home. The clubs directed players to clean out their personal items from the clubhouse, cut off payment for the players' hotel rooms and meals, and sent them off with a non-redeemable one-way airplane ticket to their destination of choice.

A last-ditch proposal by the MLBPA was shot down by the owners, and with the season scheduled to start on Wednesday, April 5, with the traditional opener in Cincinnati, baseball stadiums across the country were empty. Owners called on the players to take the field while still trying to hammer away at a deal, but it didn't happen. The idea of bringing in an impartial arbitrator was also squashed, as John J. Gaherin, the owners' negotiator, announced that the owners had zero interest in putting the issue into the hands of a third party. As the work stoppage dragged on, even President Richard Nixon intervened, to trying to help the parties come up with a solution. But as the two sides and a federal mediator prepared to meet in Washington, D.C., Greg Luzinski, Larry Bowa, and several members of the Phillies traded in their baseball gloves and bats for basketballs and squash balls at Chestnut Hill Academy on the first Sunday of the '72 season. "They were probably doing stuff like that because it's not like it is now, where they have all these fitness centers," Chris Wheeler said. "They didn't have any of that stuff. Guys showed up to spring training in those days to get in shape because they had to work during the winter. They had jobs. They'd go out and play basketball games for $100 against some high school faculty, so the money just changed all that stuff. It's completely different."[2]

During the strike, the Phillies barred the field to their players. In terms of baseball workouts during the strike, a few of the players lived in the Willingboro, New Jersey area, and Wheeler surmised that they probably got together on their own with bats and balls. "They weren't allowed to do anything formally at the ball park," Wheeler said. "Bowa and Luzinski were pretty tight and I think they just worked out and did some things. You didn't have the organization that you have now too, with all the trainers. You had one trainer. It's not like you had all the fitness drills. They probably didn't do a whole hell of a lot."[3]

Philadelphia was supposed to be in St. Louis for an NL East battle against the Cardinals on the first weekend of the season. Instead, they were left wondering when they would return to the diamond. "It was tough because we didn't make the kind of money guys make now," Bowa added. "These guys that are playing now, they have no idea what guys went through, going through strikes. Some guys had to get jobs, and you worked out on your own because you didn't know when it was going to start. You didn't want to get caught with your pants down, so a group of guys would go hit at a high school. That's one of the reasons this union is so strong because they went through a lot of strikes, a lot of player stoppages."[4]

Indeed, the union has made astronomical strides in the 40 years since 1972, when Carlton made just $45,000. According to baseball.about.com, the payrolls for opening day rosters in 2009, as compiled by *USA Today*, showed that the average player salary was $3.26 million, a four percent increase from 2008 when they pulled down $3.14 million. "As these guys get their money now, you see utility players making a million and a half and they're saying, 'Wow, pretty good,'" Bowa said. "But it was because of guys, even before I got there, that believed in the union. At that time, Marvin Miller was the head guy and he was a tough negotiator, and Donald Fehr came on and he also did a good job. I'm all for guys making money, but I like those guys that know the history and know why the salaries are where they're at right now."[5]

Finally, after a 13-day work stoppage lasting from April 1 to April 13, the strike did end. Players returned to the field when, according to an article by Bruce Keidan in the *Philadelphia Inquirer*, the owners agreed to contribute $5,940,000 to the players pension fund in the coming year and to earmark $500,000 of the "excess" revenue generated by the fund in the last year for higher pension payments. Owners also agreed to add salary arbitration to the collective bargaining agreement. Meanwhile, as the attention turned back toward the actual ballgames, Phillies traveling secretary Eddie Ferenz had his work cut out for him getting everyone to Chicago for the season opener.

While the Phillies had 13 players in Philadelphia and two in St. Louis, which was an easy plane trip to the Windy City, others were back home in California, some were in Florida, and even one (Willie Montanez) had returned to Puerto Rico. As all the players around the major leagues reconvened, however, they did so knowing that, instead of looking at a 162-game schedule, they would see their season shortened by at least six games. National League teams would play anywhere from a 153- to 156-game schedule, while American League squads would play seasons ranging in length from 154 to 156 games. It was decided that the games which were lost around major league baseball during the work stoppage would not be made up because the owners refused to pay the players for the time they were on strike. That meant, under terms of the settlement, that every major leaguer lost nine games of pay, which computed to roughly five percent of his annual salary.

When the 1972 season did finally get underway, Lefty did not disappoint. In his first three starts, Carlton went 3–0 with a remarkable 0.69 earned run average. Making it all the more impressive was that he did it against three future Hall of Famers — the Chicago Cubs' Ferguson Jenkins, the St. Louis Cardinals' Bob Gibson, and the San Francisco Giants' Juan Marichal. Jenkins

Through his first six outings with the Phillies in 1972, including starts against Hall of Famers Ferguson Jenkins, Bob Gibson and Juan Marichal, Steve Carlton put together a fantastic 5–1 record with a 1.73 ERA.

took a no-decision, while Gibson and Marichal suffered their first losses of the year. Carlton "was going up against the best every time," Luzinski said. "When they pair them up, he's going to go against the best. I feel sorry for those guys on the other side because there's teams that will face Lefty with their best pitcher going and [they] obviously didn't fare as well."[6]

Many pitchers might not have their best stuff in their first couple of appearances with a new team as they adapt to different surroundings. Roy Oswalt, a long-time ace for the Houston Astros before being traded to Philadelphia in July of 2010, went 0–1 with a no-decision and a 4.38 earned run average in his first two starts with the Phillies, but then compiled a 7–0 record with a 1.28 ERA in his next 11 outings. In Carlton's case, being traded in the off-season, in addition to knowing a couple of players on the Phillies' roster, probably worked to his favor. Mike Krukow, who was a teammate with Carlton in Philadelphia during the 1982 season, noted that when players are traded in the off-season, it's different than being traded in the middle of a season.

"You've got time to catch your breath, pack up and start your plans because immediately, you have to start thinking logistics," Krukow said. "If you have a family, it's a little difficult because often times your kids are in school someplace, or you have a lease or a home someplace. So there's logistics you have to deal with to get out of a town and get into a new town and get a new apartment or whatever. So that's extremely distracting. But in regards to going from one clubhouse to another, you have to remember that baseball is a very small world. And by the time you've been in the big leagues for five or six years, chances are there's somebody on that team they're getting traded to that they've played with and they know. So the transition is a lot easier when you have friends. And as a team that's receiving the guy, you do your best to make him feel comfortable. You offer realtors' names or he lives with you for a couple of days so he gets his feet on the ground. So there's a pretty good support group you're coming into because everybody's been through it. Everybody kinda wants that guy to get to the comfort zone as quick as he can obviously, so he can produce better. It's all positive because you're going someplace that wants you."[7]

Lefty was certainly having no problem producing positive results in his first several starts with the team. The only question on Saturday, April 15, was whether or not the conditions in the Windy City would even allow Lefty to show his stuff. The forecast in Chicago was for thunderstorms and showers, and players were bracing for soggy, slippery footing on the Wrigley Field playing surface. It wasn't inconceivable that the start of the Phillies' season would be pushed back yet another day. But play they did, however, and Carlton earned the decision in a 4–1 conquest of the Cubbies. That fact that he pitched the way that he did was even more remarkable considering that he hadn't pitched in about two weeks. Stamina was a big concern for the pitchers, and on a day when the starting pitchers would have been happy to throw six innings, Carlton actually threw eight innings of four-hit, two-run ball. The score was tied 2–2 through eight innings, and then Ron Stone pinch-hit for Lefty in the top of the ninth and delivered a two-out single. After Larry Bowa followed with his first hit of the day, the Cubs summoned lefty reliever Steve Hamilton from the bullpen to face Tim McCarver, and the Phils' No. 2 hitter in the lineup lofted a fly ball that right fielder Jose Cardenal misjudged, allowing two runs to score. Joe Hoerner then pitched a scoreless inning of relief in the bottom of the inning to nail it down. "Hoerner came up with one of the great lines about Carlton," Bruce Keidan said. "He said, 'He's not that good, he's just lucky.' I said, 'What are you talking about?' Hoerner said, 'He only pitches on the days when the other team doesn't score.'"[8]

The Cubs did score two earned runs against Carlton, but it wasn't enough. Lefty allowed just six base runners over eight innings, while striking out five in what would be the first of his 499 games pitched for the Phillies. "With Lefty on the mound, it always felt like that was our best chance to win a game, and when he had a lead he rarely gave it up," Tommy Hutton said. "It almost seemed like we played better when he was on the mound."[9]

The fact that Carlton and Jenkins were the aces on their respective staffs certainly motivated them to pitch well when they received the ball in those starts. "Oh, of course," Jenkins said. "I pitched more against Bob Gibson than anybody else because the Cardinals were in our division. So that was the fun part (pitching) against Drysdale and Marichal. I mean, the number one pitcher always faced the number one pitcher on the other team. I didn't get an easy patsy when I was out there pitching ... In my career, I never beat Drysdale, but I pitched against him about eight or nine times. The same with Gibson. I beat Gibson quite a bit, I beat Carlton, and he beat me. But it's just the fact that the number one pitcher is going to perform against the other number one pitcher. That was the fun part."[10]

Carlton's outing against Jenkins in the season opener was just one of seven match-ups in '72 that he had against future Hall of Famers. "There were a lot of thumbs that were put in ice water," Cubs star center fielder Rick Monday remarked. "In that same '72, we had Fergie Jenkins pitching for the Cubs and Fergie was out of the same mold. He did not give an inch and he would find a way, even on those days that maybe you don't have your best stuff."[11] St. Louis Cardinals star Joe Torre concurred that there were not a whole lot of nights off for the hitters during that era. "You had the Sandy

Koufaxes and Jim Maloneys and Marichal, Gibson, Drysdale, Bob Veale," Torre said. "You had a ton of number ones all over the place. And Lefty came up through the right organization and just saw the way Bob Gibson conducted himself, and I think he really learned a lot from Bob."[12]

Burt Hooton wasn't the number one for the Cubs in '72, but he definitely pitched like an ace on Sunday, April 16, throwing a no-hitter in cold, drizzly weather as the Cubs beat Dick Selma and the Phillies by a 4–0 score. If not for the conditions, however, the Phillies would have been on the scoreboard courtesy of Luzinski, who gave fans an early glimpse of his power. "That was the game where Bull hit a ball out into the street and the wind blew it back," Wheeler said. "It was freezing cold that day. But I'll never forget that ball. It looked like it was way out.... Only at Wrigley. It can give you a cheap one or take one away from you like that."[13]

After splitting two games in the Windy City, the Fightins headed back to Philadelphia for their home opener on Monday, April 17, against the Cardinals. Despite the strike, Veterans Stadium still hosted 38,182 fans, the largest Opening Day crowd in the majors to that point in '72. For those who came through the Vet's turnstiles, they received the opportunity to see a pre-game show featuring not only 1,200 mummers and a fireworks display, but also "Kiteman," who was the subject of a lot of press in the days leading up to the opener. The original Kiteman, Jeff Jobe, was forced to cancel due to a scheduling conflict caused when the home opener was pushed back due to the players' strike. With Jobe planning to be in Mexico, Paoli's John Williamson was going to step in as the pinch-flier, with his plan to get airborne outside of the stadium, reach an altitude of 300 feet, and soar over the center field fence with the game's first ball. Then he, too, canceled after determining that his stunt was going to be too dangerous, and Richard Johnson, of Cypress Gardens, Florida, became the second pinch-flier for Bill Giles, the Phillies' vice-president in charge of business operations. Ultimately, Johnson, wearing water skis, launched himself off an upper-deck ramp in center field and promptly made a crash landing as part of the Opening Day festivities.

For Dan Baker, that was a day he will always remember. A 1968 graduate of Glassboro State College, he had written to the Phillies for several years inquiring about summer work. Finally, he received a dream job behind the microphone. "Opening Day was special to me because it was my first game as a major league PA announcer," Baker said. "Kiteman made his debut. Bill Giles always had a unique way of delivering the first ball."[14] Chris Wheeler could only smile and shake his head when recalling Kiteman's act. "Giles always had some crazy Opening Day act like Kiteman," Wheeler laughed. "That would have helped make the big crowd too."[15] Many of the Phillies' players were quoted in the *Philadelphia Inquirer* as saying that they expected boos from the players' strike to disappear pretty quickly, and that fans would probably just be glad to have baseball back. The crowd for the Phillies' home opener against the St. Louis Cardinals rewarded their optimism. Unfortunately for the Philadelphia faithful, St. Louis broke a 3–3 tie in the top of the ninth inning on Ted Simmons' RBI double to left-center and Dal Maxvill's sacrifice fly, and held on for a 5–4 win.

The next night, Carlton was back on the mound on just three days' rest to face his former teammate, Bob Gibson. In the sixth inning, Deron Johnson's RBI single drove in Willie Montanez, who tripled, and that was the only run Carlton needed in a 1–0 win. It was the first time in more than two seasons, a span of time covering seven decisions, that the Phillies beat Gibson. Lefty tossed his first of 30 complete games, struck out five and yielded just three hits, while allowing no Redbird runners to advance past first base. Gibson, meanwhile, gave up 11 hits in eight innings, including two each to Bowa and Doyle, who climbed over the .300 mark. But the Phillies stranded eight runners on base and could not add any insurance runs for Lefty. Meanwhile, Cardinals Hall of Fame pitcher Gibson reached a milestone in that game when he fanned Luzinski for his 2,584th strikeout to eclipse Bob Feller and Warren Spahn for fourth place on the all-time list. Walter Johnson, Jim Bunning, and Cy Young were the only pitchers with more K's than Gibson at that point. But Gibson's loss to Lefty was part of a stretch in which the Cardinals' great would go on to lose his first five decisions. He eventually bounced back to finish the season at 19–11 with a 2.46 ERA. As well as Gibson pitched, though, Lefty was even better, particularly against the Redbirds. He went 4–0 with a 0.50 ERA against the Cardinals in '72.

Asked if Carlton seemed more motivated to face his former team that season, Luzinski said, "I don't think it was any different than pitching against anybody else, to be honest with you. He played with [Gibson] and I'm sure he knew that Gibson was a great pitcher, and that obviously he's going to try to keep the Cardinals down as much as he can runs-wise because of his opponent pitching. But I don't think that stuff bothered Steve. Steve was a competitor in his own right. That's why he's a Hall of Famer because he was a special person who was able to control his emotions and mentally have it put together where he could do things."[16]

Wheeler added, "You know, he wasn't like that (to be more motivated for one particular team). I can honestly say that about him. Every night to him was, the opponent was the hitter. He just had that kind of tunnel vision. It wasn't like he went, 'Oh so-and-so is on the mound, it's Tom Seaver,' he wouldn't think like that. He thought all the time about the hitter. He used to talk about that all the time, that all he thought about was who's at home plate, and if he was right-handed or left-handed. He didn't even think about if it was Dave Parker or Johnny Bench or something like that. He talked about the right-handed hitter or the left-handed hitter and, 'I was trying to do this,' and that's the way he was."[17]

Legendary *Philadelphia Inquirer* columnist Bill Lyon, however, suggested that Lefty was definitely more motivated to face the Redbirds. Lefty had spent the first nine years of his professional career with the St. Louis organization, so he had a history with them. That, in addition to knowing the St. Louis hitters, played to Carlton's advantage, according to Lyon. "There's no doubt he was, what's the word that is popular today ... amped," Lyon said. "He was amped to face the Cardinals, as is pretty commonplace, I think, with most people who get traded, in any sport. And yeah, it had to be a tremendous help knowing the Cardinals' batters, knowing where the holes were in their swings."[18] Asked if he had ever heard Carlton say that he was more amped to face the Cardinals than another team, Lyon said, "My recollection is that he was fairly diplomatic about it. It wasn't one of those [situations where he was] strutting around saying, 'I showed those SOBs. I stuck it up their ass.' For one thing, that was not his way, and he wasn't doing a cock-of-the-walk strut. At least not for public consumption."[19]

Pitching against his former team, the St. Louis Cardinals, in 1972, Steve Carlton earned four wins while taking no losses.

Willie Montanez made a tremendous running catch, although controversial, on a fly ball by Ted Sizemore to end the game, leaping to make the grab only to see the ball hop out of his glove. But he snagged the ball again before it hit the ground to secure Lefty's complete-game gem.

Although the Cardinals believed that Montanez trapped the ball, it was no surprise to see the

Phillies' center fielder and others making big plays behind Lefty, as they were always on their toes with Lefty working so quickly. This game, in fact, ended while there was still some daylight, with Carlton and Gibson finishing the game in a mere one hour and 33 minutes. Due to the fact that Lefty wasted no time when he was on the hill, it was no understatement to say that his teammates loved playing behind him. Overall, he pitched 12 games in 1972 that lasted less than two hours. And even while starting three contests that went to extra innings, the average duration of Lefty's 41 starts was just two hours, 11 minutes. "We played solid defense for him because he worked very quick," Don Money said. "He got the ball and there was no milling around out there. I remember he and Bob Gibson pitched one game, and I think the game was over before it got dark, in Philly. It was over, like, five minutes until nine and the game started at 7:30. It was unbelievable. Both of those pitchers got the ball and went about their business — none of this milling around, let me think about this for awhile. And when you do that, you throw strikes, you're on your game, the fielders are on their game. And look at his numbers ... over 300 innings and 190 hits. Wow, c'mon on. [He went] 27–10 and you won't see that no more because guys don't pitch like that no more."[20]

When Marty Bystrom joined the Phillies as a rookie in 1980 and helped the club win its first World Series championship, Lefty was a good role model for him in that respect. Bystrom, too, was a quick worker, but few set the pace that Lefty did. "He had awful good stuff and he worked quick, which made the defense stay on their toes," Bystrom said. "Defensive players like pitchers that work quick, and it wasn't uncommon for him

Steve Carlton threw three or four different pitches for strikes, including a devastating slider, as he notched 45.8 percent of Philadelphia's wins in 1972. That shattered the mark formerly held by the New York Americans' Jack Chesbro, whose 41 victories in 1904 represented 44.6 percent of his team's wins.

to throw a nine-inning game in under two hours. I can remember a Sunday day game, I think he pitched nine innings and it was, like, an hour and 37 minutes. So the defensive players love that and they're a little bit quicker getting to the ball, that kind of thing, because he keeps them on their toes. When a guy is really, really slow, it just drags and guys get bored."[21]

As much as Carlton liked to get the ball and just throw his next pitch, he equally disliked anything that disrupted his concentration. His battery-mates knew better than to make a lot of mound visits when it was Lefty's turn in the rotation. "When pitchers walk around the mound, they shake off, they step off, they call the catcher out ... basically, they don't have a game plan, they don't know what they want to do or how they want to pitch a certain guy," Larry Bowa said. "But he knew exactly what he wanted to do before the game even started."[22] Larry Shenk echoed Bowa's comments by saying, Carlton "didn't want stuff that interfered with his focus. When Lefty pitched, he didn't want mound visits, he didn't want pitch outs. He said he saw the catcher's glove and that's all he saw. Later, he put earplugs in to knock out the noise. He just wanted to focus."[23]

No one understood Lefty better than Tim McCarver. The two of them were teammates in St. Louis from the time that Lefty came up with the Cardinals in 1965 until McCarver was shipped to Philadelphia in October of 1969. Then after being reunited in Philadelphia in 1972, McCarver started in 12 of Lefty's 14 starts before being traded to the Expos in June. Back-up catcher Mike Ryan started in Carlton's other two starts. It was a superstition that led Mike Schmidt and Tug McGraw to ride together to the stadium during their playing days with the Phillies. Along the way to the Vet, they would pull into the Wawa convenience store to buy a milkshake. Some thought it could have been superstition early in Lefty's career that led him to wanting McCarver as his battery-mate. "They were so in sync with each other," Larry Shenk said. "Lefty was very particular about his catchers. He didn't want a lot of interference, a lot of slowing down, a lot of going over signs, talking about hitters. 'Give me the ball and let me throw it.'"[24]

Rich Hebner, who was teammates with Carlton and McCarver in Philadelphia during the 1977 and '78 seasons after signing with the Phillies as a free agent, observed the relationship. It "must have been back from the St. Louis days, and obviously he must have caught a couple of games that he won early in his career and they said, 'Hey, he's my catcher.' I've seen that before. I've seen that pitchers like to pitch to certain catchers and Lefty liked Timmy. Timmy had a nice career hanging around with Carlton.... They were good friends too. It worked out good. I know Timmy caught a lot of wins catching behind him."[25]

It extended beyond just superstition, however. Chris Wheeler said that the two developed a good rapport together starting with their days together in St. Louis, and that Lefty trusted McCarver. Together, they won a World Series with the Cardinals in 1967, when the Redbirds defeated the Boston Red Sox in seven games. They also went to the Fall Classic again in 1968, where they fell to the Detroit Tigers in seven games. Joe Hoerner was the closer on that St. Louis team before getting traded to the Phillies in a package with McCarver in October of 1969. "Timmy's older than Lefty, but they became good friends and Timmy talks about how early on, Lefty was very stubborn about some things and Tim had the ability to just take him and talk to him," Wheeler remarked. "Back in those days, guys didn't get offended like they do now. You could tell a guy, 'Hey, that's wrong. This is the way you should throw your slider, you should do this, that, or the other thing.' So they developed a rapport in St. Louis that then of course continued over here."[26] That rapport only got stronger after the Phillies reacquired McCarver in the summer of 1975, just a week after he had been released by the Boston Red Sox. He then caught Lefty for the next four-plus years until he was released by Philadelphia in November of 1979.

"When Timmy came back, Lefty still had some great years with him and they were very good together," Wheeler said. "Timmy was an excellent caller of the game. He had trouble throwing a little bit later in his career, but he could call [a good game] and Lefty trusted him. He really trusted him. And like most great pitchers, they don't want catchers out there talking to them too much. They want to have a feel for what they want to do, put down their fingers and leave it at that. And they were good that way. Lefty wouldn't shake him off too much ... I think it was more of a comfort level those two had developed for a long time."[27]

Plus, as Wheeler pointed out, it wasn't like others did not do the same thing. In fact, Hall of Famer-to-be Greg Maddux and catcher Javy Lopez were teammates for many years with the Atlanta Braves in the 1990s, but they rarely worked together. Instead, it was Eddie Perez and others behind the plate when Maddux took his turn in the rotation. "All those years, Maddux had a different catcher and nobody said that much about it," Wheeler said. The Carlton-McCarver tandem "became so well known I think because of Lefty's personality. Maddux would go talk to the media after the game whereas Lefty wouldn't. But you look up every year and Greg Maddux had another guy catching him. Javy Lopez was there for how long, and Maddux didn't let him catch him."[28]

During the 1972 season, there was another player, in addition to McCarver, catching Lefty. John Bateman came to the Phillies in a trade that

June, and Carlton did not shake him off much either. Bateman played for three teams in his 10-year career, with Philadelphia being his final stop, and Wheeler said that Carlton worked very well with Bateman. "Lefty, for whatever reason, became very comfortable with John Bateman that year," Wheeler said. "John Bateman was a journeyman guy who really didn't swing the bat much, maybe the slowest guy you ever saw, but he was a good catcher for Lefty. He was very good defensively. He probably called the game the way Lefty wanted. Pitchers don't want to be out there shaking off. They don't like that. And Lefty worked so fast. He wanted you to put the sign down and let's go. 'Be prepared, know what I want to throw, and let's go from there.' And I think he and Bateman clicked."[29]

Bob Boone came up at the end of the 1972 season, and although Bateman continued to catch all of Carlton's games that year, Boone eventually became the man behind the plate. But for awhile, Lefty did not click with Boone the way that he did with McCarver and Bateman. Wheeler thought that Carlton and Boone were just too much alike in many ways. "They were both really cerebral and they were both really stubborn," Wheeler said. "Lefty had his way he wanted to do things and Booney was getting to the point where he was getting more involved in the game because he was becoming a better major league player and catcher. They kinda butted heads and Timmy and Lefty were like two old pals. They understood each other. It just worked for them. But it changed. Bob Boone and Lefty were fine after a period of time, and he caught him obviously in '80 and won a World Series with [Boone] catching [Lefty]. But it took a little while. I don't want to put words in Booney and Lefty's mouth, but I think both would agree at that time, they were probably both a little stubborn about things.... Both of them had their own way of doing things."[30]

In April of '72, however, Boone was still a few months away from making his major league debut. It was McCarver who was catching Lefty when he hurled a one-hit masterpiece while striking out 14 in a 3–0 shutout of Juan Marichal and the San Francisco Giants on Tuesday, April 25. His 14 strikeouts tied a club record for left-handers in a nine-inning game, although it was still four shy of the club-record 18 batters that lefty Chris Short fanned in 15 innings against the Mets in 1965. That marked Lefty's single-game high for strikeouts in '72, and it was one of seven double-digit strikeout games for him that season. His "slider was unbelievable ... it spun like a fastball, and the hitters saw it as a fastball, and it was a breaking ball," Wheeler said. "They would check swing all the time at it, if they didn't swing and miss."[31]

The Giants, however, were not the only team that Lefty baffled in that magical 1972 season, however. In addition to dominating the Redbirds with a 4–0 record in 1972, Carlton was 3–0 with a 2.53 ERA in four starts against the Giants; 3–1 with a 1.54 ERA in four starts against the Cubs; 3–1, and a 0.79 ERA against the Dodgers in four starts; 2–1 with a 2.57 ERA in three starts against the Padres; 2–1 with a 1.44 ERA in three starts against the NL East-champion Pirates; 2–1 and a 2.12 ERA in four starts against the Braves; 3–0 with a 0.67 ERA in three starts against the Expos; and 2–0 with a 4.13 ERA in three starts against the National League champion Reds. The only teams that he did not have a winning record against in '72 were the New York Mets (2–4, 3.54 ERA in six starts) and Houston Astros (1–1, 1.56 ERA in three starts).

At Candlestick Park in late April, the Phillies gave Carlton all of the support he needed in the fifth inning against Marichal, as Luzinski and Don Money earned leadoff walks, Mike Anderson sacrificed, and Denny Doyle smacked a sacrifice fly to center field to put the Phillies in front, 1–0. In the eighth, the Phillies added two insurance runs, with Carlton, a .201 lifetime hitter, right in the middle of the rally. With one out, Lefty singled and Larry Bowa doubled to right field. After Willie Montanez drew a two-out intentional walk from Marichal to load the bases, Deron Johnson stroked a two-run single to right field to push Philadelphia's lead to 3–0. While Lefty went 1-for-4 at the plate that day, it was on the mound where he grabbed the headlines. With the exception of San Francisco third baseman Chris Arnold, Carlton fanned each hitter in the Giants' lineup at least once. That day, San Francisco's power-packed lineup included the likes of Bobby Bonds, Dave Kingman and Ken Henderson in the middle of the batting order, with Willie McCovey and Willie Mays available off the bench.

The Giants' only hit was Chris Speier's leadoff single to center field in the bottom of the first inning. Tito Fuentes forced Speier, as Don Money scooped up a grounder and threw to Denny Doyle at second. Fuentes was then erased by McCarver on an attempted steal. In addition to Lefty having great stuff Fuentes said, he was also very smart and set up hitters to his advantage. "What didn't he do?" Fuentes asked. "He was so comfortable — good fastball, good slider to the right-handed hitters [which was] easy to eat you alive, and good control for a left-hander. I was not too bad a hitter from the right side, but what Steve did which was very smart was he used to set me up ... fastball or slider, especially that slider going inside to let me pull. I hit it, but I hit it foul. Then the next pitch, I expected the same thing, inside, and I hit it good. So then I'm feeling good. Then after that he started working outside. He was very, very smart — he knew what he was doing."[32]

Phillies reliever Wayne Twitchell had a close-up view of Lefty's one-hitter while hanging out in the bullpen at Candlestick Park. But there was no need for Twitchell or any of his teammates in the bullpen to even think about warming up that day. "I never saw a baseball game like that," Twitchell said. "I saw a couple of no-hitters, but I never saw anything like that. The first batter of the game hit the ball between [Carlton's] legs for a base hit up the middle. That was it. I think it was just a get-ahead fastball and Speier hit it between his legs. Then it looked like he was pitching against a South Philadelphia Little League team. And it was a total mismatch."[33]

Speier was not a good hitter against pitches low and in, so his game plan against Carlton was to lay off of the slider and wait for the fastball. "I was a first ball, fastball hitter," Speier said. "I sat on my strength, and my strength was hitting the fastball. And for me, I didn't care if it was the first pitch or the fifth pitch in the at-bat. But Carlton is that type of pitcher that when all those things start working, it's pretty difficult. Just like the good ones today. If they have two or three of their pitches working for them, it's going to be a battle, and that's how he was, a tremendous competitor."[34]

Giants manager Charlie Fox had seven pure right-handed batters along with two switch-hitters, second baseman Tito Fuentes and left fielder Ken Henderson, in the starting lineup that day, but Lefty's dominant slider neutralized San Francisco's batting order. "He was a pretty intimidating left-hander and I don't think there were too many left-handers that would hang in on him with his slider, and he had a curve ball," Speier said. "And plus, he was throwing the ball in the low Nineties with his fastball and not afraid to throw inside. So any time you get that pitcher of that quality with the command of his stuff, he's going to shut down any lineup."[35]

Years later, Speier received an up-close look at just how intimidating Lefty could be following a game in Philadelphia. "We were playing here in Philadelphia and I was kinda struggling at the plate and facing him," Speier recalled. "And I hit a ball really, really well to right-center and [Gary] Maddox went and ran it down. I'm thinking double, and so I'm a little bit upset to say the least when he catches the ball. So as I'm coming back across the field, near the mound, I kinda do a little spit on the mound and he sees that. It wasn't until after the game, we happened to be in the same place, and I saw him sitting across from me and just staring at me. And I had heard stories about his training regimen with Gus [Hoefling] and karate and everything, so I got visions of him coming over and just breaking my neck. So I meekly go over to him and I apologized. I said, 'It wasn't about you. I'm just struggling right now, I was upset that I didn't get a hit. I didn't mean anything by it. Please accept my apology. I have the utmost respect for you, *Mr. Carlton*' ... He was fine with it."[36]

That intimidation no doubt played a factor as Carlton retired the next

15 batters in order after Speier's base hit, including 11 K's, until Arnold worked a free pass on a 3–2 count with one out in the sixth inning. Arnold was the only San Francisco base runner to advance as far as second base, following a sacrifice bunt by Marichal, but then Lefty stranded Arnold by getting Speier to hit an inning-ending fly out to Willie Montanez in center field.

During the season as a whole, Carlton held opposing batters to a .207 average in 1,244 at-bats, including just .186 with men on base. Overall, Lefty completed the game by retiring the final 11 batters he faced. He faced just one batter over the minimum, and he struck out the side in the second inning, when he got Kingman, Ken Henderson, and Garry Maddox swinging, and again in the fourth inning, when he caught Speier looking and then got Fuentes and Bobby Bonds swinging. Defensively, Money and Bowa were perfect on a combined five chances behind Lefty, and Carlton allowed only five fly balls to the outfield and a pop up to McCarver in foul territory. "It was a game that you watched two great pitchers hook up," Larry Bowa said, "and you knew early in the game that there wasn't going to be a lot of runs scored, playing in that cold San Francisco climate out there. To watch him go through that lineup was something special. It was probably one of his better games that he pitched."[37]

Although Lefty never threw a no-hitter, Larry Shenk recalls a time that he threatened to do just that. On May 5, 1980, Lefty yielded just three walks through the first seven and two-thirds innings on his way to striking out 11 in a match-up against the Atlanta Braves. Finally, with two outs in the top of the eighth, Bill Nahorodny stepped to the plate and stroked a single to center field. Carlton went on to finish with a three-hitter in that game while defeating Rick Matula and the Braves by a 7–3 score. "That was a very dominating performance that time, but he had a lot of them," Shenk said. "He was just overpowering people. He was so focused compared to any athlete I've ever known."[38] Overall, Lefty used that focus to throw six one-hitters in his Hall of Fame career, a modern National League record when he retired in 1988. The others occurred on the following dates:

- June, 19 1968, when Carlton blanked the Cubs 4–0. Lefty's effort was part of a stretch in which Chicago went 48 straight scoreless innings to tie a major league record set in 1906.
- September 27, 1975, when Carlton allowed only a sixth-inning double to Felix Millan en route to an 8–1 rout of right-hander Randy Tate and the New York Mets.
- June 5, 1979, when Carlton held Houston to just a seventh-inning single to left field by Jeff Leonard as he picked up the decision in an 8–1 Phillies victory over right-hander Rick Williams and the Astros.

- July 4, 1979, as Lefty handcuffed Lee Mazzilli, Joel Youngblood, and the New York Mets in a 1–0 win. New York lefty Andy Hassler yielded only five hits to Philadelphia, but Carlton was better, taking a no-hitter into the seventh inning before Elliott Maddox spoiled it with a one-out double to center field.
- April 26, 1980, when Carlton set the NL record with a 7–0 whitewashing of the St. Louis Cardinals in a game that saw John Fulgham take the loss. Lefty, who allowed only a second-inning single to left field by Ted Simmons, went on to finish 6–0 in 1980 against his former team, becoming the last pitcher in the 20th century to win six games in a single season against one team.

Wayne Twitchell considered Carlton's performance against the Giants in 1972 the best he had ever seen. "Any time, any pitcher, I never saw a game like that," Twitchell said. "There are games where guys pitch one-hitters or two-hitters or no-hitters and whatever stuff. But this game after that base hit, it was like there was nobody up there. They didn't have a prayer. That game has always stuck in my mind. It was probably the greatest degree of mismatch that I ever saw. He just threw the ball right by them."[39] Bruce Keidan was seated in the press box at that game and he, too came away impressed. "It was certainly right up there," Keidan said. "It was a very dominating performance. He had more than a few that year and a lot of them were against the other team's number one pitcher. It used to match up more that way than it does now."[40]

In the next day's *Philadelphia Inquirer*, Keidan wrote that Lefty "mesmerized" the Giants' lineup in his personal shootout with Marichal, who was San Francisco's ace. As a member of the Cardinals, Carlton lost each of his five decisions at Candlestick Park against the Giants. But Lefty put an emphatic end to that streak, striking out pinch-hitter Willie Mays and Chris Speier looking to cap a contest which lasted just one hour and 47 minutes. Despite the headline matchup, only 6,092 fans showed up at the refurbished

Philadelphia Daily News sports writer Bill Conlin wrote that Steve Carlton's one-hitter over Juan Marichal on April 25, 1972, was the best performance of his Hall of Fame career. Lefty never threw a no-hitter and finished with six one-hitters.

stadium, one which often featured cold conditions and winds whipping hot dog wrappers across the field. "When Carlton was at his best, he was unhittable," Keidan said. "He had probably the best slider in the major leagues, he had a great fastball — he had four pitches that he could throw for strikes, whenever he wanted to. And mentally, he was one of the strongest. So much of pitching is mental, and he had one of the strongest minds of any athlete I ever met."[41]

♦ 5 ♦

CATCHING THE FEVER

Carlton's one-hitter against the Giants kicked off a West Coast swing in which the Phillies won seven of 10 games in San Francisco, San Diego, and Los Angeles. Overall, the Phillies were 9–5 in the month of April and were tied for second place with the New York Mets, just a half game behind the first-place Montreal Expos atop the National League East standings. The Phillies ended the month with a doubleheader sweep of the San Diego Padres behind the complete-game efforts of Barry Lersch and Billy Champion. Lersch, who lost 11 straight decisions in 1971, cruised to his victory with a newly-developed knuckleball.

Still, Phillies general manager John Quinn knew that his ball club needed help on the pitching staff if it was going to be able to compete over the long haul. And Quinn was taking advantage of the Phillies' west coast swing to try to land an ace to join Carlton at the top of the rotation. According to reports in the *Philadelphia Inquirer*, he had his eyes focused on the San Francisco Giants' 34-year-old Juan Marichal and the San Diego Padres' 24-year-old Clay Kirby. Marichal, who was making $140,000 with the Giants in '72, had his best days behind him. He had won 20 or more games in six of seven seasons from 1963 to 1969, and he went 18–11, with a 2.94 ERA in 1971. Kirby, meanwhile, was coming off of a 1971 season in which he went 15–13 with a 2.83 ERA, but he would never win more than 12 games in a season after that and would be out of the big leagues for good following a 1–8 season with Montreal in 1976. Either pitcher, though, would have given the Phillies more credibility in the short term, but unfortunately for the Phillies, Marichal and Kirby would never wear the red pinstripes. Reports indicated that Quinn was willing to offer only straight cash for those pitchers, and both the Giants and Padres said, "Thanks, but no thanks." Chris Wheeler said, "I remember Clay Kirby's name being kicked around as a guy they that they liked. I don't remember the Marichal rumors, but Kirby was a big right-hander that threw real hard."[1]

Still, with the season just a couple of weeks old, and thanks to the efforts of two of their own unheralded pitchers, Lersch and Champion, Philadelphia already accomplished what it did just one time throughout all of '71, which was to take both games of a twinbill. With that, the Phillies capped their best start to a season since 1964, a year well known to Philadelphia for the Phillies' historical collapse over the final 12 games. The *Inquirer's* Bruce Keidan was no doubt feeling good about his prediction for a fourth-place finish for the Fightin Phillies. Despite their solid start, however, all was not rosy for the Phillies. In the final game of their series against the Giants, Deron Johnson sustained an injury while sliding into the knee of San Francisco shortstop Chris Speier. Already off to a slow start, batting just .205 in his first 39 at-bats, Johnson would go on to miss 18 straight games because of a nerve injury which numbed his left leg from the knee down. Tests revealed that Johnson only had 15 percent of his normal foot function, and although the Phillies' first baseman could walk, he was unable to flex his foot. Neurologists told him that the only possible therapy was rest.

Certainly, this was not the kind of start they had envisioned from Johnson batting out of the cleanup hole. The muscular, 6-foot-2 inch, right-handed slugger had a big year in '71 with 95 RBIs and a career-best 34 long balls, the most ever by a Phillies first baseman. In July of that season against the Montreal Expos, he became the first player to hit three home runs in one game at newly-opened Veterans Stadium.

Johnson's best years had come from 1964 to 1966 when he put together three straight seasons of 20 or more home runs with the Cincinnati Reds, including a career season in 1965 when he clubbed 32 home runs and drove in 130 runs. Still, Johnson proved that he still had power left in '71 by finishing fourth in the National League in home runs and eighth in RBIs.

Philadelphia, which had a surplus of talent at first base with rookies Tommy Hutton and Greg Luzinski, actually made efforts in the off-season prior to '72 to trade Johnson. Nothing panned out, and he was still on the Phillies' roster when spring training got underway in Clearwater. Then after some prolonged negotiating with general manager John Quinn, the nine-year veteran, while still at home in San Diego, finally agreed on a contract for a reported $80,000, a significant raise from the $60,000 he was making in 1971. But it would not turn out to be the kind of year that Johnson and the Phillies were hoping for, as he was slowed by his injury problems for most of the season. Although he returned to hit .333 in September and October, he finished the season hitting just .213 with nine homers and 31 RBIs in 96 games.

The pitching, however, was the most surprising aspect to the Phillies' fast start. With Carlton, Dick Selma, Woodie Fryman, Barry Lersch, and Bill

Champion in the starting rotation to begin the season, the Phillies did not lose a single series until mid–May. In fact, through the first month of the season, Selma was the only starter with an ERA higher than 3.00. Still, his 3.32 earned run average was respectable, and Carlton (1.59), Fryman (0.82), Lersch (1.20), and Champion (2.57) were also enjoying early season success. Many thought that Philadelphia's arms, outside of Carlton, would only be average, but the pitchers were surpassing those expectations. Pitching coach Ray Rippelmeyer was earning kudos for the pitchers' strong work, and as Keidan wrote, the pitching was good enough "to make Billy Penn's statue scratch its head in wonderment."

Not even Billy Penn would have figured that the Phillies' starting pitchers would throw ten complete games in the team's first 20 contests. When the Phillies beat the Dodgers 2–1 in Los Angeles on May 1, with Selma outpitching Claude Osteen, it marked the Phillies' fifth straight complete game. Through the Phillies' first 18 games, Philadelphia was allowing an average of 2.9 runs per outing, while putting up 3.7 runs of their own. The only negative to that string of performances was that Philadelphia had the National League's most under-worked bullpen; guys like Ken Reynolds, who yielded just one hit and no runs in his first four innings of relief duty, and lanky right-handed rookie Wayne Twitchell, who was showing that he could be a strength in short relief, were usually inactive bystanders.

Phillies fever was catching among fans in the region. Even 11,703 fans came through the turnstiles on May 8 in dreary weather conditions to watch the Phils play a meaningless exhibition game against the Baltimore Orioles. Plus, they had to like the fact that they were winning without several of their hitters putting up the numbers they expected. Over the first two weeks, Mike Anderson and Don Money were both hitting below the Mendoza line, while Tim McCarver (.234) and Johnson (.205) weren't much better. What the Phillies were doing, though, was getting timely contributions from a lot of different people at the plate. In their first 14 victories, there were 10 players who slugged game-winning hits. Overall, the Phillies banged out 121 hits over their first 14 games, a span that included Burt Hooton's no-hit gem in the second game of the season at Wrigley Field.

Lefty suffered his first loss of the year on April 29 in San Diego, with Padres hurler Steve Arlin tossing a five-hit shutout. Arlin and Carlton pitched a scoreless duel through six and a half innings, and then Bob Barton's bases-loaded single in the bottom of the seventh gave Arlin all the runs he needed in a 4–0 San Diego shutout. Carlton had extended his scoreless innings streak to 26 straight before the Padres rallied for two runs in the bottom of the seventh inning.

Tim Flannery, who had an 11-year career with the Padres starting in 1979, certainly knew the excitement that Barton was feeling after he delivered his clutch base hit against Lefty. "It was an honor to face him," Flannery said. "I hit a little home run (in San Diego), and I mean little because it hit the top of the fence and it barely went over. And I ran and got the ball, and I still have the ball, and I'll never tell anybody that it was Steve Carlton probably in the last month of his career. I'll always say it was the other guy because he was an animal. In ten years in the major leagues, I only hit nine home runs. So I tried to keep them all. But to have one off a guy like Steve Carlton.... It's always fun to say that to guys when they go, 'You hit a home run off of Carlton?' and then I go, 'Well, I did, but he was about done at the time.' But I still am very honored. It's still Steve Carlton."[2] For his career, Flannery finished with two hits in five at-bats against Lefty, although all of his plate appearances against Carlton were late in the pitcher's playing days. "I had no problem being a platoon player when he was in the prime of his career," Flannery said. "A lot of us would sit over here and watch him pitch and it was like, 'Oh my God.' He was an amazing competitor, strong as can be, prepared, and he took it very personal."[3]

Arlin, though, did not have the option of getting a day off on April 29; he was probably dreading the idea of facing Carlton. After all, his teammates had scored just two runs or fewer in 16 of his 22 career losses in the big leagues, so he surely felt like he had to put up goose eggs in order to win ballgames. And the Padres' 26-year old right-hander was actually doing a pretty good job of that early in his career. In his 11 wins in the majors up to that point, Arlin, who formerly pitched in the Phillies' minor leagues system before being picked up by the Padres in the 1968 expansion draft, had thrown six shutouts. Arlin "pitched a heck of a game," Carlton told reporters afterward. "I've already forgotten this one. I'm already concentrating on the next win."

Those words sounded prophetic when Lefty bounced back four days later to throw a complete-game six hitter in a 5–1 win over the Dodgers' Bill Singer, making for a happy plane trip home for the Phillies from the west coast. Don Money's two-run double to left field in the top of the third inning drove in Tim McCarver and Willie Montanez to give Carlton and the Phillies a 2–0 lead. But the Dodgers were within one, 2–1, until Tommy Hutton's RBI single and two unearned runs in the eighth inning finally gave Carlton some breathing room. Back at the Vet, he also twirled a gem in his next start, going the distance against San Francisco's Ron Bryant and benefiting from second baseman Terry Harmon going 4-for-4 with three runs scored in an 8–3 victory over the Giants at Veterans Stadium. The May 7 game improved his record to 5–1. Through his first six starts, Lefty was rolling along with a tremendous ERA of just 1.73, and his teammates were playing well behind him. The Phillies loaded the bases against Bryant in the bottom of the third inning, and then after Larry Bowa hit a sacrifice fly, Harmon delivered a two-run single to highlight Philadelphia's four-run rally. Harmon, who improved his early-season batting average to .458, also singled and scored on Willie Montanez' two-run double in the fifth to help the Phillies break it open, 6–0. That was more than enough for Lefty, who would fashion an impressive 9–2 record with a 1.73 ERA in 13 day games during the 1972 season. Fuentes managed to go 1-for-4 in the Giants game while playing second base, but for his career, he batted just .176 against Lefty, with nine hits in 51 at-bats, including six K's.

Like so many hitters of that era, Lefty just had Fuentes' number. "The only thing I remember is a home run I hit off of him," Fuentes said. "That's all. I hit the home run off Steve in St. Louis. I let him talk about when he got me out. I talk when I got him, that's all. He knew how to pitch me. He beat me. He got good control because if the slider was over the plate, I would have hit it. But he gave it to me inside, and then when I swung, I pulled it out. So then I was feeling good, I said, 'I hit it good.' Yeah, but foul ball. And then he got me two strikes and no balls. Then after that, what? He's got a fastball outside that he can work with it, then he got a curve ball too, and he's also got a fastball that he can overpower you. So the only chance I had is if I can get the first pitch and hit it fair.... He was good. He was too good, really. At that time, [Sandy] Koufax was number one of course as a left-hander, and Steve was number two, easily."[4]

That win over the Giants improved Carlton's record to 5–1, making him the National League's first five-game winner and tying him with the Detroit Tigers' Mickey Lolich for the most wins in the major leagues. The fact that Lefty went unbeaten in four starts against San Francisco during the 1972 season did not go unnoticed by Chris Speier, who was one of the Phillies' biggest nemeses that year. "That just shows the quality of pitcher he was," said Speier, who had eight RBIs in 12 games against Phillies pitching in 1972, with two home runs. "I mean, his record shows that he's going to shut down most offenses when he's on. He's a big strong guy and you knew that at any given time, he's not afraid to go in there and throw one at you, throw one behind you, throw one up and in to have the factor of intimidation to get you off the plate."[5]

While taking two of three against the Giants, Philadelphia also raised its mark to 13–7 on the season. During the 1971 season, it took until the Phillies' 36th game of the season to earn their 13th victory, when they improved to 13–23 on May 20 with a 1–0 win over the New York Mets behind Rick Wise.

In 1972, the win over the Giants kept them in a virtual tie for first place with the New York Mets (12–6) atop the National League East standings. If not for the Mets' come-from-behind 8–6 win in 10 innings over the San Diego Padres, the Phillies would have been in sole possession of the top spot, instead of 17 percentage points behind. For his part, Carlton was just happy to get the win and move on toward his next game. While visions of pennant fever were dancing in other people's heads, Carlton knew that it was way too early to be looking at the standings and admiring the Phillies' spot at the top of the heap. Lefty's refusal to look at the standings turned out to be smart because the dark clouds were coming. The Dodgers followed the Giants into town and the Phillies finally lost their first series of the season. Although Dick Selma claimed to have his best stuff of the season, it did not translate into a victory in the series opener, as the Phillies lost 6–1 to Don Sutton.

One night later, on Friday the 13th of May, back-to-back throwing errors by Carlton and Anderson on the same play led to a two-run third inning by the Dodgers, and Los Angeles, behind Claude Osteen, knocked off the Phillies, 3–1. For Osteen, it was just his ninth win in 26 decisions against Philadelphia, while Carlton fell to 8–3 against Los Angeles. Combined, Sutton and Osteen held the Phillies to just 12-for-65 hitting (.185) in the Dodgers' back-to-back victories. "We moved to Philadelphia in the summer of 1972," *Philadelphia Inquirer* Hall of Fame columnist Bill Lyon said, "so I arrived here just about in the middle of Carlton's unbelievable season. The Phillies had sought their rightful level by then. That 9–5 start? That's called fools gold. You've got to figure that the teams they were beating had something to do with that too. That maybe they weren't so hot. Or maybe they were going to be hot later, but at the time, the Phillies caught them at a precipitous moment."[6]

Woodie Fryman, who set a club record with 44 and two-thirds scoreless innings at home in 1968, answered with a 4–0 shutout of Jenkins and the Chicago Cubs to improve his record to 2–1. Fryman struck out seven and scattered six hits, while getting offensive support from Mike Anderson and Willie Montanez, who each hit home runs. They needed a quality game from Fryman to beat Jenkins. In fact, it was a rare outing that Jenkins did not beat his former mates. Up until that point, the Cubs' ace was 19–5 against the Phils, including eight victories in a row. During the 1971 season alone, Jenkins beat Philadelphia all six times that he pitched against them. "I had a good record against the Phillies since the trade, but I knew most of the players on the team, so I knew how to pitch them," Jenkins said. "That was the nice part of it. Regardless, I didn't try to prove that they did a wrong trade. Trades are part of the game."[7]

So are home runs, and Greg Luzinski provided the hometown Phillies fans with a special treat one night later, on May 16. Facing Burt Hooton in the fourth inning of a game against the Chicago Cubs, the Bull launched a long bomb in the bottom of the fourth inning to dead center field and hit the Liberty Bell, located with the Phillies' display on the 400-level façade. That legendary home run was the only run for Philadelphia in an 8–1 loss. "I faced Hooton in Triple-A. He was a star coming out of the University of Texas and he had good stuff," said Luzinski, who led all Phillies with 10 upper deck homers in his career. "He was the first one that I supposedly faced with a knuckle-curve ball, and that was a big pitch even in Triple-A for him, and he had a fine career. But the balls you hit the furthest are the balls you just touch off. You've got a great slugger here in Ryan Howard and he'd tell you the same thing. He's a present-day player with the Phillies that is probably going to set records with them. But if you ask him the same thing ... I just touched it off, I didn't really feel it, and it went a long way."[8]

As a team, however, Philadelphia was not going very far, and it would soon get very ugly for the Phillies.

♦ 6 ♦

TAILSPIN TAKES OVER

Despite allowing Luzinski's mammoth blast, Burt Hooton was generally a thorn in the side of Philadelphia in 1972. After no-hitting the Phillies in the second game of the season, he baffled the team on just three hits on May 16. That, combined with Chicago's 3–2 win over Carlton the next night, enabled the Cubs to take back-to-back games. "Burt Hooton pitched very good against us," Larry Bowa said. "I remember Greg Luzinski hit a couple balls that would have been way out (in Hooton's no-hitter), but the wind was blowing in and the balls ended up going nowhere. But he pitched good against us. We weren't that good of a hitting ball club at that time."[1]

Hooton's second victory over Philadelphia that season started a tailspin that saw the Phillies drop 10 straight and 19 of their next 20. Not only did the Phillies hit a miserable .207 as a team during that slump, but they also showed their lack of power, clubbing just seven home runs in that 20-game stretch. Tommy Hutton hit three of those — his first three in a Phillies' uniform — while playing at first base for the injured Johnson. The Phillies acquired Hutton in the off-season from the Los Angeles Dodgers in exchange for Larry Hisle. Up until then, he had been toiling with the Dodgers' Spokane Indians in the Triple-A Pacific Coast League for six years, but he made Philadelphia's big-league roster as a utility player, expecting to give Johnson an occasional breather at first while also providing depth in the outfield and as a pinch-hitter. Johnson's injury, however, thrust Hutton into the everyday lineup. "Deron Johnson strained a calf muscle in San Francisco in May and allowed me the opportunity to get in the lineup on a regular basis," Hutton said. "It was a great chance for me and I tried to make the most of it. I did have mixed feelings (playing because of Johnson's injury), but after all the time in the minor leagues with the Dodgers, this was my first real shot."[2]

Hutton impressed the Phillies' brass that spring not only with his glove, but also with his bat. Although he was never going to draw comparisons to

Willie Stargell as a slugging first baseman, Bruce Keidan wrote during spring training that "Hutton is the kind of hitter who can stand up from a seven-course dinner and go out and slap line drives in his tuxedo." Asked about the description of him that he lacked power, but was strong with the glove and hit a lot of line drives, Hutton agreed. "That's accurate and probably the reason I never became a regular at the Major League level. I made myself a good pinch-hitter (79 career pinch-hits); I was a very good defensive first baseman and could play all three outfield positions. I'm proud when I look back on my career of over ten years in the Major Leagues and even more proud of being able to be teammates with the likes of Steve Carlton, Mike Schmidt, Bob Boone, etc."[3]

Hutton went on to finish the '72 season batting .260 with four home runs and 38 RBIs in 381 at-bats. "He was not a long ball threat, as such," Bill Lyon said of Hutton, who also sang and played guitar at the El Cortez Hotel in Las Vegas during the off-season. "And yes, he was not a bad defender because he was a good all-around athlete. For one thing, he was a really nice guy — one of those guys in the clubhouse who was media-friendly. He was pretty good, kind of a wiry guy, a pretty good all-around athlete. He was a good guy and a pretty solid baseball player."[4] Up until that 1972 season, his major league experience consisted of just 58 plate appearances, including 56 with the Dodgers during the 1969 campaign. But his 443 plate appearances in 1972 marked a single-season high for his 12-season career. "You always want to do better, but looking back on my rookie season in 1972, it wasn't all that bad," Hutton said. "I did make the Topps All-Rookie Team that year."[5]

Utility man Pete Koegel, who was drafted by the Kansas City Athletics in the fifth round in 1965 and traded to the Phillies with Ray Peters for Johnny Briggs in 1971, also played eight games at first base in 1972, in addition to four games at third, two in the outfield, and five behind the plate. At 6-foot-6 inches and 230 pounds, Koegel, whose brother, Warren "Moose" Koegel, was a Penn State All-American lineman and a center for the Oakland Raiders, looked like he could have had a career in the NFL as well. Koegel, though, was not the only one who had double XL jerseys in his locker. Byron Browne (6-foot-2, 190), Roger Freed (6–0, 190), and Joe Lis (6-foot-0, 175) were among the others playing for Philadelphia who looked intimidating, and they might have challenged Mark McGwire during batting practice. But they failed to give the team the offensive boost it desperately needed.

"They were all great big guys," Chris Wheeler said. "Look at the size of them. But they couldn't play. They just weren't talented. But they used to put on some of the most awesome batting practice shows you'll ever see. And then the game would start, and they'd start throwing them sliders and everything.

Roger Freed, By Browne, Joe Lis, some of those guys were some of the greatest BP hitters I've ever seen. They'd be great in a home run hitting contest. But when the game started, they were not good players. They were trying to fill in with Bowa and Luzinski, and they weren't ready yet. They were getting there, but they weren't ready. And we didn't have any pitching."[6]

The Phillies found all different kinds of ways to lose during a prolonged skid. Their anemic offense mustered only three hits off of New York Mets' left-hander Jon Matlack, a West Chester native, in a 7–0 whitewashing that occurred with Lefty on the hill on May 30. They were actually even worse in a 4–1 loss to the Expos on May 24, managing only one hit — a third-inning triple by Mike Anderson — against righty Carl Morton, who brought a 1–4 record into the game but needed just 90 pitches to turn aside the Phillies. A week or so later, the Phillies wasted a quality start by Fryman while extending their misery to 17 innings in a game that featured 11 pitchers as a part of a 6–3 setback to the "Big Red Machine." Then in a game that the Pirates tried to give away to the Phillies on May 26, with the Bucs committing four errors, the Phillies lost by a 6–4 score. In another game against Pittsburgh, Philadelphia took a 4–3 lead into the ninth inning, then brought in Joe Hoerner with a runner on first base and no outs, and ended up falling by a 6–5 decision.

"We had a whole bunch of young guys, including myself, learning to play in the big leagues," Willie Montanez said. "It was a different game in the big leagues. That's what happened. We had the talent, but we just didn't click. That team finally clicked in 1976, but I was out of there by that time. I left in '75. At that time, in '71, '72, and '73, we were learning how to play as a team and how to play in the big leagues."[7] Hutton said the Phillies' early success in 1972 was just smoke and mirrors. "We just weren't that good," Hutton said. "Even with a pretty good start, Lefty didn't get on a roll until a little later."[8]

Philadelphia's bad play was one thing, but the Phillies also got a dose of bad luck when second baseman Terry Harmon sustained a broken jaw on a pitch from the Mets' Jerry Koosman that struck him in the face. Harmon, who was swinging a hot bat (.389) while platooning with Denny Doyle, was taken from the field on a stretcher; X-rays revealed the fracture. It wasn't just the hitting that went south for the Phillies after their solid start, however. The starting pitching, which had surpassed all expectations in the early going, began to show its true colors. In Philadelphia's first 20 games, its rotation went 11–3 with a 1.89 earned run average in 147 and two-thirds innings. Only five times did the Phillies' starters yield more than two earned runs through May 7. But the pitching was polar opposite to that over the Phillies' next 25 outings, when their starters compiled an unsightly 5.45 ERA in 148 and two-thirds frames.

Dick Selma was the poster boy for the starting pitchers' struggles in May and June. In five starts, beginning with his May 12 outing against the Dodgers, the 28-year-old was 0–4 with a 9.70 ERA. Philadelphia was hoping that Selma would be closer to the pitcher who went 12–10 for the Padres and Cubs in 1969. Instead, Selma failed to pitch past the fifth inning in any of those five starts. Finally, after yielding five earned runs in just 2 and two-thirds innings in a 6–1 loss to the Mets on June 1, Selma was demoted to the bullpen while Ken Reynolds stepped into his spot in the rotation. It was in the bullpen where Selma pitched exclusively during the 1970 and '71 seasons, making 90 combined appearances in relief. He was the Phillies' closer in 1970, registering 22 saves and a 2.75 ERA. "I thought Dick Selma was best suited for the bullpen," Hutton acknowledged. "His personality and stuff warranted pitching there."[9]

It wasn't that Selma didn't have experience pitching out of the rotation. The five-foot-11 righty made a combined 38 starts with the New York Mets over four seasons from 1965 to '68, and he had a single-season high 28 starts with the Padres and Cubs in the 1969 season. But heading into the 1972 season, Selma had made 169 of his 235 career appearances out of the pen. "When we got him, if I'm not mistaken, I said, 'Well, we've got Dick Selma as a righty and Joe Hoerner as the lefty out of our pen,'" Don Money said. "And then whatever the instance was that they wanted to make him a starter, now you're trying to stretch a guy. Back in those days, your relievers pitched a little bit more than they do today, especially late in the game. So now you're taking a two or three-inning guy and you're trying to stretch him into a starter — a five, six, seven-inning guy. It's difficult as it is, but some bodies don't bounce back as quick. A reliever can pitch today, pitch tomorrow, maybe get one day off and pitch two more days. With starters, they're throwing their 100, 110, 120 or 130 pitches back in those days. So maybe they were asking a little too much from him. But who knows? In hindsight, everybody will say, 'Maybe we should have just left him a reliever.' But maybe they didn't have any other starters. But we were a very young team."[10] Asked how much of a factor Selma's failed comeback as a starter was in the Phillies' struggles in 1972, Larry Shenk said, "It had to be because we weren't deep. As I recall, he was pretty much a one-pitch pitcher. Fastball. He didn't have much breaking stuff."[11]

If Bruce Keidan had a vote, he would have put Wayne Twitchell into the starting rotation. Keidan thought that Philadelphia was using Twitchell in the wrong role, that the lanky right-hander with an A-plus arm should have been a starting pitcher. In the strike zone, he was deadly. The problem however, was that Twitchell didn't find the plate with consistency. In 16 innings with the Phillies in 1971, Twitchell had struck out 15 batters, but he also issued 10 free passes. And when Lucchesi gave him a quick hook after walking the first batter he faced in a tie game against Pittsburgh, it was further proof to Keidan that short relief was not the role for Twitchell. "I was actually a little taller than Steve Carlton and since my earliest remembrance of anything athletically speaking, I could always throw things," Twitchell said. "I had probably 30 full-ride scholarships to play football as a quarterback. I could toss that thing around a little bit also ... [but] I never had the best control. A lot of times, a young pitcher who can pitch with a live arm corresponds with throwing the ball 95 miles an hour. He can be a little more erratic, rather than, as Jamie Moyer pitches, kinda throwing darts. You're giving 100 percent and your coordination sometimes isn't perfect. You're trying to throw the ball on the corner and you're missing by six inches and that's part of the deal."[12]

Chris Short was doing a solid job of hitting the corners in the 1964, '65 and '66 seasons when he finished with three straight seasons of 17 wins or more, going 17–9, 18–11 and 20–10, respectively, for the Phillies. He was Philadelphia's best left-handed pitcher before Carlton came along, and the team was hoping that he could rebound from a 7–14 campaign in 1971. Short was hoping so too, and he arrived in camp looking ready to go. He weighed in at 206, which was ten pounds lighter than the previous season. But his new look wasn't limited only to his weight loss. Short was also sporting some long locks past his shoulders. But unfortunately, the 34-year-old didn't have a new back. Disc problems limited Short to just two games and ten innings in 1969 before undergoing an operation in June of that year. In 1970 and '71, he pitched in a combined 67 games, with 60 starts, but then the back problems flared up again in '72. "He was about done then," Chris Wheeler said. "He had back problems. I don't think he ever had any arm problems his whole career. He probably could have kept on going for a long time, but his back blew out on him. He wasn't the same guy. He wasn't the guy I knew in '64, '65, '66."[13]

That wasn't good news for the Phillies, who were expecting Short to help anchor the pitching staff. In the end, the 34-year-old Short pitched in only 19 games in '72, all out of the bullpen, and finished with a 1–1 record and a 3.91 ERA. His longest outing was a three-inning appearance against the Mets on June 1, and he recorded his only win eight days later after pitching one-third of an inning in relief in a 4–3 win over the Braves. "I've got to think that they were probably counting on him that year, but physically he couldn't do it," Wheeler said. "He just couldn't make it."[14]

Unfortunately, in Don Money's short time with the Phillies, he never got to see the same Chris Short who was dominant in the mid–1960s. "We were a young team and he was an established pitcher," Money added. "I think it was three years in a row that he won 17 or 18 ball games for them prior to that. And then all of a sudden, if you're expecting him to win 15 as one of your top pitchers.... Off the top of my head, I would say injuries probably cut it short for him."[15] At season's end, Short was released by the Phillies, and he signed with the Brewers on November 16, 1972. The '73 season was his last one in the big leagues as he went just 3–5 with a 5.12 ERA with the "Brew Crew." "You talk about a great guy," Wheeler said. "He was everybody's foil. Just a wonderful guy."[16]

But Short's bad back aside in '72, the Phillies also had serious offensive issues as well. The Phils were mired in their worst slump since 1961, and if not or a 2–1 victory over the reigning World Series champion Pirates on May 27, Philadelphia would have made a run at the 23 straight losses, which as *Inquirer* columnist Frank Dolson wrote, "Gene Mauch's Calamity Nine did in 1961."

Money, using a 39-ounce bat that he received from his friend, Pittsburgh Pirates third baseman Rich Hebner, drove in the winning run in the 12th inning, and then Short struck out Hebner on an overhand curve in the bottom of the inning to end the game and halt the Phillies' 10-game losing streak. Brandon picked up the win with one and two-thirds scoreless innings in relief of Billy Champion and Joe Hoerner. Hebner and Money became good friends as roommates in the Pirates' system and remained close even after Money was traded to the Phillies on December 15, 1967, along with Harold Clem, Woodie Fryman, and Bill Laxton for Jim Bunning. Hebner, when asked if he had mixed emotions when Money drove in the game-winning run with his bat, said, "No, he's a friend. He could have struck out, but he got a hit ... I was young and it was tough losing a friend to another club, but that's part of the game."[17]

As it turned out, however, the Phillies failed to gain any momentum from the win, as they went on to lose their next nine. Not even a move to wear their first-year powder blue uniforms during a few home games could save their demise. When the Phillies returned from their highly successful west coast swing in early May, Philadelphia owned a solid 8–4 record away from the Vet. Philadelphia's new threads, according to an article by Keidan, were the "fashion hit" of the '72 season. So when the Phillies lost four of their first seven games back in the City of Brotherly Love, Dick Selma brought up the idea to wear the powder blues at the Vet. His brainstorm met with favor around the clubhouse, and the Phillies adopted a plan to wear the new uniforms at some home games. That strategy lasted all of one game, however. The Braves ripped Philadelphia, 15–3, with the Phillies wearing their road blue uniforms, becoming the first National League team to score 15 runs at Veterans Stadium. So the Phillies scrapped the idea.

"I remember we wore those blue uniforms and we got our butt handed to us and I said, 'OK, I don't think anybody's going to wear those anymore,'" Don Money said. "But that was just to let the fans see them at home instead of on TV, and it was just one of those things. Did we lose 15-to-whatever because of blue uniforms? No. They just pounded us around the ball yard that night. That's just the way it was."[18]

As fashionable as the Phillies' blue uniforms were, they were not the only ones sporting flashy new threads. The San Diego Padres introduced an unforgettable style, breaking out their uniforms with mustard yellow and brown trim. And like the Phillies, the Padres had their own struggles that year en route to a 58–95 last-place finish in the NL West standings. But while the Phillies might have looked like sharp-dressed ball players on that June night in Philadelphia, the ploy to reverse their luck was unsuccessful. "At the time, we wore the blue uniforms because we wanted to change that [losing streak]," Larry Shenk said.[19] Money said that the club was trying to find something to gain a little bit of hope. "When you lose that many, you try anything," Money said. "You try to do anything just to break the habit. Whatever we did that year, things didn't work out quite the way we expected."[20]

That failed experiment was similar to the Phillies' short-lived idea to don all-burgundy uniforms in 1979. The "Saturday Night Specials" lasted all of one game, however, as the Phillies were on the short end of a 10–5 shellacking by the Montreal Expos. Pitcher Larry Christenson started the game and was knocked out after just four and two thirds innings. After that, the only other time those burgundy uniforms were seen on a baseball diamond was when Mike Schmidt wore it on the MLB All-Star Tour of Japan at the end of the 1979 season. "We got beat that night and that's the last time we wore them," Shenk laughed. "LC was the starting pitcher and he still moans at the fact that there was a picture of him in the burgundy uniform."[21]

Similarly, the Phillies' PR director also couldn't help but to think of the 1994 season, when the team wore blue hats with a red Phillies P during day games, again with no success. Philadelphia went 0–4 in those games. The Phillies were just coming off of their special run to the National League pennant in 1993, but even with fan favorites Curt Schilling, John Kruk, Darren Daulton and Lenny Dykstra sporting the new threads, it wasn't working for the Phillies. "We decided we'd wear them for only day games," Shenk said. "And we came off the field after our fourth straight loss, [John] Vukovich was a coach then, a great guy, my good friend ... [He threw it] in the trash can and said, 'That's the last we're going to see of those, boys.' And that's the last we saw of them. Players are superstitious."[22]

Indeed, whether in their home whites or their road powder blues, it didn't matter. The Phillies were just plain bad. By the end of May, they were 16–24 and 13 games off the pace in fifth place behind the front-running New York Mets in the NL East standings. With only a .400 winning percentage on the first day of June, the Phillies were better than just three other teams in the National League — the St. Louis Cardinals (16–25), San Diego Padres (16–26) and San Francisco Giants (15–31). "We just opened Veterans Stadium in '71, the year before Steve Carlton and I started, and there were some good young players," Dan Baker said. "I believe there was a lot of optimism for the future. I think the Phillies thought that by the mid-seventies, they could be a contender. But I don't think they were under any illusions about contending in the early seventies. Clearly, getting a talent of Steve Carlton's magnitude was a step in the right direction, but they needed a lot more. But Greg Luzinski and Larry Bowa were on that ball club, and I think Mike Schmidt and Bob Boone came in September of that year. People knew that the Phillies signed a lot of good talent and were in the process of developing it. I think throughout baseball, they knew that the Phillies were an organization on the rise, but we weren't there yet."[23] As Bruce Keidan noted, they had some players in place who were going to be All-Stars down the road, but they did not have anybody in their prime, with the exception of Lefty. "Take a guy like Luzinski," Keidan remarked. "Luzinski was going to be a very good player for a very long time. Bowa was a really great defensive shortstop and his head was constantly in the game. But then again they had Denny Doyle at second base as I recall. He wasn't going to set the world on fire. He wasn't an All-Star second baseman."[24]

On a road trip through Montreal, Pittsburgh, and New York from May 22 to June 1, the Phillies were just 1–9, which still ranks as the 17th worst road trip in team history. Over those 10 games, the Expos, Pirates and Mets combined to outscore the Phillies 53–23. Only twice in that stretch did Philadelphia manage to score more than three runs in a game. Clearly, the Phillies needed a lot of help in both the pitching and hitting departments. "They just didn't have much talent," Bill Lyon said. "They were equal opportunity [in pitching and hitting]. [Carlton] would have stood out on a good team even, but this made him all but unhittable and unbeatable. I think in a way, he was thought more highly of because that team around him was so bad. If he'd been playing for the '28 Yankees or the '76 Cincinnati Reds or something like that ... I don't know other players that would overshadow him, but they would get a greater share of the limelight. Whereas with the Phillies, with that team, it was Carlton and nobody else. Or a Carlton and a bunch of who-that's."[25]

After being swept by the Reds from June 2 to 4, the Phils fell into last place for good with a 16–28 record (a .364 winning percentage). Philadelphia general manager John Quinn was the first casualty of the Phillies' swoon, as he was dumped during that series in favor of Paul Owens, who was promoted from his position as farm director. "Obviously, when you get going in April, a lot of teams get off to good starts, some get off to slower starts," Luzinski said. "I mean, we didn't have the horses to go 162 games. Talent-levels, we ran into better ball clubs compared to ours."[26]

Outside of Carlton's 27 wins, no other Phillies pitcher had double-digit victories. Bucky Brandon finished second on the team in wins in '72 with a 7–7 record. From there, Wayne Twitchell had five wins, while Bill Champion, Woodie Fryman and Barry Lersch all finished with four. "That's a pretty big gap there," Don Money said, "but it was a magical year for Carlton."[27] All but six of Brandon's 42 games came in relief, and two of Brandon's wins were in relief of Carlton when Lefty picked up no-decisions. It's Brandon who has the distinction of being the last player before Lefty to wear number 32 on the back of his jersey. Brandon, while pitching for his fourth team in five years, wore 32 with the Phillies in 1971, then gave it up to Carlton for the 1972 season. There was no mention of whether Brandon received a case of beer, as John Kruk did from Mitch Williams in 1992 for trading number 28 to the "Wild Thing," but Philadelphia eventually retired number 32 at the end of Lefty's Hall of Fame career.

Bill Champion, who started in 22 of his 30 appearances, won his first three decisions, and then earned only one more win the rest of the way after May 5. After beginning the '72 season 3–0, Champion finished up 4–14 with a 5.09 earned run average. "Champion and Lersch came up through the system, so they were going to take their lumps because they were young kids," Bowa said. "But they were very serviceable."[28]

Fryman was 2–1 on May 15 following his 4–0 shutout of Fergie Jenkins and the Cubs, but then he went just 2–9 before the Detroit Tigers purchased him from the Phillies on August 2. Overall, Fryman was just 4–10 with a 4.36 ERA for the Phillies, including 17 starts. Ken Reynolds took the ball for 23 starts in 1972 and compiled a 2–15 record with a 4.26 ERA. "I was still so much a fan in those days that I wasn't a baseball guy," Chris Wheeler said. "I remember I went to spring training that year and I'm watching these guys throw on the side and I said, 'How can anybody hit them?' And then the season started and they got hit. So I didn't know. I was 26, 27 that year and I had no idea what I was watching, except that [Carlton's 72 season] was special and he was special."[29]

Out of the bullpen, Brandon and Selma (2–9, 5.56 ERA) led the Phils with 36 appearances apiece. After going 1–6 with a 5.27 ERA in 56 one-third innings in ten starts to begin the season, the 28-year-old Selma was 1–3, with a 5.95 ERA in 42 and one-third innings in relief the rest of the way. Unfortunately, he wasn't able to find the form that enabled him to save 22 games and post a 2.75 ERA for the Phils in 1970. Wayne Twitchell (5–9, 4.06), lefty Mac Scarce (1–2, 3.44), Barry Lersch (4–6, 3.04), Bill Wilson (1–1, 3.30), lefty Chris Short (1–1, 3.91), and lefty Joe Hoerner (0–2, 2.08) all made 15 or more relief appearances for the '72 Phillies. Twitchell earned three of his five wins after joining the starting rotation after the All-Star break in July. The Phillies' staff as a whole yielded 8.5 hits and 3.4 free passes per nine innings. Only the Montreal Expos (579) and San Diego Padres (618) allowed more total walks than the Phils' 536 in the NL. Only the Houston Astros (580), Padres (589), and Atlanta Braves (654) gave up more earned runs than the Phillies (571).

"You look at the roster the next couple of years, it was totally changed over," Greg Luzinski said. "So it was obvious that we weren't at the talent level that we should be and we built through the minor leagues, so a lot of guys were coming up within the next two or three years."[30] Indeed, of the Phillies' teams that won three straight NL East Division titles from 1976–78 and then the World Series in 1980, only shortstop Larry Bowa and left fielder Luzinski were regulars on the 1972 squad. Luzinski's .281 batting average led the Phillies in '72, but it wasn't enough. Philadelphia was ninth in the NL with 1,240 hits and just 98 home runs, and it was 11th out of 12 National League teams with only 42 stolen bases. Fielding-wise, the Phillies were in the bottom third of the National League with 116 errors and 381 double plays.

Hope, however, was on the way. Mike Schmidt, who replaced Don Money at the hot corner in '73 in the first full season of his Hall of Fame career, came up at the end of 1972 and batted .206 with one homer and three RBIs in 13 games. Also arriving was catcher Bob Boone, who accrued 51 at-bats in 16 games as a 24-year-old at the end of '72, then replaced John Bateman as the regular in 1973. Tim McCarver also caught 45 games for the Phillies in 1972, and was then traded to the Montreal Expos on June 14 for Bateman before returning to Philadelphia in 1975 and becoming Carlton's personal catcher. Exchanging McCarver for Bateman was Owens' first trade since succeeding Quinn as GM.

"The brain trust of Ruly Carpenter and Paul Owens and Dallas Green and Bill Giles certainly had that vision (to let the prospects play)," Boone said. "They let us all play. In those young years, we got beat up pretty good. It probably will never be done again. It was done in a real family way — throw them in and let them get good, and then we started getting good. Paul Owens made some tremendous acquisitions. We really changed when we got Garry

6 ♦ Tailspin Takes Over

Maddox, and then he added Ron Reed and Tug McGraw. We kept fiddling with the first basemen and then we finally got Pete Rose. It was really ten years in the making to build that World Series championship. And it was five years before we got good. We were in the playoffs where we were losing as far as not getting to the World Series. But it took about four or five years until we started getting good. Certainly, the Carlton trade was one of the great trades of all time."[31]

Larry Bowa, of course, was one of those who survived the Phillies' futility in the early 70s. "The only thing that was good about the early 70s," Bowa said, "was they told everybody we were going to rebuild and we've got a pretty good core group of guys that you're going to see some good teams coming up here, and eventually it did."[32]

Denny Doyle received the majority of starts at second base for the Phillies from 1970 to 1973 until Dave Cash took over for the next three seasons, arriving in Philadelphia in a trade with the Pittsburgh Pirates for Ken Brett. Willie Montanez moved from center field in 1972 to first base in '73, replacing Tommy Hutton, and Del Unser became the regular center fielder in 1973. Garry Maddox, nicknamed "The Secretary of Defense," came to Philadelphia on May 4, 1975, in a trade with the Giants for Montanez, and then spent the next nine seasons in Phillies pinstripes. Schmidt "came up at the end of that year," Chris Wheeler said. "Bowa was playing that year. So we had some good players, but they were young. Willie Montanez, I think, was there. They weren't ready yet and you could see that we had some talent, but it wasn't the type of team that could win consistently because we didn't have pitching. We had [only] one pitcher that was consistent."[33]

◆ 7 ◆

CARLTON SLUMPS

Even Carlton, though, was not without his bumps in the road during the 1972 season. Through his first six starts, Carlton was 5–1 with a 1.73 ERA. Things were going well for Lefty, and there was no indication that the Phils were headed for a 97-loss season. But as the Phillies began to fade in mid-May, Carlton fell into a funk of his own. From May 13 to June 3, Lefty went 0–5 with a no-decision and compiled an ERA of 4.78. Sparky Lyle, who was a teammate of Carlton's in 1980 and 1981 with the Phils, pitched for the New York Yankees in 1972. But even while toiling in a different league, he was surprised at Carlton's tough stretch. "I can't even imagine he had a five-game losing streak, honestly. He was that good," said Lyle, who had a tremendous season of his own in 1972, saving 35 games to equal the major league record and set a new American League mark.[1]

Lefty was certainly good in a couple of those losses, but suffered the hard-luck decisions. On May 13, Carlton allowed just two earned runs and struck out six in seven innings but lost, 3–1, to Claude Osteen and the Dodgers at Veterans Stadium. Osteen helped his own cause in that game with an RBI single in the fourth inning. Four days later, Carlton ran into more hard luck in a 3–2 loss to the Chicago Cubs. He allowed just three earned runs and struck out eight in a complete-game effort. Philadelphia led 2–1 after six innings, but the offense could not overcome Carmen Fanzone's solo homer in the seventh and Jose Cardenal's eventual game-winning RBI hit in the ninth. The Cubs mustered only six hits against Lefty, one of those a two-out base hit to center field by Rick Monday in the top of the fifth inning. But even though Monday batted .375 in 40 lifetime at-bats against Carlton, he never felt comfortable digging in at the plate against Lefty.

"That came as the biggest shock I've ever had," Monday said of his .375 average, "because truly, to this day, I did not enjoy going to home plate to hit against him. This shows you [his] dominance. I'm at second base and

Lefty is pitching and Larry Bowa comes up to me and he goes, 'You love hitting against him, don't you?' And I went, 'What are you, nuts? There's nobody outside of an asylum that would feel good about hitting against him.' And he goes, 'No, you're hitting really well against him career-wise.' And I went, 'I can't be.' He goes, 'No, you are. We looked at your numbers today.' I said, 'I don't care what the numbers show. I hate every second of it.' That's what the experience was like to face him, for a couple of reasons. One, he was extremely talented, obviously. But two, you could always see the competitive fire burning in him. I don't care if he was up 7–0; he was not going to let a run score. I don't care if it was a 5–4 game, I don't care if he was losing 7–0. It was the competitiveness that allowed him to win that many games with the club."[2]

In the next day's newspapers, even with the Cubs winning 3–2 to hand Carlton his second straight loss, Cardenal had high words of praise for Lefty. In the winning clubhouse, you might have expected Cardenal to be talking about Billy Williams' double to right-center to start the winning rally in the ninth inning or about his clutch, one-out single to center field as the Cubs quickly hurried for their flight out of town to St. Louis. Instead, the conversation was about the big left-hander who toed the rubber for the Phillies, and the trade for Rick Wise that brought him to Philadelphia. "To me, Steve Carlton is the best left-handed pitcher in the National League," Cardenal was quoted as saying. "To me, they [the Phillies] stole it. Rick Wise is a good pitcher but I never believe St. Louis trades Carlton for Wise man-for-man."

On May 21, the losing streak for Carlton reached three in a row when he fell to Tom Seaver and the New York Mets. "Tom Terrific" gave up three earned runs in seven innings, but the Phillies couldn't capitalize, losing 4–3 in front 57,267 fans, the largest baseball crowd ever in Philadelphia at that point. Pitching against Carlton certainly brought out the best in Seaver, just as it did for Ray Burris, who pitched for the Mets in the 1979 and '80 seasons after toiling for the Chicago Cubs for seven seasons. "I didn't dislike pitching against Carlton," Burris said. "To me, I felt in order for me to get good at this game, I had to go up against the best at that time, and he was one of the best at that time. He just came at you, he attacked you. He never threw the slider for a strike on a consistent basis and that's when he got guys swinging and missing. He threw his curveball for strikes and he was just a horse. Guys back in those days pitched for a long time. You think about Nolan Ryan pitching for 26 seasons and the amount of innings he pitched — 300 and some innings a year — that's a lot of innings. And guys took care of themselves better back then. But they also had a mental toughness and that's what Steve had."[3]

Willie Mays, who joined the Mets in a trade from San Francisco on May

12, had a lot to do with Seaver winning that late–May game, as he went 2-for-4 with a game-winning, two-run home run in the eighth inning to lift New York to the one-run win. Incidentally, that was one of only two home runs that "The Say Hey Kid" hit against Carlton in his career. Overall, he batted only .177 against Lefty all-time with 11 hits in 62 at-bats. Mays was in the twilight of his career by that point, but it was moments like his game-winning blast against Lefty that explained why the Mets brought him aboard. Hall of Famer Johnny Bench pointed out that Mays' presence in the New York clubhouse surely took a lot of pressure off of the younger players' shoulders, as well. "If young kids were trying to find their way, it really gives some kind of calmness to the clubhouse and they don't have to be the guy," Bench said of Mays, who finished with eight home runs and 19 RBIs for New York in 1972. "It takes the load and pressure off of them and what they're doing."[4]

Steve Carlton is shown connecting on a pitch against the New York Mets at Shea Stadium. Lefty had 23 hits and scored six runs for the Phillies during the 1972 season.

Carlton was trying to find his way out of a three-game losing streak when he faced Pittsburgh in his next start. Unfortunately, however, things did not get any easier, as he fell to .500 at 5–5 with a 6–4 loss to the Pittsburgh Pirates at Three Rivers Stadium on May 26. Gene Alley broke a 4–4 tie with an RBI single in the seventh and Dave Cash tripled in the eighth to extend his hitting streak to 19 games before scoring on Roberto Clemente's RBI single, as the Phillies lost their tenth game in a row. But in Carlton's defense, these were no patsies that he was facing. In fact, the 1972 Pirates finished first in the National League in hits (1,505), doubles (251) and triples (47), while placing third in total runs (691).

7 ♦ Carlton Slumps

Four days after that loss to the Pirates, Lefty had his shortest outing of the season, lasting just four and one-third innings while giving up six earned runs on eight hits and three walks in a 7–0 loss to the New York Mets. Rookie Jon Matlack tossed a three-hitter and Rusty Staub finished 4-for-4 with four RBIs to lead the Mets' offense. For the season, the Mets were the team that gave Lefty the most fits. Overall, he was 2–5 with a 3.54 ERA against New York in '72. Against the rest of the National League, Lefty did not lose more than one time to any team. But even through the end of that '72 campaign, Lefty was only 12–15 against the Mets in his career. Although the Mets were a team on the rise in 1972, they were not at the level of the Reds or Pirates in the National League, two teams against whom Lefty posted a winning record. "That's one of the things about baseball is there are some things for which there is no logic, no rationalization," Bill Lyon said. "No rhyme, no reason. Logic would have told you that he'd struggle against a really good team and then feast on the bad ones. I think it's been that way ever since they invented the game and I know it's still that way today."[5]

Lefty fires a strike against the New York Mets at Shea Stadium in Queens. The Mets were one of only two teams in the National League that Carlton did not have a winning record against during the '72 season.

Although the Mets finished third in the National League East that season with an 83–73 record, under skipper Yogi Berra, they did have talent on the pitching staff. Led by Seaver, who was 21–12 with a 2.92 ERA in 1972, the Mets had four pitchers, all under the age of 30, with double-digit wins. Matlack finished 15–10 with a 2.32 ERA, Koosman was 11–12 with a, 4.14 ERA, and Jim McAndrew went 11–8 with a 2.80 ERA. All four of those pitchers were also key factors in 1973 in helping to lead the Mets to a first-place finish in the National League East and the NL pennant, prior to losing to the Oakland Athletics in seven games in the World Series. "The Mets had great pitching in those days," Chris Wheeler said. "They were one year removed from the World Series in '73. So they had [Jerry] Koosman and they had Seaver and they had Gary Gentry and those people. They had tremendous pitching, so they would get in those low scoring games with them and they could beat you with their pitching."[6]

During this tough stretch, Lefty talked after a game about his concern for "lost rhythm," which was contributing to him allowing late-inning runs. In his four losses to the Cubs, Dodgers, Pirates and Mets, Lefty had yielded seven runs in the seventh inning or later. There was no question that Carlton wasn't the same pitcher that had started the season 5–1 with his new team. But Greg Luzinski said that whether you're a hitter or a pitcher, rhythm is an important part of your game. "He talks about throwing downhill a lot," Luzinski said. "He was like six-foot-six, so he was a big guy on the mound. It's like a hitter. If you don't have the right rhythm, you don't pick up the ball as well. His release point was probably a little different, which if you don't start making your pitches — in the big leagues, you've got to make pitches. If you don't make your pitches, you're going to find guys that hit them."[7]

With Carlton, the problem was that he was gripping the outside of the ball, which led to his wrist dropping off to the side and losing snap from pitches. He was quoted telling reporters, "I've had a lot of trouble staying on top of the ball and I've been making some bad pitches. My rhythm has been bad." To compensate for his struggles, Lefty unconsciously left a third finger creeping up on the ball, leading to him throwing a three-finger fastball. But with the help of Phillies pitching coach Ray Rippelmeyer, Lefty eventually made an adjustment in his delivery, dealt with some pitching fundamentals and righted the ship.

"I kind of equate it to golf," Marty Bystrom said. "You can't see yourself swing, you can't see yourself pitch. And it's very easy to develop some bad habits, and a lot of times you know what you're doing wrong, but you can't fix it. That's where a good pitching coach comes in handy when you have your bullpen session in between starts and you can work on things. But I think in his case, with his slider being his out pitch, he really had to keep the fingers on top of the ball, and if he gets down on the side a little bit, then it's just not going to have as sharp of a break. Sometimes it's just one of those things you go through during the season. I mean, God, he won 27 games that year out of 59 [team victories]. So it was crazy, what a great year."[8]

As adept as Carlton was at making adjustments, however, Larry Shenk said that he didn't immerse himself in the techniques of pitching. Shenk recalled that the Phillies brought Carlton back after his career to work with some of Philadelphia's minor league pitching prospects. Unfortunately, though, it did not produce the results they wanted. While there was certainly no one better to speak with the farmhands about focusing on the mound, Shenk said that Lefty is not a technical baseball person. "He had a great arm and a great slider and a great fastball and he was a great competitor — just like Ted Williams was an awesome hitter," Shenk said. "But Williams knew hitting. He had hitting theories. Lefty doesn't have pitching theories. Somebody said, 'How do you throw your slider?' He said, 'You hold it like this and throw the shit out of it.' The only other description I heard is that you take it like this (gripping the ball) and then you throw it like you're pulling down a blind. I think I was in the presence of Dick Ruthven one time and he said, 'How do you throw that slider?' [Carlton said], 'You take it like this and throw the shit out of it.'"[9] Bystrom was not in the presence of Carlton, Ruthven and Shenk at that time, but had also heard Lefty's explanation for throwing that fearsome slider. "That's what he used to say," Bystrom said. "But I think he had really good mechanics. And good mechanics produce consistently throwing strikes and throwing the ball where you want to throw it. So maybe he didn't focus on those — really when you're on the mound, you're not focusing on your mechanics. You're focused on your target and you're just letting it go. So I wouldn't say that he had terrible mechanics. He was pretty smooth."[10]

Indeed, Wayne Twitchell said that when Lefty was in rhythm, it was like watching a machine run. A native of Portland, Oregon Twitchell compared current Phillies star pitcher Cliff Lee to Carlton. With Lee pitching in the Pacific Northwest with the Seattle Mariners in the first half of the 2010 season, Twitchell watched many of his starts. Similarly to Lee's style, Twitchell noted that Carlton's motion was the same every time and that he looked machine-like. "That's the best description I can give you," Twitchell said. "He was just mechanical, everything was perfect. It was like watching pistons and an engine or something, basically. It was repetitive. Same motion, same thing over and over and over and over, where not all pitchers can do that."[11]

But the frustration for Carlton to find that machine-like rhythm continued in his next start against the Cincinnati Reds on June 3. Philadelphia took a 5–0 lead through three innings on Tommy Hutton's home run and Larry Bowa's two-run triple. But the Reds rallied from behind and eventually won 6–5 on Julian Javier's tenth inning single. Ken Reynolds suffered the loss for the Phillies and Lefty took a no-decision. Johnny Bench's 13th home run of the season, leading off in the top of the seventh inning against Carlton, not only helped the Reds get started on their comeback, but it put his name in the record books. With seven dingers in five games, Bench tied an NL record set by the St. Louis Cardinals' Jim Bottomley in 1929. "I remember the seven home runs in five games because Vin Scully said, 'Well, he did it again,'" Bench smiled. "So that was one of my great memories, that Vin Scully was actually talking about me on the radio. But I got three off of [Carlton] twice, and his wife even yelled and told me to leave him alone one time."[12]

The first of those occasions that Bench hit three against Carlton came on July 26, 1970, as the Reds hammered Lefty and the Redbirds, 12–5. Then he did it again on May 9, 1973, in Cincinnati's 9–7 victory over the Phils at the Vet. Bench also happened to achieve a major milestone against Lefty on May 4, 1983, when he collected his 2,000th career hit in a 9–4 Cincinnati loss. He "couldn't get Bench out," Larry Shenk said. "He had trouble with him."[13] Talking about Bench's success against Lefty, Bowa recalled conversations that he had with some of the Reds' players regarding that topic, including shortstop Dave Concepcion. "The only guy I remember that hit him was Bench," Bowa added. "Johnny Bench used to own him. He would go back and look at the home runs that he hit off of him. I remember a lot of times talking to guys on that team [like] Dave Concepcion when he came up. [Bench] said he saw something in Carlton that he knew almost every pitch that was coming. The other guys on Cincinnati would say, 'Well, tell us.' And he said, 'It's just something I see.' Even Steve would be the first to tell you. He never gave hitters credit, but he'd say if you talk to him now that Bench wore him out."[14]

For his career, Bench batted .298 against Lefty, going 37-for-124 overall. Although Carlton struck out Bench 20 times, the Reds' slugger belted 12 home runs and seven doubles against the Phillies' ace. Nobody hit more home runs against Lefty than Bench, with Gary Carter hitting just one fewer (11). "It was just one of those guys that would give you trouble," said Reds pitcher Ross Grimsley, who pitched in Cincinnati from 1971–73 before going on to Baltimore, Montreal, and Cleveland. "That's just like you look at Mark Belanger hit well against a lot of the better pitchers. I don't know if the pitchers let up on them some, I doubt it. People ask me, 'Who was the hardest hitter to get out?' And I go, 'Well, pick a team,' because every team had somebody that I had trouble with. It was just a matter of not letting those guys beat you."[15]

The Reds, though, did beat the Phillies in that June matchup. And just a few hours before Carlton's winless streak was stretched to six straight starts, the Phillies terminated Quinn's run as the general manager. The 64-year-old Quinn, who was hired to the post in 1959, learned of his fate during lunch at owner Bob Carpenter's house in Delaware. Quinn came to Philly with an impressive resume, having led the Boston Braves to the pennant in 1948 and then the Milwaukee Braves to a World Series championship in 1957 and another NL pennant the following year in. After being lured to Philadelphia in January of 1959, Quinn assembled Phillies' rosters that posted six straight winning seasons from 1962 to 1967 with a combined record of 514–456, but they never reached the Fall Classic in his tenure. He would remember the 1964 season as being the biggest disappointment, as the Phillies collapsed after building a lead of six and a half games with just 12 left to play.

In the end, as the Phillies began to struggle after their fast start and it became evident that they did not have the horses, the fact that Quinn was unable to improve a last-place team with a trade at the winter meetings in Phoenix likely put him on thin ice. Quinn was coming under fire in recent months, and the day after the Phillies' general manager was relieved of his duties, *Inquirer* columnist Frank Dolson wrote, "It was clearly time for a change. And, finally, grudgingly, painfully, Bob Carpenter made one Saturday morning." Dolson penned that the long-suffering baseball fans in Philadelphia, along with the young players and their manager, deserved more than Quinn was able to bring them during recent seasons. Plus, Quinn certainly did not help his cause with an ill-timed phone call to Frank Lucchesi in which he blasted utility player Ron Stone following a loss at Veterans Stadium. Reporters were seated nearby Lucchesi and could hear the general manager shouting into the telephone, "That SOB Stone don't belong here. That SOB can't play Triple-A..."

But according to Keidan's story in the June 4 issue of the *Inquirer*, Quinn was a model of decorum on his way out the door, saying, "My only regret is that I haven't been able to produce a pennant-winner for two fine gentlemen — Bob [Carpenter] and his son Rudy ... I think we have great potential, both here and in the farm system."

With the team going bad, many might have thought that Lucchesi would hit the unemployment line before Quinn did. But it did not turn out that way. As Keidan wrote in a column, Quinn had lost the ability to function with the cool objectivity of a modern GM and placed too much value on questionable talent. Lucchesi, meanwhile, was a cool operator with the press. He was open, friendly, and accessible, earning him the reputation of a media darling. "I don't think it was unusual (to replace Quinn before Lucchesi)," Larry Shenk said. "Paul Owens came in, what, '65? He was the heir apparent and the Carpenters just decided to make the move then ... We were in the new ballpark, attendance the first year was great here at the Vet, but then the performance was not great. And Paul Owens was a guy that believed in player development and scouting and that was the direction that they went because that's what produced the '50 team too — player development."[16]

Certainly, Lucchesi needed no introduction to his new boss, Owens, with whom he roomed in the late fifties in spring training in Clearwater. Owens, was still unaware of the change when he pulled into his parking spot at Veterans Stadium before the Phillies' game against the Reds that day. He finally learned of the news when Bob Carpenter caught him on the telephone a short time later. Eventually, the move became public when it was announced during a press conference in the tenth inning of the Phillies' loss.

In general, fans that had become frustrated with Philadelphia's downward spiral welcomed the general manager shuffle. Owens, however, was not exactly a household name yet among the Phillies' faithful, or with a CBS Network analyst who referred to him as "farm director Jim Owens." Inside the industry, however, baseball men had the highest of respect for Owens, who climbed the ladder from being a first baseman who had signed with the St. Louis Cardinals in 1951, to becoming a player-manager, to joining the scouting ranks, to taking over as the Phillies' farm director. While serving in that latest role for six years, he produced such major leaguers as Larry Bowa and Greg Luzinski and Denny Doyle. But taking over as the general manager of the last-place Phillies had to be his toughest task to date.

One thing that Owens had going for him, however, was that he had the league's best pitcher on his roster. And in Carlton's next start, he began a streak in which he reeled off an incredible 15 straight wins.

♦ 8 ♦

DESPERATE TIMES

In 1972, the Phillies were just 13–31 against left-handed pitchers, but Carlton had six of those victories for the team. One of those came against Jerry Reuss and the Houston Astros on June 7. With Philadelphia riding a nine-game losing skid, Carlton matched up against his former teammate and became the Phillies' stopper, pitching the home team to a 3–1 win in front of just 10,712 fans at the Vet. Lefty lost the shutout on Jimmy Stewart's RBI single in the seventh inning, but that was one of the few blemishes on a night when Carlton struck out 11 while scattering five hits and three walks in seven innings. In front of their home fans, the Phillies were just 28–51 in 1972, and Carlton's win over Reuss was their first one at Broad Street and Pattison Avenues since May 15.

Just one day earlier, the Phillies used their first pick, and the third overall in the Major League Baseball annual draft, on a right-handed pitcher that Philadelphia fans would come to know well in the seventies and early eighties — Larry Christenson. The six-foot-four hurler had dazzling numbers at Marysville (Washington) High School that season. In addition to posting a 0.28 earned run average, he struck out 143 batters in 72 innings, with just 12 walks, while mainly throwing a fastball. But while Philadelphia was hoping that Christenson would breathe some life into its franchise in future seasons, the Phillies, behind president Bill Giles, reached into their bag of tricks that same day to try to breathe some life into their current fortunes. Perhaps taking their cue from the players who had their own superstitious rituals, the Phillies broke away from the norm on "Turn Around Night" to try to reverse a skid that saw them lose 18 of 19 games going into their battle against the Astros. Their unusual stunts included holding the traditional seventh-inning stretch in the third inning. "Phanavision" recognized fans not celebrating birthdays and it welcomed groups not in attendance. Only 8,237 fans showed up for the game, but those who did were greeted by ushers wearing their caps backward with their identification badges attached to their backs. Spectators had to arrive at the ballpark even earlier than usual to hear the National Anthem played, the Phillies' lineup was announced in reverse order and the players ran onto the field opposite of their normal routine. Just for good measure, the Phillies also played "Goodnight Sweetheart" before the game and not after the last out. Unfortunately, however, none of the stunts worked, as the Phillies still lost, 4–3, to the Astros.

But what the crazy ideas could not accomplish, Carlton did, pitching the Phillies to a rare victory on the following evening. After stranding 48 runners on base in Carlton's previous six starts, the Phillies snapped their slide against Jerry Reuss and the Astros despite being outhit 6–5. Philadelphia scored all three of its runs in the bottom of the sixth against Reuss. Luzinski's two-run double was the key blow, driving in Larry Bowa and Don Money to break a scoreless tie and give Carlton all the support he needed.

Bowa led the club with 67 runs scored in 1972, but it was with the glove that he was already establishing himself as one of the league's top shortstops in his first two seasons. Bowa easily could have won the National League's Gold Glove at that position in 1971 after committing only nine errors in 715 total chances. Instead, the award went to the New York Mets' Bud Harrelson, who had five more errors in 20 fewer chances. It was at the plate where the Phillies' scrappy 1965 free agent signee looked to improve his game. At a mere 158 pounds, Bowa was the smallest player in spring training camp. He did not look like a 26-year old big league baseball player. Rather, Bowa looked more like a Little Leaguer, as evidenced when a security guard stopped him on the opening day of the 1970 season, perhaps thinking he was an autograph seeker headed to the Phils' clubhouse. Even opponents treated him like a Little Leaguer, bringing their outfielders in to shallow depth with Bowa at the plate. Still, Bowa led Philadelphia with 162 hits in 1971 and batted .250 in his first two seasons on his way to a career that saw him produce 2,191 hits in 16 seasons. He still ranks sixth in Phillies franchise history with 1,798 hits.

"When I first signed, it was good glove, could run, and if he could hit .230, that would be great," Bowa said. "But I learned how to hit. If someone would have told me when I first came up that you're going to get over 2,000 hits in the big leagues, I would have laughed because as much as I worked, that's a lot of hits. Billy DeMars was our hitting coach and he really helped me out more than anybody in baseball. It was just hard work and determination and stick-to-itiveness and reading negative articles and people saying, 'He can do this, he can't do that,' and trying to turn them around. I didn't get drafted, I signed as a free agent. But I try to tell kids that if you want something bad enough and you have some kind of ability, you can attain any kind of goal you want."[1]

Bowa's goal in '72, while still learning how to become a good hitter, was to be more selective at the plate and increase his walks total out of the leadoff hole from the 36 he had in 1971 in 650 at-bats. That, in turn, would also allow him to steal more bases after swiping 28 a year earlier. Bowa certainly did a lot of good things that season, such as compiling a team-high 12-game hitting streak. He also broke up a no-hit bid by Jerry Reuss on June 18, smashing a leadoff double into the left-field corner in the top of the ninth at the Astrodome. It was one of only three hard-hit balls off Reuss, who went on to post a 10–0 victory. And Bowa set a National League record with five triples in an eight-game span in June. But the Phillies' fiery shortstop mentioned in spring training that he felt like he had to score at least 100 runs to help the Phillies finish with a .500 record or better. Unfortunately for Bowa and the Phillies, it didn't happen. The Phillies' leadoff batter actually fell 33 runs short of that goal, but that probably had as much to do with the fact that the Phillies were a last-place team and did not score a lot of runs, period.

"We weren't very good," Bowa acknowledged. "We weren't very disciplined at the plate. When you first come up, it's different. You get all the hype and the hoopla before you get there and everything, but until you go through a couple of seasons and get close to 1,500 or 2,000 at-bats, it's a constant adjustment period. Trial and error, making adjustments every at-bat, facing tough pitching every night. In the minor leagues, you didn't face good pitching every single night. But you go into New York and you get Seaver and Koosman and Matlack and Gentry and guys like that. It was every night you had to battle. It was tough."[2]

Bowa, a switch-hitter, was batting .333 the first week. But then he dropped off to .246 at the end of the first month while battling a pulled muscle in his right leg. Unfortunately, he struggled to hit the ball to the opposite field and was never able to really recover, as he ended the season hitting .250 in 150 games. Bowa swatted a career-high 13 triples, but saw his numbers drop in walks (32) and stolen bases (17). "I don't think you're ever happy with a season," Bowa said. "I think I could see things happening that were coming around. I learned how to switch-hit, really, at Triple-A. I was all right-handed and Bob Skinner, who was the manager in Philly, told me one spring, 'You can be a utility man the rest of your career if you want to hit just right-handed or you can go down to Triple-A and learn how to switch-hit and be an every day player.' I wanted to play everyday, so I went down and learned how to switch-hit."[3]

A little lower in the batting order, Greg Luzinski wasn't a switch-hitter, but instead a feared power hitter from the right side of the plate. And in his first full season in the big leagues, he put up solid numbers with 18 home runs and 68 RBIs. Compared to the first full big-league seasons of some of the best-known sluggers in the game, the Bull was in good company. In comparison to those with at least 300 at-bats, Luzinski smashed more home runs than Hank Aaron (13), Johnny Bench (15), Yogi Berra (14), Jimmie Foxx (13), Hank Greenberg (12), Gil Hodges (11), Al Kaline (4), Mickey Mantle (13), Stan Musial (10), Babe Ruth (11), Al Simmons (8), Willie Stargell (11), Hack Wilson (10), and Carl Yastrzemski (11), and he equaled Willie McCovey and Mel Ott, who both hit 18.

"It was shortened obviously by the strike," Luzinski said of his rookie season. "The numbers might not have been what they have should have been. But it was my first year. I improved after that. I was just getting my feet wet for the first time for a full year. Plus I was learning how to play left field in the big leagues. I never got back to first base where I started out."[4]

On Thursday, June 8, Luzinski picked up his team-leading 23rd RBI of the season with a 2-for-3 night at the plate while helping the Phillies knock off the Houston Astros, 7–2. The next day, the *Philadelphia Inquirer* couldn't help itself, invoking some sarcasm in its headline, "Phils Push Win Streak All the Way to 2." Thanks to six innings of solid work from Bill Champion, the Phillies not only earned a series win over the Astros, but they won back-to-back games for the first time in more than a month.

Luzinski actually was one of the few players in Lucchesi's lineup that was not platooning at that point. The others were Bowa and Don Money, partly because the Phillies did not have any other third basemen. Terry Harmon and Denny Doyle were sharing time at second base. Also platooning were Tim McCarver and Mike Ryan behind the plate, Tommy Hutton and Pete Koegel at first base due to Deron Johnson's injury, and Roger Freed and Oscar Gamble in right field, with Mike Anderson struggling. Willie Montanez, too, endured a sophomore slump after a tremendous rookie season and began platooning with By Browne in center field. At one point, Montanez was benched for not hustling. In a 17-inning, 6–3 loss to the Reds on June 2, Montanez failed to slide in a crucial play at the plate. And while batting just .217 in early June, the Philadelphia boo-birds were giving the likeable Montanez an earful. "They did (boo me), but remember, that was in Philadelphia," Montanez said. "They booed Santa Claus one time over there. I wasn't doing a good job. I hit 30 home runs (in '71) and the next year I hit 13, so that was a big drop. It was part of the game. But they did like me after I started hitting the ball. They were on my side again."[5]

Despite the treatment he received from the Philly fans, Montanez did not use the boo-birds as an excuse for his struggles. Although he acknowledged that he heard the fans, he tried not to let it affect his play between the white lines. Instead, he continued to try to find the form that enabled him to set the Phillies' rookie record for home runs in a single season. "If you start thinking about that, you dig your own self a hole," Montanez said. "Yeah sure, I ain't going to say that it didn't bother me and all that ... but baseball is difficult enough to play without having to worry about those things. It's not an easy game. You'd better get a base hit. If you don't get it, get back into that dugout quick. But if you concentrate too much on that booing, that's not good."[6]

With Deron Johnson hobbled and headed for the disabled list from June 15 to July 1, it wasn't a stretch to figure that Montanez and others were putting more pressure on themselves to pick up the slack. Johnson was one of the few veterans on the team, so he was a natural leader for the squad. Without him in the lineup, the Phillies had an obvious void. "They were young guys," Larry Shenk said. "Luzinski was young. Montanez was young. Anderson was young. Even in '76, Paul Owens went out and got Dick Allen because the Bull and Schmitty were still young in terms of experience in the middle of the lineup. But we didn't have that kind of leadership, or veteran, in '72. Deron was. He was a good role model. Luzinski and Johnson were very close too.... The veteran guy that they all looked up to was Deron Johnson. He took Bull under his wing, telling him, 'This is how you behave in the big leagues,' and he was a nice man."[7] Larry Bowa agreed that Johnson was a tremendous help for the younger players on the squad. "When you have a couple veterans and those are the guys that you rely on in your offense and then one of them goes out, it puts a little more pressure on the younger guys," Bowa said. "No question about that. Those guys helped a lot of us guys out, just teaching us how to act at the big league level and just handling your business the way you're supposed to handle it. We had some good older guys. Deron Johnson, who was an unbelievable guy to have on your team, helped the young guys a lot."[8]

Montanez's slumps in '72 aside, however, he was a colorful personality and a popular player in Philadelphia. He was known to flip his bat and do other stunts on the field. "That was the way I played," Montanez said. "I wasn't trying to show anybody up or anything like that. That was my style of playing."[9] While some might have felt that Montanez was a bit of a hot dog, others knew that it was just his way of having fun and enjoying the game. "I remember we had a picture of him playing first base and he's got his glove over by the guy's belt, like he's holding onto the belt," Shenk said. "He's left-handed, the base runner's off the base, and I think he had his fingers in the guy's belt and you could see it. He was a crazy character — a good fun-loving guy."[10]

Unfortunately for Montanez and the Phillies, however, the 1972 season was not too much fun. The Phillies' hopes in 1972 hinged in large part on their young, but talented threesome of Luzinski, Montanez, and Anderson in the outfield. Luzinski, though, was the only one who lived up to the billing. Montanez never really got on track and Anderson spent the majority of the 1972 season at Triple-A Eugene in the Pacific Coast League. "It's funny," Shenk said, "because baseball people thought that Denny Doyle was going to be a star and Larry Bowa may never make it. And Mike Anderson would be a star because he was a multi-talented athlete and Bull was just a pure power hitter. And it went the other way."[11]

The Bull certainly had a lot of people speaking highly of him in 1971 during a season with the Eugene Emeralds in which he batted .312 with 36 home runs and 114 RBIs while playing first base to earn a promotion to the big leagues. But when Philadelphia failed to trade its first baseman, Johnson, in the off-season, Luzinski suddenly found himself trying to learn a new position. Although Luzinski was a confident man, he wasn't without his anxieties about moving to left field. Early in spring training, when Frank Lucchesi asked to speak to his budding star in his office about switching positions, the Bull showed up holding a bushel basket. In the Phils' Grapefruit League opener against the Boston Red Sox, however, Luzinski did not need that bushel basket. He did just fine with his Rawlings glove despite a bright sun and high sky, making a sliding catch on John Kennedy's line drive and then throwing out fleet-footed Reggie Smith at the plate following a bloop single by Cecil Cooper.

As a matter of fact, if the Bull had concerns about playing left field, it didn't show at the plate either. Luzinski finished the spring batting a sizzling .429 with two long balls and then carried that into his first full season. Even in May, as Philadelphia was dropping like a rock in the National League East standings, the Bull was putting up impressive stats with six home runs and 17 RBIs and a .295 batting average. Those were the kinds of numbers that the Phillies were hoping Luzinski would produce when they made him their number one selection in the June 1968 free-agent draft. But Philadelphia fans had to endure some nervous times as they waited for him to choose between signing with them or signing with one of more than 50 universities who wanted him to play college football. Growing up at Notre Dame High School in a suburb of Chicago, Illinois Luzinski had earned All-State honors not only in football as a linebacker and fullback, but also in baseball as a first baseman/outfielder. But in the end, the Bull told University of Southern

California football coach John McKay and his other college football suitors that he was going to play professional baseball.

"[Bull] was built like a lineman and had a lot of power," Bill Lyon said. "He had a very short, compact stroke. It's like, the most dangerous punch in boxing, they say, is the one from about six inches away. That applied to him with a baseball bat—nice, short, crisp, and compact. And as a result, the shorter the swing like that, then the less likely you were to go into a horrific slump. There are fewer things that can go wrong. A perfect example of that now on the Phillies is their second baseman [Chase Utley]."[12]

Carlton and Luzinski were two of the Phils' few bright spots, as the Bull was not only showing some pop, but also hitting consistently despite no one getting on base in front of him. Like the Bull, Mike Anderson was also a hot-shot prospect going into the 1972 season. Although he was overshadowed by Luzinski, the quiet 20-year-old brought impressive credentials of his own to the table, with a .334 average and 36 home runs at Eugene in 1971. Anderson struggled in 26 games after being called up to the majors in September, but he acknowledged later that he was nervous. He felt like the jitters were out of the way for his rookie year in '72, which was good news for the Phils, who were counting on him to play the bulk of games in right field.

In one of their final games of spring training, Anderson received a scare when he was drilled in the left ear with a fastball from Cincinnati's Clay Carroll, and was taken off the field on a stretcher and rushed to the hospital. However, he was in the starting lineup batting seventh when the Phillies opened their season against the Cubs at Wrigley Field on April 15, and he went 2-for-4 against Fergie Jenkins and two relievers. But he finished with just six more hits for the rest of April and ended the month hitting just .167. His struggles with the low outside pitch continued in May, in addition to a strong, but inaccurate arm in right field, and he began losing playing time to Roger Freed and Ron Stone. Anderson, a prospect with all of the tools who was dubbed a "can't-miss" player by Owens, did miss in '72 and was eventually optioned to Triple-A Eugene on June 2. "Anderson never made it. Mike got beaned in spring training and never was the same after that," Larry Shenk said. "That was scary. But Mike had a lot of tools."[13]

Anderson finished that season batting just .194 in 103 at-bats in Philadelphia and accumulated the majority of his at-bats (309) at Triple-A. Roger Freed, a major disappointment in '71, received the majority of starts in right field for the Phillies in 1972, batting .225 in 73 games. Anderson came back to hit .254 from 1973 to 1975 for the Phillies, with a career-high 145 games played in 1974. But he never blossomed into the superstar that Philadelphia had envisioned.

In Montanez, despite his struggles at the plate in '72, the Phillies still had one of the National League's most talented center fielders with his speed and athleticism. The fact that Montanez became a decent outfielder was a credit to his athletic abilities. His natural position was actually first base. But with the Phillies having an over-abundance of first baseman, he received a taste of right field after being called up in September of 1970 and then continued to play that position in winter ball in his native Puerto Rico. Making the transition from first base to the outfield was just the start of problems, however. It also exacted a physical toll. After breaking his leg in 1969, it was no easy chore patrolling center field on the hard turf at Veterans Stadium. "That was painful playing center field on artificial grass," Montanez said. "It was rough. But I had to make a living, so I went out there. I played with my ankles taped over my whole career."[14]

Montanez appeared well on his way to making a good living after a tremendous showing in his first full year in the majors. Unfortunately for the Phillies, however, Montanez never came close during the '72 season to duplicating his offensive numbers from '71, when he finished second only to Earl Williams of the Atlanta Braves in Rookie of the Year voting. After a putting up a season in which he hit 30 home runs with 99 RBIs, Montanez might have figured to have a little leverage with his contract going into the next season. The Phillies' second-year star, who made barely more than the major league minimum of $13,500 in his rookie year, was looking for a contract worth $30,000, while Quinn was offering $25,000. Eventually, after Montanez held out for a week or so in spring training, the two sides settled in the middle at $27,500. "Montanez was an under rated player," Bruce Keidan said. "He was colorful and sometimes that overshadowed the fact that he was really a fine player."[15]

Although Montanez was late arriving in Clearwater, he played winter ball in his native Puerto Rico in the off-season, which helped prevent some rust. He had a decent April average-wise, batting .276 with five runs scored out of the third spot in the order behind Bowa and McCarver, but he had just one RBI and no home runs. Montanez finally hit his first long ball on the first day of May against Claude Osteen in a 2–1 Phillies win, but he batted just .218 during the month (22-for-101) to drop his average to .236. Opposing pitchers exposed a weakness in Montanez by throwing him soft breaking pitches, and the Phillies' center fielder finished the season hitting just .247 with 13 home runs and 64 RBIs in 596 plate appearances.

"The pitchers got used to you," Montanez said. "There were a lot of smart people in the league and [the pitchers] changed their pattern on me. They changed the way they pitched to me. They threw more breaking balls and stayed away more and I had to learn to hit the ball to left with a line on it. I became a better hitter that way. At first, they challenged me. The first year around, they challenged to see what he got. And then I had to make adjustments. In '72 and '73, I had to make that adjustment to the way they were pitching to me."[16]

Montanez did make the necessary adjustments in 1974 while hitting .304 after returning to first base. He also hit .286 in 20 games for Philadelphia in 1975 before being shipped to San Francisco in May for Garry Maddox. Although he hit just 33 more long balls for the Phillies after his brilliant 30-home run rookie season, he obviously still had value with other teams around the league. The Phillies capitalized on that when they acquired one of their key pieces to the 1980 World Series championship in exchange for Montanez.

Bill Champion was traded from the Phillies at the end of the 1972 season, but not before lifting Philadelphia to its series win over the Astros in early June. Then Chris Short's one-pitch win in relief of Ken Reynolds and Barry Lersch, a 4–3 conquest of Atlanta, successfully opened a series against the Braves. Atlanta responded with a 15–3 drubbing one night later to snap the Phils' modest three-game winning streak. But Carlton took the ball on June 11 and took care of business, giving Philadelphia its second straight series win with a 3–1 complete-game victory over future teammate Ron Reed. Atlanta's two-hole hitter Ralph Garr and cleanup man Rico Carty were the Braves' only two batters in the starting nine who were hitting over .300 entering the game. But Garr took an 0-for-4 collar while starting in right field to drop his average to .299.

For his career, however, Garr was a terrific .375 lifetime hitter against Lefty, collecting 21 hits in 56 at-bats. But like many other left-handed hitters, he wasn't fond of stepping into the batter's box against Carlton. Garr, who was traded from the Braves to the Chicago White Sox in 1975, made that perfectly clear several years later during a spring training game in Clearwater, Florida. Jerry Martin, a teammate of Lefty's from 1974 to 1978, recalled a humorous incident involving Garr when the White Sox traveled to Jack Russell Stadium for the second time in the spring. As an established superstar, Lefty never made any bus trips to pitch on the road, and had already pitched against the White Sox in their first visit to Clearwater. Prior to their second game, Garr walked past several Phillies players sitting in folding chairs and started up a conversation.

He "was a real good player and one of the funniest guys I've ever been around in the game," Martin said. "No left-hander really liked facing Lefty, but 'Gator' didn't like facing him either, and I don't blame him. The White Sox just took the field to hit, and here comes 'Gator' walking up and we knew what he was going to ask. He said, 'Hey man, how are you guys doing today?' We said, 'Alright, 'Gator.' How are you doing?' He said, 'Man, who's toeing the rubber today?' He was walking along and somebody said, 'Lefty,' and he froze. He said, 'Man, that guy don't make any road trips. I came all the way over here for this?' He just started walking out in center field shaking his head. That was funny, man. We knew what he was going to ask and it just so happened Lefty was pitching again."[17]

On that June day in 1972, Lefty certainly brought his good stuff to the mound against the Braves. There were 32,468 fans who came to the Vet wondering if Hammerin' Hank Aaron could add to his home run total. In the Braves' rout one night earlier, Aaron clubbed a sixth-inning grand slam for his 649th career home run, moving him ahead of Willie Mays on the all-time home run list. His 14th career grand slam also tied him with Gil Hodges for the National League record. But Carlton held Aaron to a harmless 1-for-4 night while striking out nine and allowing just one run on eight hits and one walk. Amazingly, Lefty went 19–8 in '72 when his turn came up in the rotation after a Phillies loss.

"I can't remember that something turned the corner (when Carlton was 5–6), except all I remember was that he just started to win games and pitch complete games one after another," Chris Wheeler said. "Our team was going this way (lowering his hand) and he was going this way (raising his hand). It was like two ships in the night. And yet the team was going so bad and he would keep winning. Of all the guys I've been around, other than (Pete) Rose, he had the most incredible concentration powers I've ever seen. He didn't talk to you before the game. That was back when he talked to the media.... He didn't talk. I mean, he'd say 'It's win day, boys. It's win night, boys.' That was all he'd say and you just left him alone. But he was all business. All business."[18]

'Win day,' in fact, became a familiar saying for the Phils on days that Carlton pitched throughout his entire career. Carlton used the phrase. And his teammates used it. In fact, Larry Shenk said that it might have been Larry Bowa who started the 'win day' refrain. "After he rattled off so many games, I said, 'Today is win day,'" Bowa acknowledged. "But he would come in and he goes, 'You guys know what the job at hand is.' And he would find any way to get it done. It didn't matter if we lost eight in a row before that. We really felt we could win when he took the mound. Everyone thinks that he wasn't that good in the clubhouse and all. He was great in the clubhouse. But the days he pitched, you just stayed away from him. He was in a zone and didn't really want to be talking to people or anything. But after the days he pitched, and leading up to the days he pitched, he was great in the clubhouse."[19]

That customary "win day" saying was long established by the time Gary Matthews came to the Phillies on March 25, 1981, in a trade with the Atlanta

Braves for Bob Walk. Carlton and Matthews were teammates for three full seasons in Philadelphia, and "win day" remained en vogue throughout Sarge's tenure there. Years later, after Matthews joined the Phillies' broadcast crew, he still recalled the positive vibes in the clubhouse on the days that Lefty pitched. "Every time he pitched on his outing, you won," Matthews said. "That year they lost 97 games, he won 27. He was a Cy Young Award winner, so obviously they got used to that. So when I came over, we continued. We felt that every time he was on the mound, we were going to win. So we just called it 'win day,' but that was there before I got there. They had some bad teams back then."[20]

June 16 against the Astros in Houston was not a win day for Carlton, but Lefty certainly did all he could. Carlton shut down a Houston lineup that included Lee May, Bob Watson, and Jim Wynn, pitching ten scoreless innings on six hits while striking out 12. Only two Houston base runners advanced as far as second base, until the ninth inning. But Carlton's efforts only led to frustration as he received no offensive support. "You had trouble seeing his slider because it was so tight," Bob Boone said. "There was no arc in it. It got to the plate and then broke, and he had tremendous command of it. He had tremendous command of all his pitches. He concentration, his toughness were what made him so great. He had phenomenal ability [to adjust]. If he made a mistake with a pitch, he'd correct it with the next pitch."[21]

Meanwhile, Philadelphia's offense, led by John Bateman (3-for-5), Larry Bowa (2-for-4), and Tommy Hutton (2-for-4), managed 13 hits against Houston's Don Wilson and Tom Griffin. But they stranded 13 runners on base and the score remained 0–0 after ten innings. Finally, Wynn's home run against Dick Selma leading off the bottom of the 11th inning lifted the Astros to a 1–0 win in a game played in two hours and 51 minutes. "It was probably a multitude of things (causing the Phillies' struggles in 1972)," Wayne Twitchell said. "But I do remember in '72 and '73 and even into '74, we didn't score runs in bunches. We were nothing like the Phillies were (in 2008 and 2009)."[22]

Remarkably, the Houston game was the first of three times in '72 where Carlton pitched into extra innings. He only won one of those, beating the Padres, 3–2, in San Diego in 11 innings on July 19. Lefty also threw all 11 innings in a 2–1 loss to Phil Niekro and the Atlanta Braves on August 21, snapping Carlton's 15-game win streak. One might have thought that Carlton would have grown frustrated with the Phillies' ineptitude in 1972. But Luzinski didn't believe that to be true. "I think he probably knew through conversations with Paul Owens, who did a lot of background work and behind-the-scenes work for John Quinn before taking over, that we were on the upswing and there was help coming through the minor league system and through key trades and that we'd soon be better," Luzinski said. "Obviously, our team, until we got to 1980, was built from the inside, with valuable assets coming from the outside. But basically, it was all farm players, people that went through Reading."[23]

Larry Bowa said Lefty's focus was just on pitching every fourth day and controlling only the things that he could control. "That's one thing," Bowa said, "he never let things that he had no control over affect the way he pitched. He had no control over how young we were or what we were going to do. He just went out there every fourth day and did his job."[24]

His 346 total innings pitched in 1972 were tops in the National League, easily ahead of the next two closest pitchers. The Cubs' Fergie Jenkins was second with 289 and one-third innings and the Braves' Phil Niekro finished third with 282 one-third innings. The Chicago White Sox's Wilbur Wood led the Major Leagues with 376 two-thirds innings pitched. "The one thing about Steve was, usually if he started it, he was going to finish it," Bowa said. "He probably cracks up at these quality starts, that people say, 'He led the league in quality starts.' It's a joke, really."[25] The fact that the Phillies did not have a very good bullpen in 1972 was also a factor. "You wouldn't take him out," Chris Wheeler said. "He was so good, and it's not like nowadays where you build up the back of your bullpens with stars. What were the alternatives? They didn't want one of those guys necessarily who was fresh as opposed to a tiring Steve Carlton because Lefty was still so dominant. And he didn't throw that many pitches. He'd get ahead of hitters. He had a fastball he'd run away. He didn't pitch inside with the fastball, he pitched away with it mostly, he threw his breaking ball, and he had a little curve ball that he'd throw once in awhile. But it was basically fastball, slider, and that was it."[26]

The Cubs' Rick Monday noted that although he didn't have the perspective of a pitcher, an everyday position player goes to the ballpark less than half of the team's 162 games feeling in tip-top form. There were many days that they had to grind out, even playing in front of Wrigley Field's enthusiastic bleacher bums. So considering the number of innings that Lefty pitched in 1972, Monday knew that it took a special person to achieve that level. "I can tell you from a center fielder's standpoint, you play 162 games and there may be 50 to 75 games that you go out there, if you're lucky that many, where you say, 'Wow, I feel really good today,'" Monday remarked. "I don't know what it's like for a pitcher. But I would imagine, when you get down into August and September, and as many innings as Lefty worked, and those pitchers of that era worked, you had to be strong internally, not just a gifted pitcher. And I think that's what helped him be a cut above everybody else that may have had the same type of ability. But what's the makeup of the person? He was not fun."[27]

Tim Raines played behind a tough ace in Steve Rogers early in his career in Montreal, so he was familiar with the mindset that Carlton had in his starts. Rogers threw 129 complete games in a 13-year career with the Expos from 1973 to 1985. So he and Carlton were cut from the same mold in a lot of ways. "Back in the day, you saw a lot more complete games and guys like Carlton didn't want anyone to screw their games up," Raines said. "They'd rather be out there pitching until the game was over. If they lose, they lose. They don't hand the ball over to anyone else and say, 'You're going to save this game for me.' He's the best pitcher on your staff, so you keep him out there. Regardless if you have a closer, and back then I don't think they had closers, but I don't think anyone was a better pitcher than him at that time. In the ninth inning, the tenth inning, the 11th inning, it doesn't matter. He's still their best pitcher out on the mound, and he's probably one of those pitchers that wanted to finish what he started. And he did most times. He was just a good pitcher. He was good."[28]

With the Phillies obviously headed for another disappointing finish in the National League East standings, they were looking to make a splash prior to the trade deadline in June with a major acquisition. Paul Owens, who indicated that none of his players were untouchable, told reporters that he was in serious discussions with six or seven clubs. According to a Frank Dolson column, the six Phillies players who were worthy of major trade talk were Carlton, Montanez, Bowa, Luzinski, Money, and Hoerner. Houston Astros right fielder Jimmy Wynn was high on Philadelphia's radar. In fact, one serious rumor making the rounds had the Phillies offering to send Montanez to the Lone Star State in a swap for Wynn. But in the June 13 issue of the *Philadelphia Inquirer*, Houston vice-president and general manager H. B. (Spec) Richardson was reported as saying "no way" to the deal.

Owens suggested that in addition to a right-handed starting pitcher, acquiring a quality hitter was also atop the Phillies' wish list. After all, the Pope knew that the Phillies' tailspin in which they lost 19 of 20 from May 16 to June 6 had as much to do with the Phillies not getting key hits as it did with pitching. That would help to explain the speculation that Larry Bowa was on his way to Pittsburgh for slugger Bob Robertson. At the time, while Bowa was still young, he said those rumors did not bother him as much as they did later in his career. "Early in my career, there were some rumors that I was going to Pittsburgh and Atlanta," Bowa recalled. "As I got older, it bothered me a little bit obviously. But I think the more you play, then the more you understand that that's part of baseball. Paul Owens was the kind of general manager that, I don't know if he tried to keep you on your toes or what, but he would always plant some stories and not let people get real comfortable. He wanted you to stay hungry."[29]

Outfielder Gene Clines and infielder Rennie Stennett of the Pittsburgh Pirates were two other players in whom the Phillies apparently expressed interest. Plus, one report said that besides Wynn, such pitchers as Los Angeles' Don Sutton, Houston's Larry Dierker, and Montreal's Carl Morton were potential players that the Phillies could acquire. Prior to the Phillies heading out on a 16-day road trip through Cincinnati, Houston, Atlanta, Montreal, and Chicago beginning June 13, Owens instructed Eddie Ferenz to give the players just three and a half days of meal money, taking them up until the trade deadline on June 15. Philadelphia's general manager had been working the phone lines diligently since taking over for Quinn on June 3, communicating with at least 12 different teams in the days leading up to the deadline.

But the major trade that Owens and the fans were hoping for never happened. Instead, the Phils only made a couple of minor deals that figured to have little impact. On June 14, the team dealt McCarver to the Expos for John Bateman in a one-for-one trade of catchers. Then one day later, Philadelphia, still desperate for a right-handed starting pitcher, sent Joe Hoerner and Andre Thornton to the Atlanta Braves in exchange for righties Jim Nash and Gary Neibauer. With McCarver and Hoerner leaving town, the Phillies dumped some salary, as the two players combined to make more than $110,000 that season. But as *Lancaster Intelligencer Journal* sports editor Al Benshoff wrote in a column, the McCarver-Bateman trade was a "bit of a shock." Although Bateman might have been a defensive upgrade on McCarver, the Phillies, Benshoff wrote, weakened themselves in the hitting department, an area where the Phillies needed help. Plus, not surprisingly, the trade was not a real popular one with Lefty, who also was a teammate of McCarver's from 1965 to 1969 in St. Louis.

"It was more of a mental thing with Steve—Timmy caught mostly every one of his games," Larry Bowa said. "Pitchers, especially, they get in a comfort zone with somebody behind the plate, and especially when you're having success like he was ... I don't think he was at a point where he was really upset. But he wasn't real happy, put it that way. Guys react, they go, 'What are we making this trade for?' or something like that. As great as he was, he could have pitched to anybody."[30]

Benshoff also penned that the Hoerner-Nash deal was "rather disturbing." While Hoerner was one of the top relief pitchers in the National League, and a valuable commodity for the Phillies, Nash was far from being the pitcher that he was in 1966 with the Kansas City Athletics, when he finished 12–1 with a 2.06 ERA as a 21-year-old rookie. Yes, Nash was still only 27 at the time of the trade, eight years younger than Hoerner, but he had been dealing with arm troubles in recent years. In 1972, he had been demoted to the bullpen and was only 1–1 with a 5.46 ERA on a Braves team which had its own pitching issues. Neibauer was also just 27 years old, and he showed promise at Triple-A Richmond in 1971 while posting a 13–9 record. But his ERA (7.37) in 1972 with the Braves looked more like Barry Bonds' hat size, as he allowed 14 earned runs, 27 hits, and six walks in 17 and a third innings.

Plus, by subtracting McCarver and Hoerner from the roster, both of whom had played for St. Louis Cardinals teams that hoisted the World Series championship trophy, it could also be argued that the Phillies let two players get away who knew how to win. But the best move that the Phillies made was the trade they never made. *The Atlanta Constitution* was reporting a deal between the Braves and Phillies that would have sent Carlton to Atlanta for outfielder Rico Carty and Nash. Owens was hoping to obtain a solid bat for the Phillies' lineup, in addition to a starting pitcher, and the *Atlanta Consitution* reported that Philadelphia's general manager was on the verge of making a deal with the Braves. "I do remember that, but I wasn't aware we were going to trade Carlton. We got Nash later on," Shenk said. "There were no rumor mills back then on the Internet."[31]

One other rumor making the rounds, though, involved Carlton, McCarver, and Willie Montanez going to the San Francisco Giants for Juan Marichal and another pitcher, likely to be Ron Bryant. Bruce Keidan's response to those reports about the Phillies trading Carlton was that they were total nonsense. He said that those rumors were the result of reporters looking for an off-day story or off-day column. Many would have agreed with the *Philadelphia Inquirer*'s beat writer that moving Carlton would have been a horrible trade for the Phillies on more than one level.

"That would have been sending a pretty clear message, wouldn't it?" Keidan said. "It would have been really stupid because not only was he the best pitcher in the National League, in my estimation, but he paid for himself. The crowds at home were significantly better when he pitched, and the crowds were significantly better when he pitched on the road. He was a difference maker at the box office. I would have been amazed if they had done that trade. He wasn't old. He didn't sign a contract with the Cardinals and that's why he was traded from the Cardinals. No, there was never any serious talk unless you would have overwhelmed them with three really strong players."[32]

Bill Lyon echoed Keidan's sentiments, saying, "It would have been unimaginably devastating. Without him in '72, they might have made a run at the 76ers' record for ineptitude that stands to this day. Nine wins and 73 losses. I mean, no one has broken that yet. It would have been similar to that. Who else was going to win 27 games? I mean, all the rest of them could only win 32. It would have gone from being arguably the best trade they ever made in their history to being the worst. There would have been no in-between."[33]

♦ 9 ♦

Protecting His Teammates

The headline in the *Philadelphia Inquirer* on Monday, June 26, thundered, "Phils' 1-2 punch? Carlton and Bateman!; Battery KO's Expos, 1-0." As might be expected, the Phillies and the Expos staged their version of a beanball game and Carlton was right in the middle of it. For three innings, it was just a quiet battle between two teams who weren't going anywhere, buried in the NL East standings. Then, Philadelphia first baseman Joe Lis was plunked on the left forearm on a two-out pitch thrown by Expos pitcher Ernie McAnally in the top of the fourth inning. It took Carlton just one pitch to retaliate in the bottom of the frame and set off some fireworks.

Carlton, who was convinced that Montreal skipper Gene Mauch had ordered McAnally to hit Lis, was known for his slider, but one can easily assume that Lefty did not use a breaking ball to nail Montreal shortstop Tim Foli in the batting helmet on his first pitch of the inning. As Lefty and Foli started toward each other, both dugouts emptied. According to reports, Mauch, the former Phillies boss, threw the first punch when he swung an overhand right at Carlton. The Phillies' left-hander avoided full contact by throwing up his right arm and taking Mauch's fist on his shoulder. "I was playing third," Don Money said, and Carlton "warms up and the ball goes around the infield. So I got it at third base and I was standing about 20 feet away and said, 'OK, Steve, let's go, bud.' You're heads-up for the bunt and you're playing in and the first pitch ... boom. It was the furthest thing from my mind. I wasn't even thinking about that."[1]

The next thing Money knew, Mauch had quickly emerged out of the Expos' dugout. It wasn't long after that Montreal's skipper started jawing with Lefty on the mound. All the while, Money and others were starting to drift toward the center of the diamond. "Then Mauch either jogged or started toward the mound and that was probably the dumbest thing he ever did," Money said. "We didn't win many games, but we didn't lose any fights. I'm telling you. We had some big puppies on that club, especially on the pitching side. Pete Koegel was with us, Jim Nash, Joe Lis was a little short but stocky. I mean, we didn't lose any fights. And Mauch got pretty well smacked around that night. But Carlton plunking Foli was the furthest thing from my mind. I'm just sitting there trying to figure how to get some hits and try to catch the ball."[2]

Bowa said that the altercation was probably one of the best fights he has ever seen in baseball. "It lasted a while," Bowa said. "It wasn't just holding guys back. Guys were swinging and everything. That was a free-for-all."[3] The Phillies' shortstop said that when a team knows its pitcher is going to throw at an opposing batter, it spreads through the dugout. In this particular situation, nobody said a word. "They knew that Carlton, being the professional he is, was going to take care of business," Bowa said. "I'm sure he was aiming at Foli's shoulder or something. And I remember Foli going down and then trying to get up three times, and before you knew it...."[4] Bowa didn't have to finish his sentence. With Nash at six-foot-five, 230 and Koegel at six-foot-six-and-a-half, 230 leading the way, the Phils were well-armed for fisticuffs. "The one thing we had in '72, we weren't very good, but we had some monsters on that team," Bowa said. "I'm talking about big dudes. That was one team you didn't want to mess with."[5]

Mauch was eventually tossed from the game, but not before he and first base coach Larry Doby exchanged heated words with catcher Jason Bateman, the Phillies' recent acquisition from the Expos. "I remember the clubhouse at Jarry Park was in left field," Bowa said. "Gene Mauch had his legs so crumbled — I mean, he was at the bottom of the pile, guys were punching him — and it must have taken him ten minutes, to walk to the clubhouse after he got kicked out. The game was held up about 10 minutes and he wouldn't get on a cart or anything. He walked from the dugout all the way down the left field line to the clubhouse and he could hardly walk."[6]

Chris Wheeler, too, called it one of the best fights he has ever seen. "The guy that got beat up the worst was Mauch," Wheeler said. "Mauch went out and took that swing at Lefty and he missed him. Oh my God. The joke was that half the players that beat him up were his own players. He had to limp all the way down to the clubhouse and I remember him dragging his leg and the crowd cheering him when he was thrown out."[7]

Unfortunately, Foli was taken from the field on a stretcher, but X-rays at a hospital later proved negative. Then when play finally resumed, Bateman led off the top of the fifth with a home run, accounting for the game's only run. Carlton dug in next, and when McAnally's pitch came close to Lefty, the Montreal hurler was ejected from the game. Both Carlton and McAnally were fined $50 for their parts in the beanball incident, an automatic penalty after home plate umpire Dick Stello had warned both hurlers for hitting an opposing batter with a pitch. McAnally received an additional $100 fine for ignoring that warning. The aftermath from that brawl also had Mauch serving a one-game suspension.

Although Carlton clearly meant to protect his teammates, Carlton was quoted afterward as saying that he regretted hitting Foli in the batting helmet. "I'm sorry I plunked Foli on the head," Carlton reportedly said. "I was trying to get him in the ribs, but the ball got away from me. After all, this was Mauch's type of game. He can't expect to throw at our guys without nothing happening in return. He gave the order to hit Lis.... You have to retaliate to protect your teammates."

The effects of the melee that resulted after Lefty retaliated were still evident at the airport after the game. At the Montreal airport, the Phillies were waiting to board their plane for a trip to Chicago to play the Cubs in their next series. At the gate right next to them were none other than the Expos, heading to St. Louis to play the Cardinals, and Mauch looked like he had just stepped out of the boxing ring. "Darned if the Expos aren't right next to us when we were boarding," Wheeler said. "There was no problem with the players, but I remember looking over and Mauch looked like a tomato. I mean, he had welts on his face. We beat the shit out of him. We went to the airport, and we were in one boarding area and they were in the other. We were flying commercial in those days. You didn't have charters. You were waiting for your flight. And wherever they were going, we were going somewhere and they were right next to us. Mauch, oh my God, they beat him up bad."[8]

Even before that incident at Jarry Park in Montreal, Lefty and Mauch had a history with one another, stemming back to Carlton's days with the Redbirds. It was just one year earlier, in fact, that Carlton surrendered a long ball to Rusty Staub while facing the Expos. In Staub's next trip to the plate, Lefty nailed him in the back, which resulted in heated words being exchanged between Carlton and Mauch. Lis did not believe that McAnally was throwing at him, but as far as Carlton was concerned, it didn't matter. In the dugout, Lefty looked at Frank Lucchesi for confirmation to retaliate. Lucchesi did not oblige, but Carlton was his own boss. And although he did not get a chance to retaliate at Mauch, the Phillies' 1–0 win over the Expos was good enough. "Beating them by 1–0, that makes it perfect," Carton told reporters after the game. "That makes up for not getting to hit Mauch."

That game against the Expos was a perfect example of why Carlton was so well respected in the clubhouse. Lefty was going to make sure that he protected his guys, and according to Gary Matthews, that's one of the reasons that Carlton was loved by his teammates. "He would always protect you," Matthews said. "So if you got hit, he would hit two of their guys. You didn't have to be worried about being intimidated by the opposition because he would not stand for the opposition to throw at his guys who would play every day. That's really the main reason (that he was a popular teammate)."⁹

In the clubhouse, Carlton was generally quiet, but well liked by all of his teammates. Of course, Lefty played during an era when hitters often didn't talk to pitchers and vice versa. This was a routine that Matthews learned early on his career. "We didn't talk to pitchers too much back in those days at all," Matthews said. "We were taught that by [Willie] Mays and the rest of them. One of the reasons we didn't talk to them that much was because if they're on the opposition or they get traded, they're going to have to knock you down. So it's pretty hard to be around guys that you know that's eventually going to bing you one or two times. The same with Bob Gibson. He never talked to any of the hitters. Neither did Steve Carlton. So it wasn't a big deal."¹⁰

Even around other pitchers on the staff, though, Lefty was quiet, but very supportive. By having a uniform number (33) consecutive to Carlton's 32, Twitchell lockered next to Lefty on the road, so he often saw the demeanor of Carlton. "There'd be times where he'd win or lose and we'd be sitting there and he'd look over at me and say, 'I want you to come out to dinner with me,'" Twitchell said. "We'd go out and have dinner and we'd drink a couple of beers and BS a little bit. He'd be talking about the game a little bit. But he wanted to just clear his mind of that. [His attitude was] you can't do anything about it anymore and he wanted to go on to his next game.¹¹ Twitchell, too, called Lefty a great teammate. "As far as I'm concerned, there's two kinds of leaders," Twitchell said. "There's the vocal leaders and there's the leaders by example. He was the latter, obviously. But you couldn't ask for a better example."¹²

"In the clubhouse, he was fine," Sparky Lyle added. "If you ask him for advice or anything like that, he was normal. I couldn't tell you what happened between him and the media. I don't really know. But it had to be something that he lost his trust in them or whatever the (heck) happened. And that was one thing about him, that hey, if you messed up as far as being a friend of his or something like that, you weren't every going to get him back, that's for sure. But I wouldn't be that way."¹³ One report mentioned that Carlton was always bringing a box of peaches into the clubhouse for the team. "I don't know about bull(crap) like that," Lyle said. "But I think he was a great teammate. Everybody liked him. I don't know of anybody that didn't like him that played with him."¹⁴

Teammates, however, knew to give Lefty his space on days that he pitched. Rich Hebner signed with the Phillies on December 15, 1976, to replace Dick Allen at first base after playing nine seasons in Pittsburgh. But it didn't take him long to realize how intense Lefty was when it was his turn to pitch. "He was a good teammate. The day he pitched, though, I'd be afraid to walk by him," Hebner said. "I was on his own team. I was afraid to look at him. I thought he'd chew my head off. Lefty got very focused the day he pitched. He was very focused and he stayed focused his whole career and that's why his numbers are so good."[15]

"Extremely social off the field with teammates, but not necessarily with fans," Tommy Hutton said of Lefty. "To this day, when my wife and I go to Durango, Colorado (we've had a place there for 15 years), I'll give Lefty a call. If he's in town, we'll usually get together for drinks or dinner in downtown Durango.... He was a tremendous teammate. Lots of fun in the clubhouse, enjoyable to go out with for dinner and an unbelievable competitor. But you didn't talk or mess with him on the day he was pitching."[16]

Walking up the tunnel from the dugout at Veterans Stadium, Lefty lockered in the far right-hand corner of the clubhouse, and teammates knew better than to ask him about dinner plans — or anything else — on the nights that he pitched. "Richie said it perfectly, you just stayed away from him," Twitchell said. "Everybody just kinda stayed away from his corner of the clubhouse that day. You didn't say much to him, just 'Go get 'em' or 'Good luck.' It wasn't a day to sit down and have a conversation about your golf game or whether you're going to go fishing over the winter or whatever."[17] Twitchell added that if Lefty won his start, he was approachable after the game that night. If he lost, people continued to stay away from him. "That was kinda his time and he would go do his own thing," Twitchell said. "Then the following day, again he was back preparing for his next start."[18]

As focused as Lefty was on game days, however, he was known to be perfectly relaxed, friendly and easy-going during the next two days. Carlton then began to change a bit on the day before his next start, becoming withdrawn to himself as he started to concentrate and get ready for the task in front of him. Then on the day of his start, he was quiet, intense, and totally within himself. "His preparation was totally amazing," Twitchell said. "The things I learned from Steve Carlton were his preparation for a game, and his intensity was just amazing. Maybe as good or better than any pitcher I ever played with. And he also had good stuff. He had a good fastball and a good slider."[19]

"He was totally prepared, totally focused, and yeah, what Hack [Hebner] says about him, you didn't even bother [to talk with him]," Chris Wheeler said. "The day he pitched, we all knew it. 'Hi Lefty,' 'Hi.' That was enough.

You didn't go up and talk to him before the game. Then after the game, not to the media but to us, he'd chirp like a magpie after the game. He was great. He'd do whatever you wanted him to do.... When he had that stuff with the media, he wouldn't come in and yell at guys and intimidate them. He wasn't like that. Deep down inside, he's a great guy. I'm prejudiced because I love him so much personally and like I said, we've had a great relationship all these years."[20]

As Wheeler noted, however, Lefty didn't have much to say to the media for most of his career. It wasn't that way in 1972, when Carlton was very gracious with his time toward reporters. He was also gracious away from the stadium. Officials from the Brandywine Race Track in Wilmington, Delaware, brought him down to the track, where Lefty was honored with a race being named after him, and then he presented a trophy on the track and signed autographs. Carlton was also non-stop in the off-season, doing the circuit of sportswriters banquets and appearing at other Phillies promotions. "He was our story in '72 and he did everything we ever wanted him to do," Larry Shenk said. "It was endless. He did everything that winter and came down with bronchitis and never got on track in '73. I think he was ill in spring training (because) he did too much that winter."[21]

Indeed, after dealing with his sickness in the off-season and into spring training, Lefty endured to a tough start en route to a 13–20 finish. The next thing he knew, Carlton began receiving negative headlines. According to Joe Flower's *SPORT* magazine article in 1983, references to Lefty's "esoteric interests" upset him. Longtime friend Tim McCarver was reported in that article as saying that Carlton felt "some private things, some theories on life" that were discussed with reporters in '72 were used against him in the next two years. Flower's report explained that Carlton eliminated daily clubhouse interviews by 1975. Lefty's contact with the media became more rare, according to the article, and then he granted his last full interview to Stan Hochman of the *Philadelphia Daily News* for a story printed on July 5, 1979.

Larry Shenk said, "I don't remember what year it was, Lefty said to me he didn't want to talk to the media anymore because he said, 'I read the paper today and they didn't quote me accurately and they took things out of context. If I'm going to spend my talking to them and they're not going to report it accurately, why should I do it? Let them go write the story, let them write the game, let them be more creative in their writing. They don't need me.' That's my most vivid memory of why he didn't talk to the media. He was consistent. It was 'Policy is policy.' Then the media got to accept that. Where the media had a problem with that was basically, sometimes they talk, sometimes they don't talk. On the '80 team, Pete Rose was available every day to the media.

He loved that stuff. Schmitty, Bowa, and Bull were available, so Lefty was allowed to be quiet. Tug [McGraw] was media savvy."[22]

And because of the fact that Lefty was quiet, Luzinski said that his former teammate remains misunderstood by a lot of people, even today. "Lefty's a good guy," Luzinski said. "If he'd walk through that door right now, he'd sit down and talk to the press. At that time, a couple of the writers got on his personal life, his family and things of that nature, and set him off. And that's one of the things you didn't want to do."[23]

Jerry Martin, who was Carlton's teammate for five seasons until being traded by the Phillies to the Chicago Cubs in February of 1979, agreed with Luzinski that Carlton is misunderstood by a lot of people. Martin got his first look at Lefty during the '72 season while playing in Spartanburg, (South Carolina). The Phillies played their Single-A minor league affiliate in an exhibition game on an off-day, and Martin, like everyone else, could not wait to see the man that everyone was talking about in baseball circles. Eventually, Martin made his debut with the big league club in 1974 and quickly came to learn that Lefty was a great teammate. "That situation (of not talking to the media), he just started letting McCarver talk for him," said Martin, who was traded along with Henry Mack, Derek Botelho, Barry Foote and Ted Sizemore to the Cubs in exchange for Manny Trillo, Greg Gross and Dave Rader. "He's probably misunderstood by the Philly media and I guess everybody around the league when he was playing, because as a teammate, he was a great teammate. He was always talking it up. He wasn't a real loud guy, but when he said something, you listened. I think in his own way, he was kind of a leader. Guys lead different ways. He wasn't a real boisterous guy, but out of respect for him and the way he handled himself, not only on the field but in the clubhouse, he had some leadership qualities about him that rubbed off on the players."[24]

Martin hit three home runs against Carlton in '79 after being traded to the Cubs, and he was certainly listening when Lefty caught up to him one day later following the third of those long balls. Carlton, of course, was only being playful when he spotted Martin behind the batting cage prior to the game. "We're milling around the cage getting ready to go out and hit," Martin recalled with a laugh. "The Phillies are about done hitting and all of a sudden, somebody grabbed me by the neck, and as soon as he grabbed me by the neck, I knew who it was. It was Lefty. He said, 'Mud, that's it. You're not going to hit another home run off me. I'll hit you in your big head.' I said, 'Lefty, that's it. No more, Lefty.' He was just teasing me. But he was just a heck of a competitor."[25]

Bruce Keidan was one of those in the media who thought he had an understanding with Carlton. Since Lefty spent most of his career not talking to the media, many people might have perceived him as being surly or unfriendly. That, however, was not the case, Keidan acknowledged. In fact, Keidan said that he had an amicable relationship with Carlton. "Steve's thing starting in '73 about not talking to the media, it only applied for 'To the record,'" Keidan remarked. "People had the impression that he was surly to the media. He wasn't. But he was not at all surly. You could talk to him. I always got along great with him."[26]

Keidan said that he had an agreement with Lefty where, if he ever wanted to ask him something on the record or for print, he would ask up front. From there, Carlton would either answer it or not answer it. "I remember putting him on the record one time about an incident one time where a fan ran out onto the field, ran out to the mound and did a 'We are not worthy' bow," Keidan recalled. "And Steve actually laughed. He was pretty intense, but he laughed at that. I remember asking him about that. But for one thing, he had one of the world's great interpreters. He had McCarver. For another, that wasn't his general demeanor. He was not surly with people."[27]

All agree that Carlton was not surly with others. But there are those who question whether Carlton ever went on the record with reporters after the mid-seventies. Scott Palmer came to Philadelphia from Chicago in 1981 to work as a television reporter for Channel 6, and Lefty had already eliminated interviews by that time. "When I got there, Lefty was like a sphinx," Palmer said. "I was a kid reporter and we knew going in that he wouldn't do interviews, but when you're a young, aggressive reporter, you want to try. Who knows when he might say, 'Yes,' and you'd ask him. The first time, he said, 'Don't you know I don't do interviews?' I said, 'I did, but I thought I'd ask.' He said, 'Save your breath,' and then after that I never did. The news director said, 'Did you try to get him?' and I said, 'Yes, I tried, but he's not talking today.' I respected him. He was consistent. He wasn't going to pick and choose who he was going to talk to."[28]

Keidan was the Phillies' beat reporter at a time when there was a lot fewer media members covering the team. Larry Shenk said that he is thankful that Carlton never threw a no-hitter because he is not sure how Lefty would have handled the extra volume of reporters that exists in today's game. "He didn't want to talk to the media," Shenk said. "McCarver knew what was up, so he was always available to the media after the game. Booney was the same way. So a lot of times, you didn't need Lefty. But today, it's a different ball game. I mean, right now in a World Series game, the winning team, when the last out is made, there are six different interviews that go on right in front of the dugout before they get off the field. We never had that."[29]

What they did have, however, was a media room where players were asked to go at the end of post-season games. For the most part, Carlton managed to avoid being roped in front of the cameras and microphones and tape recorders. Following one particular playoff game in Los Angeles, however, he was not so lucky. "Not all the media has clubhouse passes, and (with interview rooms) you can accommodate the masses," Shenk said. "It's not to the degree it is today in volume, but in all the post-seasons—'76, '77, '78, '80, '83—I only needed Lefty once. Most of the time, Tug finished the game. So we took Tug because I knew Lefty wouldn't do it. So we're playing the Dodgers in Dodger Stadium, and I think it's the game where he hit a home run and we beat them 1–0 or something like that. So I'm in the dugout at Dodger Stadium, which is on the first base side, and Lefty comes off the mound and I said, 'Lefty, I need you.' 'Why?' I said, 'We've got to go someplace.' He asked, 'Why?' I told him, 'Just follow me.'"[30]

With that, Shenk grabbed Lefty by the belt, and together they walked up the dugout steps and over to the Dodgers' dugout on the third base side. From there, they walked past Los Angeles' clubhouse down a corridor to the interview room. "Lefty didn't say much," Shenk said. "Maybe once or twice, he said, 'Where are we going?' So we get down to the media interview room and there's this massive media, and his eyes got as big as saucers. I said, 'There's the microphone.' And he gets up to the microphone and he whispered out some answers, very short ones. He never said anything to me. After that, he went back to the club and never complained or never did anything."[31]

Carlton, however, did complain — loudly — after things went awry when accommodations were made for him to speak following his 300th career win during the 1983 season. "I went downstairs [to the clubhouse] after he finished his workout with Gus [Hoefling] and I said, 'Lefty, what are we going to do after your 300th win?'" Shenk recalled. "He said, 'Go for 400.' I said, 'I know that. That's not what I'm talking about.' He said, 'What do you have in mind? I want to communicate to the fans, but I don't want to talk to the media.' I told him, 'Well, there's a way we can do that. We could have Harry Kalas interview you after the game, and that way the fans are hearing you talk about winning 300. And I said we could even ask the writers to give questions that we could give to Harry so they feel like they're contributing.' He said, 'Well, we'll see. OK.'"[32]

But when Lefty lost to Mike Krukow and the San Francisco Giants on Saturday, September 3, at the Vet while going for win number 298, that meant that Carlton would probably achieve his 300th win on the road. Sure enough, he picked up the milestone win in St. Louis on Friday, September 23, in a 6–2 decision over Joaquin Andujar. It was the eighth win in a row for the first-place Phillies and it maintained their three-game lead over the Pittsburgh Pirates in the National League East standings. But when Carlton suffered that loss to Krukow, the plans all unraveled. "It was looking like it wasn't going to happen at home, so I thought I should tell the media, the writers, what the plans were in case some of them weren't sure if they were going to St. Louis," Shenk said. "And the next day, there were articles in the paper, 'Lefty's going to talk, but it's going to be a controlled press conference.' And the *Inquirer* had a seven-column headline, 'Lefty to speak after 300th win.' I thought, 'Oh, boy.'"[33]

Oh, boy, indeed. Shenk remembers sitting in his office at the Vet when a clubhouse attendant telephoned. "I'll never forget this," Shenk said. "The clubhouse guy said, 'Lefty wants to see you.' I knew exactly what it was. So I go down to the clubhouse and he said, 'Did you see the papers?' I said, 'Yes.' He said, 'Well, I don't want to talk. That's the problem. They're making a bigger deal out of me talking than out of us winning the game. My only concern right now is winning because we're trying to win the pennant. That's number one. Whether I talk or don't talk is not important.' He could answer a question with his eyes without saying a word. They'd go right through you. So I said, 'Fine. I understand.' So I went upstairs, and Bill Giles was the president and my boss and I said, 'Bill, I just had a talk with Lefty and (told him about the conversation). He said, 'I'll go down and talk with him.' I said, 'No, I don't think you should.' 'Why not?' I said, 'His eyes told me he wanted no part of this. He didn't want his focus to be interrupted from winning a game. I think it's best we stay away from him.' And he said, 'OK.'"[34] Not even after the Phillies won the World Series in 1980 did Lefty allow himself to be cornered by the scribes. "There was a lot of champagne in the clubhouse and all that," Shenk said, "but Lefty would go back in the weight room with Gus Hoefling and a couple other teammates and do his celebrating back there."[35]

One of the few times that Lefty broke his silence came when he was voted into the Hall of Fame in 1994. As per custom, Carlton flew into New York on a Tuesday and then attended a press conference the next day. Lefty called Shenk and asked for him to come to New York and go over what was going to happen. "So I go to New York, we're in his suite," Shenk said, "and he's got these crazy ideas of the world and all that, and he's talking to me about it, and I said, 'Lefty, tomorrow I don't think we should get into all that. I think you ought to consider what you're going to say to the media, why you are talking now, and why you didn't.' He said, 'No, you don't understand....' I thought, 'I'm not getting anywhere.' So the next day, we go down, they have the press conference, and he's up there and he's just blabbing away and answering every question. And finally, the president of the Baseball Writers Association of America looked at me and said, 'It's 25 minutes. Can we cut it off?' So I kind of waited for a question and then I said, 'We want to thank you very much,' and Lefty goes, 'Larry, no, I'm having fun with this. Let's keep going.' So I stepped back and let him go ... I think being a Hall of Famer, it's just so impactful, and I think he put everything else aside. Since then, he still prefers not to talk. It makes my job easy."[36]

Given his distrust for the media, Lefty surely would have enjoyed a trick that was played on a reporter involving catcher Bob Boone and his brother Rod during a trip to San Francisco. "In the mid-seventies, Lefty quit talking to the press, so the press would come to me looking for a Steve Carlton quote, I guess," Bob Boone said. "So we went to San Francisco, and my brother had played and gotten to Triple-A. He was an engineer in San Francisco. He looked a lot like me. He was three years younger than me. So he wore a Bob Boone uniform and took batting practice. This one writer kept pestering him. He kept asking to talk to him and Rod said, 'No, you don't want me. You don't want me.' Finally he relented and went into the dugout and talked for 20 minutes about Steve Carlton."[37] Asked what Lefty's reaction was to that, Boone said, "He would have thought it was funny, any time you can trick the press."[38]

Carlton was still only 27 years old when he came to the Phillies and was known to have a little bit of a wild side to his personality in his younger days. Many of his teammates acknowledged that Lefty liked to have fun off of the field; Shenk didn't deny that Lefty was a bit playful for a time. "He was a little bit early, which I think is typical of young players," Shenk said. "He and LC [Larry Christenson] were an entry. LC could be a little wild too — just crazy wild. Lefty didn't harm people. He wasn't nasty to people."[39]

Lefty's wild side dated back to his days as a youngster growing up in the shadows of the Everglades in Florida. He was drinking beer and vodka by age 14. Even after he made it to the big leagues, going out and having a few drinks with his teammates was Lefty's way of unwinding after pitching in a game. Carlton acknowledged to reporter John Flynn in an article for the *Philadelphia Inquirer* in 1972 that he was a "bad kid," and his interests as a teenager weren't so much on sports, but on roaming the Everglades looking for rattlesnakes and alligators. He had a cannon for a left arm even as a youngster, as he could throw a football 85 yards in the air. Despite his gifted ability to throw, however, he ignored suggestions to try out for Little League until he was 12 years old. Finally, his friend Joe Schmidt dragged him to the Little League park for a tryout and the rest is history. Lefty, a lanky six-foot-three, 135-pounder as a high school freshman, even tossed a perfect game in his first All-Star contest.

Seeing his own success on the diamond, Lefty naturally took a liking to the game, and his accomplishments in Little League, high school, and American Legion did nothing to dampen it. Basketball was his other sport, but the hoops season overlapped into baseball, and when that contributed to a subpar junior season on the diamond, he gave up roundball. The Pirates had been showing interest in Lefty until he struggled as a high school junior, but even so, Carlton wasn't thinking much of a professional baseball career as a high school athlete. Yet, when Lefty saw a friend sign with Kansas City for $18,000, that changed his outlook. Lefty was one of three children — and the only son — to Joe and Anne Carlton, and the family managed to get by on Joe's salary as a maintenance worker for Pan-American Airlines. But having gone to high school in a Jewish neighborhood, Lefty was able to see the haves and the have-nots around him, and when he was offered a $5,000 bonus contract by scout Chase Riddle of the St. Louis Cardinals in 1963, he took it. After a semester at Miami-Dade Junior College, he started his minor league career with the Single-A Rock Hill (South Carolina) Cardinals in 1964, then was promoted to Winnipeg and Tulsa. Finally, Lefty got his feet wet with St. Louis in 1965, pitching in 15 games with two starts. After returning to Tulsa and going 9–5 with the Triple-A Oilers in 1966, Carlton was promoted to the Cards' rotation for good in 1967. From there, Lefty made one start for St. Louis against Boston in the 1967 World Series, where he suffered a Game Three 3–1 loss to Jim Lonborg. He also pitched in two games for the Redbirds in the 1968 Fall Classic against the Detroit Tigers.

In his days with the Cardinals and early on with the Phillies, Lefty still had a bit of a wild side. Eventually with age, he became a little more tame, but he still liked to make people laugh. "When you were with Lefty, you had fun," Larry Shenk said. "You laughed. People didn't see that. There was an AP sports writer named Ralph Bernstein, who's no longer living. Every year in spring training, Ralph would go up to Lefty and say, 'Look, no pen, no notebook, no tape recorder. Can we talk?' 'Ralph, policy is policy.' 'OK, I thought I'd try,' and walk away."[40]

Years later, Shenk laughs about a game of hide-and-seek that Lefty played on him and Bill Giles during a few camera day promotions by the Phillies. At the time, however, Shenk and Giles probably were not smiling too much. "We had camera night and he would never come out," Shenk recalls. "We didn't have cell phones and Bill Giles called me on the dugout phone. 'Where's Lefty?' I told him I'd find out, but I could never find him. I don't know where he was. I called Bill. 'I can't find him.' He just didn't want to do that. A lot of players didn't want to do the photo day over here (at the Vet). But I remember asking him one time, 'What was your fondest memory of the Phillies?'

And he said, 'Hiding from Larry Shenk and Bill Giles,' which was his humor."[41] Pressed on those incidents, Shenk said, "There's a way at the Vet you could get underneath the stands. I think that's where he went. There's a little door back by the equipment room. I didn't go out there. But I'd go into the restroom, there are no feet in there, unless he's standing on the toilet. I could never find him. It wasn't seven, eight years in a row, but it was a couple or three times."[42]

Chris Wheeler, too, said that Lefty had a very playful side to his personality. "That phase in his life really didn't last that long. It was only a few years and then he settled down," Wheeler said. "He was a little playful for a few years."[43] Lefty might have settled down eventually, but he still had a sense of humor. "He was always fun to be around for us because he trusted us," said Wheeler, a Phillies broadcaster since 1977. "He trusted me, he trusted Harry [Kalas], and he trusted Whitey [Richie Ashburn]. We were his friends. We weren't his adversaries. He wouldn't do interviews with us, though. No way. He said policy is policy. He made up his mind that that was it and he wasn't going to do any of that sort of stuff. Lefty was interesting. You found that out later, that maybe it was better he kept quiet sometimes. But he always had his opinions on things and he loved to talk to you. We would talk after games, we did our Vegas trips and he was fun. He's a great — just a great guy. He just decided he wasn't going to talk to the media, but he was never mean to the media. They will tell you that. He wouldn't walk up and say, 'Bleep you, get the bleep out of my face.' He'd just go, 'Policy is policy.' He was never mean about it. I'll never forget about that. I'm not saying he was always polite and that he couldn't scare somebody, but he didn't try to intimidate people by yelling at them. He didn't put on a show."[44]

Mike Krukow, who started his career with the Cubs, was Carlton's teammate on the Phillies' 1982 team and noted that Lefty was completely opposite of the person that Krukow thought he was while playing with other teams. "When I got to Philadelphia, I was completely overwhelmed at what type of guy he was," Krukow said. "I just thought he was 'Mr. Machine.' He never talked to another opponent. I mean, he was a robot out there. He was just a stud. And then when I got with the Phillies, he was funny, he was articulate, he was witty, and a great teammate. He was kind of a smart ass, he had great wit. It was sarcastic. When there was clubhouse banter, which there was a great deal of on that team, he would always have a zinger or two that would get everybody laughing. He was hysterical, and I lockered next to him in the clubhouse. So we had a lot of discussions about everything. Just really a neat guy."[45]

Krukow's remarks about Lefty not showing any emotion as an opponent and refusing to talk to anybody wearing another team's colors also fit the picture that others painted of him. Tito Fuentes, when asked about the mystique of Lefty, said, "He didn't speak to nobody, he never said, 'Hi,' or nothing, so he was the kind of guy that nobody knew nothing about him. So when it was time for us to talk about him, nobody ever mentioned, it because since he was not friendly, you're not going to give him any props.... He was always the same way. It wasn't like two years he was this way and then he was this way the other year. He was always the same way."[46]

Bob Walk, a teammate of Carlton on the Phillies' 1980 World Championship and currently a Pirates broadcaster, said that there was nothing mysterious about Lefty as a teammate. The big right-hander noted that Carlton was as normal as any other teammate and that he would often go out after a game and have a beer while being social. But Walk did acknowledge that Carlton had an aura about himself with his opponents. "At that time (in his playing days), he did (like that aura). He probably doesn't care much about it now. But at the time, he enjoyed the fact that nobody knew anything about him. He thought that was cool. And it was kinda cool. He didn't deal with outsiders. Teammates, fine. Outsiders, no."[47]

Tim Flannery was never a teammate, so he could certainly relate to that aura that Carlton had. "I don't really have any good stories about him. I didn't have the opportunity to play with him, and he didn't talk, so you didn't know a lot about him. And it seems like you don't know a lot about him now either."[48] Up until he was traded to the Phillies in March of 1981 for Walk, Gary Matthews was an outsider with Lefty. But that all changed when he played for the Phillies from 1981 through 1983. During that time they were teammates, Matthews saw nothing about Lefty that led him to believe that he was mysterious. "We always felt that the people that were interviewing him were weird," Matthew said. "It wasn't him. And to this day, we feel the same way about some of the crazy questions that people ask and so on. He was a great teammate for me and the guy was a good pitcher — one of the best of all time."[49]

While many talked about Lefty as being a good teammate and having a good sense of humor, they also described him as a very private person. Even in retirement, his living conditions seem somewhat secluded in Durango, Colorado, along with being a bit unusual and mysterious. Lefty divorced from his wife Beverly, a Canadian woman he met in 1964 while pitching in Winnipeg. Together, they had two sons, Steven and Scotty. "The last time I saw him," Wayne Twitchell said jokingly, "they were closing down the Vet, and he told me he was sleeping on a rock in some cave in Durango, Colorado. Some people think that's normal. I think that's a little different. I actually questioned Steve about it and he said, 'I'm not talking to you because you wouldn't understand it.' No, I'm sure I wouldn't.... He's a fabulous guy, a fabulous teammate. But he definitely has his little quirks. A lot of baseball players do."[50]

Jerry Martin added, "He lives out in Colorado ... and I think it's a 100 and-something or maybe 200 acres. I've heard all kind of stuff about his house. I've heard it's built in the side of a mountain and all that stuff. I don't know. I've heard there's not a TV in the whole place. I don't know that either. You hear all kinds of stuff. All I know is I've always liked Lefty and I've always respected the type of pitcher he was. That's the type of guy he was — just a good guy."[51]

Jim Kaat, who was a Phillies teammate with Lefty from 1976 through 1978, said that Lefty had some unusual and opinionated ideas not only on baseball, but on life. But the 25-year big league veteran thought those ideas might have also contributed to his career being one of Hall of Fame caliber. "I think that's what made him different and maybe added to his success as a pitcher," Kaat said. "There's a fine line between being stubborn and being stupid, and Lefty was very stubborn in the right way and very opinionated. And it worked to his advantage."[52]

Lefty was certainly stubborn about having his time in the outdoors. During his playing days, he often enjoyed the camaraderie of teammates and friends on various hunting excursions. Those groups often included teammates Tim McCarver and Joe Hoerner. "Back in those days, there was camaraderie," Chris Wheeler said. "Timmy and Lefty and Hoerner, they had all been together with the Cardinals and they were friends. They had other guys go on those trips. They just liked each other. They were friends. It was a guy thing. It was a bonding thing."[53]

Sports Illustrated had hoped to take advantage of Lefty's love for hunting as a way to conduct an interview with him, but to no avail. "Lefty was an avid hunter, so *Sports Illustrated*, the Outdoorsmen section, wanted to do a story about Lefty hunting," Larry Shenk said. It wasn't happening "because that was a way of trying to get in the door. He was consistent. It made my job easy."[54]

According to McCarver's remarks to Wheeler, those hunting trips that Lefty organized were just that — very organized. He "loved to hunt," Wheeler said. "Timmy used to go with him all the time. Timmy said that typically, the way Lefty approached hunting was the way he approached everything — methodical. Everything was organized, they knew where they were going to go, they knew where they were going to stay, they knew where they were going to hunt, and they knew where they were going to go at night. It was typical Lefty. It was organized."[55]

Nowadays, Carlton has also organized his own business, Game Winner Inc., and a web site, carlton32.com, where he sells autographed balls, jerseys, and caps. Lefty still makes appearances at card shows as well. "He has a very good business manager who is really great to deal with," Shenk commented.[56] Lefty also has very good friends who are supportive and loyal. Obviously, Tim McCarver and Chris Wheeler go way back with Lefty and have shared a lot of laughs with each other. That friendship included a couple of trips that McCarver and Wheeler took to Las Vegas with Carlton. "He and Timmy and I had a good relationship. To this day, we still do," Wheeler said. "Lefty would set up Vegas trips. He was great, he liked to entertain that way. He was a gregarious guy who had a problem with a guy in the media and shut it down, didn't talk to the media. But with the people he liked, he couldn't have been any nicer. He was gracious. Like I said, he'd set up these Vegas trips, we'd get off the plane and they'd have the car waiting. You'd be all set to go at the hotel and all in Vegas. We did that two or three times, and I was lucky enough that Lefty would invite me to go along too. And Timmy was always there too. They were funny together. They had a great relationship. Timmy knew how to handle Lefty, Lefty knew how to handle Timmy, on the field and off the field, and they were great together. They talk about being buried 60 feet, six inches apart, that's Timmy's line, and there was something to that."[57] Bob Boone added, "Lefty really enjoyed life to the max. He really competed when it was time to compete. As a starting pitcher, then you basically have four days off where you're not competing."[58]

Wheeler did not say whether their trips to Las Vegas consisted of staying at Caesars Palace. But Steve Blass recalled an occasion in Vegas with a group including Carlton during the 1970 season. Blass was Dave Giusti's roommate with the Pittsburgh Pirates, and Giusti had just come to the Bucs in a trade in October of 1969 after playing one season with the Cardinals. During that time in St. Louis, Giusti had come to know many of the Redbird players, and it just so happened that the Pirates and Cardinals had a mutual off day on the west coast during the 1970 season. So a few players from both teams took advantage of the opportunity to visit the "Entertainment Capital of the World."

"Some of us from each team wound up in Las Vegas at Caesars Palace," Blass said. "I never hung around Lefty because back then you didn't fraternize. There was none of that, or minimal. But we just hung out because it was an off day, we had mutual respect, and we knew a lot of the guys. We wound up in the hallway in Caesars Palace, and they have these half busts of all these Roman gods and goddesses. And I wound up fooling around with one of the goddesses, Plaster of Paris, and for some reason, it just tickled Steve. It was entertaining to him. So on the occasional times that I will see him now decades later, we'll bring up that story and he'll say, 'You did have a good time up in that hallway,' and I say, 'Yeah, really.' It's kinda neat to have a rapport with a guy of that stature. I absolutely respect him. I was delighted to be pitching in an era that had a Steve Carlton."[59]

◆ 10 ◆

FINISHING WHAT HE STARTED

When the Phillies won the World Series in 2008, Brad Lidge was a perfect 41-for-41 during the regular season and 7-for-7 in the post-season in save opportunities. Thirty-six years earlier, the Phillies had just 15 saves as an entire staff. Lefty, himself, was his own set-up man and closer. From late June to late August, Lefty went on an impressive streak in which he finished 14 of his 15 starts. And as an indication of just how dominant he was, not only during that particular stretch, but also for the entire 1972 season as a whole, Carlton rarely had any innings in which he allowed more than one run. To be exact, Lefty was so dialed in during the '72 campaign that in his 346 one-third total innings that year, he put up a zero in 288 of them (83 percent). In 39 other frames, he yielded just one run. That means that Carlton yielded two or more runs in only 19 one-third innings during his 27-win masterpiece.

On June 29, Lefty earned the first of just two wins in six starts against the New York Mets, defeating Gary Gentry, 9–4, in Philadelphia to improve his record to 9–6. Although Lefty felt like he had a great warm-up session, he acknowledged that he did not pitch exceptionally, and the Metropolitans took leads of 1–0 and 3–1, as Ted Martinez went 1-for-2 with a triple and three RBIs. "The thing about Steve Carlton was that he could go out there and not have his good stuff, and by the time he got to the mound or pitched an inning or two, he'd have his good stuff," Sparky Lyle said. "I mean, that's pretty much why he was so successful. I think he had the best stuff that I'd ever seen a starting pitcher have time after time after time because he was so disciplined."[1]

"If you say a pitcher got lit up, that didn't happen much with Lefty," Jerry Martin added. "We had a good offensive club back when I was there in the seventies, we had pretty good offensive players and we won the division those three years in '76, '77 and '78. Lefty was the type of guy where he might go out there and give up two, three, four, maybe five [runs] in the early innings. Well, guess what? You turn around and in the eighth inning, guess who's standing out on the mound? Lefty. And now we're ahead, 6–4, or whatever. To me, that's the mark of just a true, bona fide number one starting pitcher, and I saw Lefty do that more than a couple of times. He was the type of guy that, if you get him, you'd better get him early because more times than not with a guy like Lefty, if you didn't get him early, you didn't get him."[2]

Phillies pitching coach Ray Rippelmeyer attributed Carlton's early-game struggles to him dropping his wrist while throwing sliders. During the Mets game he was one pitch away from handing the ball over to the bullpen in the top of the fourth, but he struck out Dave Marshall on a 3–2 pitch to leave the bases loaded. Even while not having his best stuff early on, however, Carlton kept his emotions in check on the mound. "He would be upset off the field—he had a temper," Bob Walk said. "But it was always important to show that he was totally under control of his emotions when he was out on the center of the diamond. He would never let anybody know that they had gotten to him. That's for sure. I think it's just if you want that aura about you as being the man, and you guys can't touch me, then if you're going to roll your eyes or throw your glove in the air or react every time something bad goes on, it kinda shows you're human. Steve Carlton back in those days wasn't human. He was the man."[3]

Steve Blass said that one thing you never wanted to do on the field was to show up an opponent. Carlton definitely had a reputation of respecting the players on the other side of the field. If he gave up a home run, he simply retrieved another ball from the umpire and went back to work. "You didn't fraternize, but you knew who everybody was," Blass said. "That was just the way it was back in that era. I don't think Carlton ever showed anybody up. He had tremendous respect for his opponents and we all respected each other. There was some pretty damn good baseball in that decade—among other decades, sure. But there was a concentration of talent and the only time that you really had something bad to say about somebody is if he embarrassed you on the field. And I never had any record of Carlton doing that. When you give up a home run, you don't watch him go around the bases. But if the batter goes around the bases like a jerk, that goes in the file. Absolutely. I think that's the number one rule in baseball that we had, and I hope it still exists that you don't embarrass anybody."[4]

In that 9–4 victory against the Mets, Lefty finished with an eye-popping 171 pitches and allowed just one run over the final five innings. When the dust settled, Lefty had struck out 13, while yielding four earned runs on seven hits and six walks. Throwing "171 pitches now is damn near three starts," Bill Lyon said. Pitch counts "would have been the antithesis to him. Here's a guy that was into martial arts, sticking your hand into a bucket full of rice, all these esoteric things that he had. To come out of a game would have been unthinkable for him. It would have been just unthinkable."[5]

Although it might not have been his best outing of the season, it didn't have to be because the Phillies supported Lefty with a season-best 17-hit attack against Gentry and relievers Bob Rauch, Buzz Capra, and Ray Sadecki. Greg Luzinski was 3-for-5 with three RBIs and two runs scored, while Don Money and Bill Robinson each went deep in the onslaught. Trailing 3–2, the Phillies took the lead for good with a four-run fifth-inning rally in which they piled up five singles and capitalized on two walks and a wild pitch. Mets manager Yogi Berra called for Rauch from the bullpen, but Lefty helped his own cause by mashing a two-strike, two-run base hit. During the 1972 season, Lefty batted .197 in 1972 with three doubles, one triple, one home run, and eight RBIs. Two of those RBIs were of the game-winning variety.

Bill Robinson ripped a solo blast leading off the fourth inning and Joe Lis chipped in with a base hit. The Phillies had been hoping that Lis and Robinson would provide the club with some much-needed power when they called the pair up from the Eugene Emeralds on June 23. Lis might have been summoned from the Triple-A club a few weeks earlier, except that John Quinn was still the GM when Mike Anderson was demoted and he favored Oscar Gamble. Paul Owens, though, was a Lis man, and the 25-year=old finally received his chance in June to show what he could do. At the time of his call-up, Lis was still recovering from being hit on the left wrist by a pitch, but he nonetheless led all of organized baseball with 26 home runs. He also had a .338 batting average and 58 RBIs with the Emeralds. Lis immediately stepped in and started ten of the Phillies' next 12 games at first base, and then when Johnson returned, he started six of the next seven games in right field. Over the remaining three months of the season, however, it was Freed, Gamble, Hutton, and Robinson who made the majority of starts in right. Lis made a number of starts back at first base in late August and September and eventually finished the season with six dingers and 18 RBIs while batting only .243 in 62 games. He also had six homers and drove in 10 runs in limited action during the 1971 season, but was traded to the Minnesota Twins prior to the 1973 season, along with Ken Reynolds and Ken Sanders, for Cesar Tovar.

The Phillies acquired Tovar as a utility infielder, a role that ended up pushing Terry Harmon out of the picture at second base in 1973. Average-wise, Harmon was actually one of the Phillies' most consistent hitters in 1972. He played ten seasons in Philadelphia, but his best year with the club came in 1972 while platooning at second with Denny Doyle. In 73 games, the 28 year-old Harmon hit .284, but finished with only two home runs and 13 RBIs. His batting average was 80 points higher than his .204 average in 1971, and he clubbed his first major league home run on August 30, an inside-the-park shot against Houston pitcher Jerry Reuss. Meanwhile, Doyle, who was also 28 years old in 1972, batted just .249 with only 26 RBIs and 33 runs scored. After not living up to his promise, he would spend just one more season with the Phillies before being sent to the California Angels in 1974 to complete an earlier deal. But Harmon and Doyle were known more for their glovework, and neither figured into the Phillies' long-term plans.

"Both of them could catch the ball. Neither one of them were big offensive guys," Chris Wheeler said. "Harmon wasn't a guy that could swing the bat. He was a pretty decent utility player, he could play all the infield positions. He choked up a lot, that sort of stuff. But I could see him and Denny catching the ball. And [Larry] Bowa and Denny played together so much that they really knew each other. When Bowa and Denny came up together, they thought Doyle was going to be the better player because he could hit a little more, he was stronger. They played together in the minors, so they really thought he was going to be the better player. Obviously, it didn't turn out that way."[6]

As a team, consistency continued to haunt Philadelphia throughout the '72 season, and after the Redbirds swept the Phillies to drop them to 24–45, Carlton took the mound on July 3 with an opportunity to be the stopper once again in a series-opening game against the Giants. He delivered by scattering six hits, while striking out seven and walking two in a complete-game, 4–2 win over Don Carrithers to improve to 10–6. "Everybody has one year that is much better than the rest, which nobody can explain because it's the same person, the same game," Tito Fuentes said of Lefty's 1972 season. "Sometimes things are working your way and you can not stop it."[7]

The Phillies managed just five hits, but that was enough for Lefty, who allowed only two solo home runs by Dave Kingman. Willie McCovey took the collar against Carlton. "His slider looked like a fastball, he consistently threw strikes, he was an intimidator when he was on the mound, and he was pretty serious," Gary Matthews said. "He'd never put the blame on anyone else. And he wanted everyone to play straight up. If they hit them in the gaps, he felt it was his fault. And his slider was his strikeout pitch. He had a good move to first base. He was a complete pitcher."[8]

But while some described Lefty as being intimidating, others disagreed with that particular word in characterizing the legendary left-hander. Dusty Baker, a star for the Atlanta Braves in 1972, was one of those people.

He "wasn't intimidating," he said. "He was just great. He was the kind of guy that if you hit him, you hit him, and he and Tom Seaver and guys like that, they didn't necessarily feel the need to throw at you just because you got a hit. Those are the guys you respect the most because you know that you're having just a tremendous battle when those guys are out there. You go to bed thinking about Steve Carlton and you wake up in the morning thinking about Steve Carlton. That's what you do when you face those great pitchers because you knew they've had two or three days to think about you. I remember Hank Aaron used to give us a theory and a philosophy as young hitters how to approach Steve Carlton and Tom Seaver and Bob Gibson and some of those guys. If you don't have a theory and a philosophy, you have very little chance of hitting those guys. And when you get your pitch, you can't miss it because you ain't going to get it again."[9]

Tim Flannery also talked about the intimidation of Lefty, from the standpoint that he simply had great stuff and was a great competitor. Asked if he was known to be a pitcher like Bob Gibson or Don Drysdale, Flannery said, "Back then, with a lot of those guys, that was just part of almost everybody's game, to knock people off the plate. He wasn't a headhunter by any means. He wasn't known for that. He was just known as a great competitor."[10]

Lefty's 11th win of the season, and his sixth straight without a loss, came on July 7 in the first game of a doubleheader against Mike Corkins and the San Diego Padres. John Bateman delivered a two-run single in the Phillies' three-run sixth inning, while Carlton scattered nine hits in yet another complete-game effort. His eight K's improved his strikeout total on the season to 174, which was tops not only in the National League, but the major leagues. Asked when he knew he was watching something special, Chris Wheeler said, "They kept swinging and missing at him. Major league hitters don't swing and miss a lot. I always say that if you want to see a pitcher who is really pitching good, watch guys that are swinging and missing. They don't do it. That year, I was just new in the game, and I was still a fan. I know a lot more now than I did then. And that ball was disappearing. I didn't know what he was [throwing], it was some kind of a breaking ball. It turned out that it was his slider that he threw that looked like a fastball. He probably got more strikes on balls than any pitcher I've ever seen because they would swing and miss at him all the time on balls in the dirt. And all the hitters would say the ball spun so tight. They'd look and see breaking ball, but it looked like a fastball coming out of his hand, so they would swing and miss at him or check-swing, and he would get tons of strikeouts on the slider. So when did I think it was special? Well, as that season went along and he kept striking everybody out and playing two-hour games. And he was pitching complete games all the time. He really almost had to because that bullpen we had wasn't too good. Lefty would start and finish and we'd win."[11]

Lefty's win over the Padres also proved to be the final win of Frank Lucchesi's career as the Phillies' manager. Philadelphia fell into another four-game skid and Lucchesi was relieved of his duties on July 10, with Paul "Pope" Owens replacing him as field manager. At the press conference announcing the change, Phillies owner Bob Carpenter said that the decision to replace Lucchesi was made on Sunday, July 9, after Philadelphia lost for the third time in a four-game series against San Diego. In Owens, the team was going with someone who had never played or managed in the big leagues.

Owens was traveling with the big league club on its road trip from June 13 to 27 through Cincinnati, Houston, Atlanta, Montreal, and Chicago, looking for answers to explain the Phils' losing ways. During that time, Lucchesi laughed while dismissing rumors that he would be replaced as Philadelphia's manager. He compared his situation to that of Gene Mauch, who remained as manager in 1961 despite his team enduring a 23-game losing streak. The *Philadelphia Inquirer's* Frank Dolson supported the embattled skipper in a column in June, noting that the Phillies' woes weren't Lucchesi's fault, that Quinn had handed him a second-division ball club, and that without Deron Johnson, the Phillies weren't even a dangerous second-division squad. Owens even gave Lucchesi a vote of confidence after Tom Seaver pitched the Mets to a 3–2 win over the Phillies on June 28, saying that Lucchesi would remain at the helm until the end of the season. But less than two weeks later, the Phillies reversed course. Losing three of four to a Padres team that was last in the National League West Division standings was apparently the final straw, dropping the Phillies to 26–50 (.342 winning percentage).

"Paul knew Frank Lucchesi [and] Frank Lucchesi was a great minor league manager," Larry Shenk said. "I think he struggled a little bit with some of the big stars in the big leagues that year, and Paul felt that the best thing to do was to put himself in the dugout and get to know what he has there and what he doesn't have so we could start over and move forward."[12] Still, the Phillies took a lot of heat in the press when they finally dropped the axe on Lucchesi. In the July 11 issue of the *Philadelphia Inquirer*, the headline above Dolson's column was 'Phillies Flop—Even in the Firing of Lucchesi.' According to reports, it was Bruce Keidan who told Lucchesi on Saturday night, July 8, that the *Inquirer* got word from an "unimpeachable source" that the Phillies were going to relieve him of his duties. The fact that Philadelphia had contacted Dave Bristol, the former skipper with Cincinnati and Milwaukee, only added credibility to the story.

Lucchesi had a hard time believing it, and after a sleepless night worrying about the news he received from Keidan, he decided to get to the Vet early on Sunday morning to ask his old pal Paul Owens about the rumor. Then upon reaching South Broad Street Lucchesi started seeing some bad signs. First, Owens showed up an hour tardy for an 11 A.M. appointment he had with Lucchesi regarding another matter, due to having friends in town. Secondly, a team cookout that had been planned in Delaware on Sunday night, of which Frank Powell (the team's assistant to the president) had reminded Lucchesi all week, was suddenly canceled. The reason Powell gave was that Bob Carpenter and Owens were not going to be able to make the event. Eventually, Lucchesi was able to sit down with Owens, arriving at the Pope's office to find both him and farm director Dallas Green on hand. It was there, according to Dolson's column, that Owens assured Lucchesi that "there's nothing going on." Owens reportedly told Lucchesi that the Phillies had contacted Bristol for information regarding an American League player that they were interested in acquiring in a waiver deal.

So Lucchesi left Owens' office feeling that his job was safe. After all, in the short time that Owens had occupied the general manager's title, he had developed the reputation of being open with the press, so there was no reason to believe that he would not be honest with his former roommate. But when the Phillies did give Lucchesi his walking papers just 24 hours later, announcing at a Monday noon press conference that Lucchesi was gone and that Owens would step in to finish the season as the team's skipper, president Robert R. Carpenter firmly stated that they had only made the decision on Sunday. He said they wanted to give Owens an up-close look at the players they had, the better to make moves and wholesale changes at the December winter meetings. As part of the shake-up, Philadelphia also let third base coach George Myatt go, promoted Billy DeMars from first base coach to third base coach, and brought super-scout Brandy Davis on board with the Phillies' coaching staff.

Chris Wheeler acknowledged that the firings of both Quinn and Lucchesi did not go smoothly. But he added that it was a vastly different era in terms of the number of media representatives that covered the team. "You had Ray Kelley and Allen Lewis and [Bill] Conlin and those guys," Wheeler said. "Conlin was still young, and all that stuff. Basically, you had no talk radio, you had no mini-cams, and you had no talk shows and all that stuff, ESPN and Comcast SportsNet. You had a couple of writers and the TV's were a non-entity. I remember back then, I was only a year into the job, but you really didn't worry that much about what the media thought. I know that's hard to believe now, but it was not that big of a deal. Clubs were more inclined to just do what they had to do and then worry about the media later. So if it was a little ragged, that's my opinion why."[13]

On top of everything else, it was also a time of transition for the Phillies' organization and the Carpenter family. "It was a bad team," Wheeler said. "Bob Carpenter was turning things over to Rudy at that time. It was the beginning of what would turn this organization completely around, with Ruly taking over the ownership, Paul Owens being the general manager, and Danny Ozark coming in as the manager, who was perfect at the time with those guys. I was part of the PR department with Larry [Shenk] and we didn't have a whole lot of media then. But Mr. Carpenter wasn't really like an owner of today where you've got to make sure you've got your ducks in a row for the media and everything. People didn't think that way like they do now. They just didn't."[14]

Lucchesi could not help but to shed a few tears at the news conference, where it was revealed that he was being demoted to a special assignment representative for the club. "He was really disappointed and very emotional," Shenk said.[15]

Bill Lyon acknowledged, however, that Lucchesi should not have been surprised at his fate. "That's the easiest solution, isn't it, when you have a bad team? Baseball people tend to be hidebound traditionalists and they operate under the theory of, 'Well, that's the way we've always done it,'" Lyon said. "So no, he shouldn't have been [surprised]. That's the old story of Birdie Tebbetts opening the desk drawer (as the Milwaukee Braves' manager). Bobby Bragan got fired as manager in Milwaukee and he found a piece of paper that said, 'Open the middle desk drawer,' which he did and the first envelope said, 'Blame it on me.' And they finished the year just as bad as they were, and started the next year and were even worse. And he opened the drawer for envelope number two and it said, 'Prepare two envelopes.'"[16]

During his managerial career in the minor leagues, Lucchesi became known for some of his colorful antics, such as climbing a light tower and managing from there after being thrown out of a game; sitting on a base and refusing to leave; and getting onto his hands and knees and covering home plate after being ejected. "Some of that wouldn't go here in the big leagues, but he was still very colorful," Shenk said. "[Gene] Mauch had left, Bob Skinner was the manager and he didn't work out. We were trying to change our image, and Frank was perfect because he loved people. Mayor Rizzo was an Italian mayor, so he and Frank hit it off."[17]

Lucchesi also hit it off with the media. Reporters who covered the Phillies could always expect a colorful personality behind the manager's desk during his tenure with the team. "After the game was over," Shenk said, "we'd just lose another game and the media would come into his office and he'd have a yellow pad there. 'I wrote down what you's are going to ask me. This is the first question you're going to ask me.' And they all loved him. He was colorful. But it wasn't big league."[18]

Lucchesi was also loved at an establishment named Palumbo's, which often attracted entertainers who went there to sing, including Frank Sinatra on one occasion. "Frank [Lucchesi] was big there," Shenk said. "As a matter of fact, Frank was in the hospital one time, and the first thing he did when he got out of the hospital was go to Palumbo's, and they introduced him on the stage."[19]

As big as Lucchesi was at Palumbo's, however, that sentiment was not necessarily shared by all of the Phillies' players. "He's a good friend of mine and I don't want to say anything negative about him, but the veteran players didn't like him," Shenk said. "He had a pre-game show and he wanted to say 'Hi' to nuns and all that stuff all the time. I don't think Lefty was fond of him. I know McCarver wasn't. I don't know about some of the other guys. But players weren't very fond of Dallas Green either. It's not that unusual."[20]

♦ 11 ♦

THE NEW MANAGER

Paul Owens was nicknamed "The Pope" because of his uncanny resemblance to Pope Paul VI. In July of '72, the Phillies just might have gotten some divine intervention with The Pope as their manager, playing .500 ball in their first 16 games after the change-over. During the remainder of the season, Philadelphia was 33–47 overall with Owens at the helm—good for a winning percentage of .413. "When Pope went down on the field, one of the main things he tried to do with his general manager instincts was to weed out the guys that he didn't want on his team—not only the players that couldn't play, but the people he didn't want in his clubhouse," Chris Wheeler said. "More than anything, that's why he went down on the field, to do a recon like that because we knew at the time we had a pretty good farm system and we thought we had some pretty good young players coming. We didn't want them to be around a lot of bad guys. I'm not saying that every guy that was moved was a bad guy. That's not true. But he went down there and just decided who he wanted to get rid of, and then things started to change, and then by '74, it got better. '73 was grim and '74 got better. '75 was pretty good and '76 ... real good."[1]

However, it wouldn't be the Pope in the manager's seat when the Phillies turned it around. The Pope had only taken over on an interim basis, and at season's end, Owens, the general manager, would name a successor for Owens, the field manager. One candidate's name mentioned during the final 80 games of the season was that of popular former "Whiz Kid," Richie Ashburn, who had helped the Phillies win the 1950 National League pennant. Phillies owner Bob Carpenter opened the door when he made the comment that the club's next manager would be "somebody that can stay around here and manage this club for the next 15 years or so, like Walt Alston has (with the Dodgers)." Later that July 10 night, while sitting in the Veterans Stadium announcer's booth, Ashburn raised some eyebrows when he remarked, "The only one I

11 ♦ The New Manager

can think of like that is me." As Bruce Keidan noted in a column later that week, Whitey's droll sense of humor no doubt contributed to that statement. But Ashburn might not have been kidding when he said, "I think what this club needs in a manager is somebody who can give it a sense of pride and a sense of dignity. And the only one who can do that is somebody like me or Robin Roberts or Andy Seminick."

The *Philadelphia Inquirer* conducted a poll with the fans that summer to determine whom they would have liked the Phillies to hire as their next manager. Not surprisingly, Ashburn, a two-time National League batting champion during his playing days, won in a landslide. "Whitey" received 33 percent of the fans' votes, easily ahead of runner-up Jim Bunning, who collected 17 percent of the tallies. Bunning, who authored a perfect game for the Phillies in 1964, was on his way to skippering the Reading Phillies Double-A team to a 70–69 finish in the Eastern League during the 1972 season. "The *Inquirer* ran a poll and [Asburn] was the people's choice. For years, he called himself the people's choice and said, 'Boys, if I had been down on that field, you wouldn't have enough fingers for those World Series rings,'" Chris Wheeler laughed. "That was one of Whitey's great lines."[2]

Finishing third in the poll was another star pitcher from the Phillies' past, Robin Roberts, with nine percent, followed by ex–Phils skipper and then–Montreal Expos boss Gene Mauch, with six percent. Others who received write-in votes were ex–Cubs manager Leo Durocher, former Phils catcher Andy Seminick, who was managing the Phils' Triple-A team in Eugene, Oregon, two-time MVP Award winner Frank Robinson, former Milwaukee and Cincinnati boss Dave Bristol, Dodgers third base coach Junior Gilliam, and Owens himself. Ashburn was certainly flattered by the fans' votes, and he was not surprised by the results either, no doubt sensing their desire for a link to a brighter Phillies era. Ashburn even received a taste of what it might be like to manage when he was named the pilot of the National League all-stars from 1952 when that classic was "resumed" in the summer of 1972, some 20 years after rain had halted the game at the start of the sixth inning at Connie Mack Stadium. Neither of the 1952 All-Star managers— Casey Stengel and Leo Durocher—were able to make it back for the renewal, in which the Nationals defeated the Americans 5–1 at Veterans Stadium, or 8–3 for the game. Despite Ashburn's success at the helm of the '52 stars, however, there were some who doubted whether Whitey would even accept the position if it was offered to him. Bruce Keidan was one of those doubters, noting in a column that Ashburn's popularity could have quickly been lost within the span of one losing season.

In fact, Wheeler and the Phillies' broadcast team encouraged Ashburn to stay in the booth for that exact same reason. "We'd say, 'Whitey, stay up here,'" Chris Wheeler recalled. "I don't know how we worded it, but the basic premise was 'You're one of the biggest heroes in this city and you'll leave this town the biggest hero.' Well, who'd have known he'd have a funeral at Memorial Hall in Fairmount Park. And we were right. He never got fired. If he had gone down and been manager, he would have gotten fired and he would have never been the Richie Ashburn that when he died, everybody loved [him] the way they did. It wouldn't have happened. I don't know if he'd have come back as a broadcaster after he had managed. Who knows? But he would have never been the same because he would have been scarred with that. I think a part of him wanted to manage and a part of him realized how good he had it up here [in the broadcaster's booth]."[3]

No one will ever know how Ashburn would have fared as a manager, but what a lot of people might not have known was that he had a bad temper. Wheeler, in fact, questioned how Ashburn would have dealt with the growing number of media representatives who began covering the club. "The media that developed later on, he would have never been able to deal with them," Wheeler said. "At that time, it would have been better because they were his contemporaries, like Ray Kelley and Allen Lewis and Bill Conlin. He knew all those guys for so long, and you didn't have the attention you have now ... I don't know. I just never saw that in Whitey being a manager, because like I said, he had a terrible temper. As a baseball guy, who knows? You didn't have the bench coach idea that you have now, and the things that guys help out with. He hated pitchers. Hated them. The only pitchers he liked were pitchers that could hit. He loved Larry Christenson. He loved Barry Lersch. He loved Lefty, everybody loved Lefty. But I mean, Whitey hated pitchers. So, I don't know. It's something that's such a hypothetical [as to how Ashburn would have done as a manager]."[4]

Keidan figured Robin Roberts to be a long shot for the manager's job, because it was Roberts who brought Marvin Miller and the Players Association together. Andy Seminick had too low of a profile in the organization, despite managing the Eugene Emeralds. Keidan's best guess was that Bunning would get the job when the Phillies finally announced their choice in October. Bunning, in fact, was on a list of seven candidates, including Owens, pitching coach Ray Rippelmeyer, Roberts, and Ashburn, as reported by the AP. The *Inquirer*'s Frank Dolson listed Rippelmeyer as a 5–2 favorite to get the job in a column on October 3, arguing that the Phils' brass liked him and that he knew the league. Bunning and Bristol — in Dolson's opinion — were tied at a distant second, both with 25–1 odds. Bristol was known for having well-drilled and well-disciplined teams, and many considered him to be the best unemployed manager available. And despite the fact that Dolson thought his strong-willed style might be too much for the Phillies' brass to control, the AP reported in mid–October that Bristol would be named the Phillies' new manager. Ultimately, according to Keidan, Bristol might have been a pawn in what the writer described as "The Great Game." Keidan was convinced that Philadelphia was ready to name Bristol as the new field boss when Lucchesi was dismissed in July, and it did not happen, he argued, because the Philies wanted to save face. Then, when the AP, specifically writer Ralph Bernstein of Philadelphia, let it leak that Bristol was the Phillies' choice, Keidan suggested that the Phillies would use the same reasoning to not go in that direction.

Whatever the case, Danny Ozark, an 11th-hour candidate, was named the Phils' new skipper on November 1. Ozark, a coach for eight years on Walter Alston's staff with the Dodgers from 1965 to 1972, was the man favored by Bill Giles. Prior to serving on Alston's staff, Ozark was a minor league first baseman in the Brooklyn Dodgers' farm system and then became a manager with the Dodgers' Class B club in 1956 and rose through the ranks. The Phillies gave Ashburn an interview for the position, along with others, but they felt that it was Ozark who was right for the job. "I think they gave Ashburn an interview before they interviewed Ozark," Chris Wheeler said. "Dave Bristol was another guy that was involved in that. They gave Whitey the courtesy of an interview, but I don't think that he was ever a real serious thought to be the manager. I just think they thought he was great at what he did, and we know he was great at what he did."[5]

Bristol, though, was considered by many to be the logical choice, and Bill Lyon acknowledged that Ozark's hiring was a surprise. "It was a big surprise, as I recall," Lyon said. "Danny was a really sweet man. And I'll tell you who Danny Ozark was. He was Charlie Manuel. The similarities between them are amazing. Danny was given the same kind of country bumpkin, rube, but just a good old country boy at heart. That's Charlie Manuel, so I thought it was strange the time that Manuel is here."[6] That country bumpkin persona was reinforced at Ozark's introductory press conference, as he said with a straight face, "When we go to spring training this year, our No. 1 issue will be to win a pennant."

Lyon also recalled another incident with Ozark. "With Danny, probably the most unfortunate thing was, when it got late in the season — I forget which season it was — they had just lost and were eliminated from the pennant race," Lyon said. "And Danny said, 'Well, at least we've still got a chance.' And it took several tries for him to finally be convinced of this immutable mathematical certainty that if you're four games behind with three to play, you've been eliminated."[7]

Although the Phillies endured two more losing seasons under Ozark in 1973 and '74, he improved their win totals to 71 in his first year, and then to 80 the following year. Philadelphia finished runner-up in the National League's Eastern Division in 1975 with 86 victories, and then won the division title three straight years from 1976 to 1978. But even early in his career with the Phils, Ozark was thinking positively. "I remember in '75, we almost won," Larry Shenk said. "We were in Allentown at the winter tour. God bless him, Danny Ozark. He got up to the microphone and said, 'We're building a dynasty in Philadelphia.' I guess he was right. At the time, we hadn't been out of last place for years. But we were getting good."[8]

The Phillies could have used some of those positive vibes during their 1972 season. The only positive aura they had that season came from Lefty, who was responsible for four of Owens' first eight wins as the manager, beginning with a 4–1 conquest of the Dodgers on July 11, giving Carlton his eighth straight victory and a 13–6 record. Eventual Hall of Famer Don Sutton yielded just four hits in six innings, but Carlton was even better, allowing no earned runs on five hits and one walk while striking out eight. The Phillies scored all the runs Carlton needed with a four-run rally in the second inning against Sutton. Three of Philadelphia's four hits against Sutton came in that inning; the Phillies also capitalized on two walks. After Willie Montanez walked and stole second, he scored the game's first run on Denny Doyle's base hit to right field. Carlton's single and Larry Bowa's free pass loaded the bases in front of Don Money, who smashed a double into Veteran Stadium's left field corner to clear the bags. That was one of Money's highlights from a '72 season in which he batted just .222 with 15 home runs and 52 RBIs.

Acquired from the Pirates in December of 1967 with three other players for Jim Bunning, Money gave the Phillies a glimpse of what he could do in 1970, batting .295 with 14 long balls and 66 RBIs. Money also ranked second among National League third baseman in fielding during the final season at Connie Mack Stadium. But then Money struggled miserably in 1971, seeing his average plummet to .223 with just seven dingers and 38 RBIs. Anything that could have gone wrong for Money that year did, as he hurt his throwing arm, and then in late May, he took a hot grounder off the bat of St. Louis' Phil Gagliano directly in the face and landed on the disabled list for a month with an eye injury. That was also the season that Money lost stretches of time with the Phillies while going to summer camp and meetings with the U.S. Marine Corps. While he was gone, John Vukovich took over at the hot corner, and then even after Money returned to the ball club, "Vuke" stayed at third and Money moved to left field in addition to playing 20 games at second base as well.

Needless to say, Money was looking forward to a fresh start back at third base when spring training rolled around in February. In Clearwater, Money told reporters, "If you would have told me last spring that I wouldn't have hit .225, I would have said you were crazy. I've got to have a better year. I sure as heck can't have a worse year." Unfortunately for Money and the Phillies, however, their hopes for a better year in 1972 never really materialized. Even with the Phillies off to their fast start in April, Money was hitting just .188 at the end of the month. He was still batting under the "Mendoza Line" in late May when Bruce Keidan wrote in a column that Money was the Phillies' "chief enigma." Keidan penned that Money "has the physical ability to be a .300 hitter. He is hitting under .200. Against left-handed pitching, he is hitting about half that." In hindsight, Money struggled with the Phillies' attempts to get him to take the ball to the opposite field more often.

Following his sterling 27-win season in 1972, Lefty slipped to a 13–20 record with the Phillies in 1973. Overall, Carlton went just 44–47 from 1973 to 1975, but then rode his incredible slider to a 165–88 record over the next seven seasons, including four 20-win campaigns.

"When I came up to the Phillies, I think I hit .229 my first year with the Phillies," Money said. "Then the next year, it was the last year at Connie Mack Stadium in 1970, and I got my feet on the ground and I was hitting .300 the whole year and I ended up hitting .295. I really felt good, and at the time I was really more of a pull hitter. I could go the other way when it was hit-and-run or stuff like that. And I remember going into 1971 that I felt real comfortable because I came off a good year and I was still only 23, 24 at the time. Then all of a sudden, I was asked to change my style of hitting. They wanted me to go the other way a little bit more, and I tried. But it just didn't work out. I tried to go the other way and it wasn't for me and I struggled in '71 and '72."[9]

Eventually, at the end of the '72 season, Paul Owens traded Money, Vukovich, and Bill Champion to the Milwaukee Brewers in exchange for Ken Brett, Jim Lonborg, Ken Sanders, and Earl Stephenson. With Milwaukee, Money had his best years as a big leaguer. In 11 seasons with the Brew Crew, Money hit .270, including a career season in 1977 in which he hit .279 with 25 round-trippers and 83 RBIs. The trade "worked out great for everybody," said Money, who is currently the manager of the Brewers' Triple-A club, the Nashville Sounds. "I went over there and played third and got my feet on the ground. I was 26 at the time and I was there for 11 years. Could it have happened in Philly? Yes, it could have been turned around. As players get older and learn the game, they get their feet on the ground and that's what happened to me. After I had the good year my second year, the third and fourth years I was trying to do things their way and it just wasn't working out. And I just got in a rut and I couldn't get out of it. And the trade was great for me and great for the Phillies and the Brewers, because I think everybody made out in the trade. I just started over new and just went on and had a pretty good career in the American League."[10]

Money, however, was not the only player who underachieved for the Phillies during that 1972 season. There's a reason that the Phillies received a very high pick again in the 1973 draft, when they took John Stearns with the second overall pick behind the Texas Rangers. "That was a real bad team, and when Carlton pitched, that team turned into a championship team, for whatever reason," Bob Boone said. "One of them was because of what a great pitcher he was, how dominant he was."[11] As Carlton proved, however, even the great ones need a little luck sometimes. His winning streak could have ended at eight in a row in a game against the San Francisco Giants on July 15. Lefty lasted just five frames in that outing, while yielding four earned runs on five hits, and he left the game with the Phillies trailing 4–0. Gary Matthews made his big league debut with the Giants during the 1972 season and collected four home runs and 14 RBIs in just 20 games. And even as dominant as Lefty was that season, it might not have been as traumatic for "Sarge" to face him as one might think. For his career, Matthews hit .328 against Lefty (22-for-67) with seven extra-base hits, including one home run. Given that Sarge was a right-handed batter and Carlton was a left-handed pitcher, it wasn't as uncomfortable for him to face Lefty as it was to go against the likes of hard-throwing righties such as Nolan Ryan, J.R. Richard, Goose Gossage and Bob Gibson. "Pitchers from the left side for the most part, even if they got you out, it was a lot more comfortable than facing the guys on the right side," Matthews said.[12]

Fortunately for Carlton, his teammates erased that deficit against the

Giants and got him off the hook with a season-high 11 runs in the top of the seventh inning against Giant hurlers Frank Reberger, Don McMahon, Jerry Johnson, Randy Moffitt, and Don Carrithers. The Phillies scored three runs before a single out was recorded, with John Bateman delivering an RBI single, Greg Luzinski working a bases-loaded walk, and Oscar Gamble scoring on a wild pitch. Denny Doyle's sac fly tied the game at 4-4, and then Philadelphia went on to score seven more runs. Willie Montanez provided a two-run double off the fight-field fence and Gamble smashed a two-run triple to right-center field. Before Carrithers finally ended the inning with a strikeout of Roger Freed, the Phillies had scored 11 runs on six hits and six free passes. Bucky Brandon picked up his fifth win of the season and improved to 5-2 with just one inning of work in relief. For Lefty, meanwhile, the streak lived on, as he picked up a no-decision in Philadelphia's 11-4 conquest.

"It happens all the time," Luzinski said. "Guys get taken out and he ends up getting a win (or no-decision) when he was down or whatever. That's just part of the game. I'm sure he lost or had no-decisions in games where he pitched well, or got a no-decision because we didn't score enough runs. Like I said, I think it will average out during the course of his career."[13]

Despite the short outing against the Giants, however, Carlton's numbers up to that point spoke for themselves. He had a 12-6 record, while allowing just 52 earned runs in 176 on-third innings for an ERA of 2.65. He also had a major league-leading 187 strikeouts. And on Tuesday, July 18, Lefty earned a deserving honor when National League manager Danny Murtaugh, who skippered the Pittsburgh Pirates to the 1971 World championship, named him to the Mid-Summer Classic. Carlton was the Phillies' only representative and joined a staff that included NL wins percentage leader Gary Nolan of the Cincinnati Reds; Bob Gibson of the Cardinals, who had won 10 straight after losing his first five decisions; Steve Blass of the Pirates; Tom Seaver of the New York Mets; Don Sutton of the Los Angeles Dodgers, and Bill Stoneman of the Montreal Expos. Mets reliever Tug McGraw was the only other left-hander on the squad besides Carlton.

"You just named some of the best," Fergie Jenkins said of Seaver, Carlton, and Sutton. "There's nobody compared to that era ... Marichal, [Gaylord] Perry, Koufax, Drysdale. The era now, they've got some guys that are decent pitchers. [The Cardinals' Chris] Carpenter is a pretty good ball player and C.C. Sabathia [of the Yankees]. I've only seen that Clifford Lee pitch in the playoffs. He's not bad. In the era I played, guys didn't get hurt. They pitched every third day, every fourth day and didn't get hurt."[14]

"You're talking about Hall of Famers," Larry Bowa said of the NL's starting pitchers in 1972. "You try to relate to guys playing now and they really don't understand the quality of pitchers that were [playing] back then. There was a four-man staff. They didn't go five innings, they went eight to nine. They attacked the zone. They had three quality pitches, sometimes four. But the one thing they all had in common [was] they were unbelievably competitive and they felt when they were on the mound that they were better than you. You could just see it in their demeanor, the way they approached pitching. It was a battle facing guys like that. It was tough."[15]

Asked if the pitchers were better in that era 40 years ago compared to today, Bowa said, "Not even close. Your number ones now would probably be at the top of the rotation. But I think where you see the difference now is your threes, fours, and fives. I mean, the depth ... when you take a look at the Mets and the Astros and the Cardinals, their threes and fours were real good. I think the thing that's tough with pitchers right now is the strike zone is so small. Back when we played, you didn't have the video cameras. Today, they're analyzing every pitch an umpire calls, and to me, that's hurting baseball."[16]

For Lefty, this was his fourth of ten career All-Star selections. He started and won the 1969 Classic while pitching for the Redbirds, as the National League defeated the American League, 9–3, at RFK Memorial Stadium in Washington, D.C. He also pitched one inning, in the NL's 1–0 win over the AL at the Houston Astrodome in 1968. Plus, he was a member of the 1971 All-Star squad that lost, 6–4, at Detroit's Tiger Stadium. Besides Carlton, Seaver was the only other NL pitcher with All-Star experience going into the 1972 game at Atlanta–Fulton County Stadium.

Prior to going to the All-Star Game, however, Lefty had two more starts on the Phillies' west coast swing. The first of those was in San Diego on July 19, and Lefty followed up on one of his shortest outings of the season with one of his longest. It was an 11-inning complete game, to be exact. Apparently, San Diego's Clay Kirby did not have a pitch count either, as he too went the distance. The Padres' hurler allowed 13 hits, but he survived the tightrope with Philadelphia stranding 14 on base. Finally, in the top of the 11th inning, Denny Doyle stroked a one-out single and Bill Robinson, a seventh-inning replacement in left field for Joe Lis, slammed a go-ahead RBI double, breaking a 2–2 tie that had lasted since the second inning and giving the Phils a 3–2 win. Carlton sealed it with a scoreless inning in the bottom of the 11th, completing an outing that saw him strike out eight while yielding just two earned runs on seven hits and four walks. Earlier, Philadelphia took a 2–0 lead against Kirby in the top of the first on Tommy Hutton's RBI ground out and Willie Montanez's two-out RBI single. The Padres pulled even with one in the home half of the first and another in the second. But that was all the Padres mustered off of Carlton.

"I think initially, did [the Phillies] think they'd gotten the better of the deal [for Rick Wise]? I don't think they did," Bill Lyon said. "The whole key to [Carlton] was the slider, and I think he kept working on it and he didn't perfect it until he was here after a year or so. That's just my theory anyway, because that was his out pitch. It's so simple — you knew what was coming. The slider low and in and then he'd tie them up with fastballs high. Up, down, in and out. It's not that hard to figure it out, but to [hit] it is something else entirely. Those were the two pitches he used probably 95 percent of the time. Fastball up, slider down. And you can be the batter and know that it's coming, but hitting it is something all together different and much, much, much more difficult."[17]

Known by teammates and opponents alike for his intense preparation, Lefty logged at least 229 innings all but one time over a 17-year span from 1968 to 1984.

The Dodgers certainly had a difficult time trying to hit Lefty on July 23, as Carlton went all nine innings in a 2–0 shutout against Tommy John and Los Angeles at Dodger Stadium. Carlton blanked the Dodgers on just five hits, while striking out six and walking one. His ninth straight victory improved his record on the season to 14–6. Carlton and John waged a scoreless pitchers duel until the Phils scored both of their runs in the top of the seventh. Greg Luzinski's leadoff single started the rally against John, followed by Willie Montanez sacrificing pinch runner Bill Robinson into scoring position. Montanez also reached base when John's throw to second was too late to get Robinson. Roger Freed and John Bateman went down on strikes, but Lefty helped his own cause with a ringing two-run triple off the right-field fence.

The Dodgers had runners at first and third in the fourth and fifth innings, but Lefty whiffed Steve Garvey to end the former situation and Manny Mota lined out to end Los Angeles' threat in the latter. At the end of the game, Carlton's 3.56 strikeouts to one walk led the NL, just ahead of Don Sutton's 3.28 ratio.

The fact that the Phillies were buried in the NL East standings made no difference in how Lefty approached his starts. "Carlton's going to pitch the same way as if he was with a contender or a last-place team," Sparky Lyle said. "That's the whole thing about Carlton. He's going to get up for those games. A lot of guys pack it in. A lot of guys could be your number one starter for a last-place team, but can they be a number one starter for a first-place team? Not many. He could do both. 'Give me the ball and I'll win this game for you.' That's what separates him from everybody else."[18]

Former ace Sandy Koufax certainly took the ball and won a lot of games for the Dodgers during his era; Lefty was now invoking memories of the Hall of Famer with his performances in 1972. But Carlton had no interest in comparing himself to Koufax, telling reporters, "If I had to choose between Koufax and myself to start one game, it would be Koufax. He had better stuff." St. Louis Cardinals star Joe Torre faced both Koufax and Carlton, and was a teammate of Lefty's at one time, so he offered an interesting perspective on the comparison between those two pitchers. "Sandy had more experience than he did up to that point," Torre said. "So I think that's where that came from. Lefty always respected that. Bob Gibson was another one that he respected. Lefty didn't need to be better than somebody else. He just needed to be better than the team that he was pitching against. He was pretty low maintenance as far as I'm concerned. I think the only time you knew he was a special guy is when you knew that in spring training, he didn't make any road trips. Usually your stars on your club don't make road trips — pitchers anyway. They'll devise some kind of game to keep them from going out and about and riding on a bus for two, three hours at a time."[19]

Bill Lyon was asked if Lefty was just being modest in his remarks about Koufax, to which he responded, "I'm not so sure. By the way, I would agree with (Carlton that Koufax's stuff was better). There was about a three or four-year period where Sandy Koufax was as good as there's ever been, lefty or righty. Two bad things happened. He was very wild at the beginning and it impeded his progress. His control was a real problem early. And then by the time he got that straightened out, all the elbow misery started. Today, I don't think he can bend his left arm. Had he had a full 12-year or 13-year or 14-year career and been healthy, boy, I don't know what his numbers might have been like. So I wouldn't be surprised if Carlton was sincere. No false modesty. He might have believed that, that he'd rather have Koufax's stuff. I'd rather have Koufax's stuff."[20]

Hall of Famer Fergie Jenkins, who joined Lefty Grove, Warren Spahn, Christy Mathewson, Walter Johnson, and Robin Roberts as just the sixth pitcher ever to post six straight 20-win seasons with his 20–12 record in '72, added: "Everybody at one time wanted Koufax because he'd done so much in the playoffs and World Series. Carlton was a winning pitcher. The guy won 300 ball games. Koufax got hurt. What did he win, 165? Comparatively so, I think that Carlton was a dominant pitcher after he left the Cardinals. So I think that if you had a game to win, I'd pick him or Gibson in his era — or myself. I never got in the playoffs. And Carlton only got [there] maybe once, twice. But Koufax pitched a lot of games in playoff competition and he beat the Yankees. Those were some of the series that everybody remembers Sandy for doing and striking out X number of guys in playoff competition, in World Series competition."[21]

Lefty's pickoff move, though, might have separated him from a number of other pitchers. In the Dodgers' 2–0 loss to Carlton on July 23, Los Angeles seemed ready to score in the sixth inning when Frank Robinson reached on an error at third base by Don Money, with Wes Parker and Bobby Valentine following him to the plate. But Carlton picked off Robinson and the Dodgers went quietly after that. Robinson was one of six base runners that Lefty picked off during the '72 season. According to Bruce Keidan, Lefty learned his pickoff move from Mets pitcher Jerry Koosman on a hunting trip; he would hang his right leg in the air while in the stretch. Hunting was one of Carlton's passions, along with skiing, and he was often out shooting guns with friends in the off-season. "Koosman taught him this move where, as he would lift his leg, he would hold it there for a long time without balking and he could freeze a runner," Keidan said. "And he used to practice that and work on that with part of his strength regimen he went through with Gus Hoefling. Carlton had one of the best left-handed moves to first base of any pitcher. He was tough to run on."[22]

Carlton was also tough on his own teammates who happened to be playing first base. Tommy Hutton said that you had to be careful not to leave first base too early on bunt plays, for fear of being picked off as well. "He had the ability to lift that right leg and pause and make a last-minute decision of throwing to the plate or throwing over to first base if he thought the runner was going," Hutton said.[23] Richie Hebner could certainly relate to that during his two years in Philly in 1977 and 1978. "I played first base for two years with him and he picked me off a few times, and I was on his own team," Hebner said. "I didn't know when the heck he was coming over. He had a nasty move. He picked a few guys off. There's not many things he didn't do right. He was a great pitcher over all those years. He was one of the top lefties ever in the game."[24]

Larry Shenk said, however, that if runners timed Lefty, they held a big advantage. "He had a pickoff move, but if you timed it right, you could run and there was no chance at getting him," Shenk said, "because he would hang that right leg and once he started going to home plate, he was slow. But if he hung it and you moved and it was still hanging, then he would get you. He'd pick guys off. But if you timed it properly, you could run on him."[25]

Despite Lefty's excellent pickoff move and all of his success in 1972, the Phillies mercifully entered the All-Stars break with a 31–57 record. They were dead last in the National League East standings, 24 games behind the front-running Pittsburgh Pirates, as Carlton headed to Atlanta for the All-Star Game. Earning his fourth selection to the Mid-Summer Classic belied the fact that Lefty was erratic early in his career. His record in his five full seasons in St. Louis from 1967 to 1971 was just 15 games over .500 (74–59). After a 17–11 season in 1969, Carlton slipped to 10–19 in 1970, and then rebounded to go 20–9 in his final year with the Cards. And following his sterling 1972 season with the Phillies, he was only average in terms of winning percentage in his next three campaigns, going 44–47. That included a 13–20 record in 1973, when he got off to a bad start following an off-season in which he battled a case of bronchitis. Lack of confidence probably contributed to Lefty's 19-loss season in 1970, when he depended too heavily on his off-speed pitches. But Joe Torre, who normally played third base and first base that season, tried to correct Carlton of that problem during a game behind the plate against the Dodgers, as he gave regular catcher Ted Simmons the day off.

"I just was noticing that he was very defensive in the way he was pitching and I had asked manager Red Schoendienst, 'Let me catch him one game,'" Torre recalled. "We were in L.A. at Dodger Stadium. And Red let me catch him. He had just stopped using his fastball because he was pitching defensively and he was throwing a lot of breaking balls. Every single pitch I called was a fastball, and he shook me off (one time) and he gave up a home run to Andy Kosco. I'm not sure if there was nobody on, one man on, but we won the game. But that was the only time he shook me off and he gave up the home run. He pitched the whole game, I think, and we just threw fastballs. I just wanted to prove to him that his fastball was his best pitch and he had to go out there and trust it again. It's like pitching around somebody. People think because you pitch around somebody, that means you're throwing breaking balls. No, it just means you're trying to stay away from the strike zone."[26]

Aside from that confidence issue, Torre noted that Lefty was still learning how to pitch during that stage of his career, which helped to explain his erratic results. "He just wasn't there. I have a young left-hander, Clayton Kershaw here, and he went out and gave up two three-run homers," said Torre of the budding star on his 2010 Los Angeles Dodgers. "And you keep saying, 'Oh,

I wish ...' Then you realize he's 22 years old. It is what it is until they sort of settle in. Lefty, you've got to remember, is this tall kid. So in being a tall kid, it's all about rhythm and trying to get your body all going in the same direction at the same time. And I think it took him a little time."[27]

It took Steve Blass a little bit of time to get on track for the Pirates as well. Pittsburgh's right-hander was only 22–23 during the 1964, '66 and '67 seasons. But then he put together a solid 1968 season in which he finished 18–6 with a 2.12 earned run average in 33 games for the Bucs. "It's such a vague term that quote-unquote, they get it, they figure it out. All of a sudden, they say, 'That's the way it looks,' and you find a way to get consistent. Everybody says they want to be consistent. But how do you become consistent. That's the key. And guys say, 'I don't know. I wasn't and now I am.' They get it. And you get on a roll and you figure out, 'OK, that works that way.' Once you get it and you figure out what works, you've got to have it happen all the time. That's how you get consistent. It's not just understanding it. It's doing it. It's the theory and then the application."[28] Torre said that winning 20 games in 1971 gave Lefty a lot of confidence, and then when he went to Philadelphia, he knew what he had to do. "The thing about Lefty is, he would compete," Torre said. "He wouldn't lay around licking his wounds. I mean, I saw him in 1970 when he was struggling and he was certainly lacking some confidence. But the '71 season and beyond, he had a pretty good idea of who he was."[29]

"It's pretty typical of pitchers, I think," Larry Shenk said of Carlton being erratic early before developing into a Cy Young winner. "Like a quarterback, it takes them some time to really get going. I remember talking to former Phillies manager Jim Fregosi one time. He said, 'Generally, it takes a pitcher four or five years to mature and get to know how to pitch and everything else, and then you lose him because you've given up on him. He becomes a free agent or you've traded him. Lefty had situations where he didn't hold runners on base well and they would run on him, but if you don't get on, you can't run."[30]

A big reason that runners didn't get on base against Carlton was due to perfecting his slider. Coming back with his slider in 1972 after not using it during the '71 season was certainly a key to his success. It was also the centerpiece to his arsenal as he put his erratic ways behind him from 1976 through 1984, when he compiled a 165–88 record with four 20-win seasons. "He was always good," Steve Blass said, "and I don't know when it happened, but when he started doing a little cutter, that pure slider inside to right-hand batters, it was over. Stop the fight, draw the drapes, it's over. He was just great."[31]

Just as important in his development was the fact that he took up martial arts, which helped him go to great heights both mentally and physically. It was in 1974 that Lefty turned to the deep conditioning and discipline of Shodokan Karate at a facility in his hometown St. Louis in 1974. Prior to that, Lefty had developed a friendship with a man he knew as Briggs, who helped him with the power of positive thinking. It was during Carlton's nightmarish 1970 season with the Cards, when he was 10–19, that he received a letter at Busch Stadium from Briggs, a 60-something-year-old, part-time night watchman who was living in Tucson, Arizona, at the time. Carlton had been pitching defensively and expecting to lose every time he went to the mound, and in Briggs' 10-page neatly-typed letter, he told Lefty that he was tired of seeing someone with such tremendous talent lose, and that he decided to write after having a vision.

Lefty told John Flynn of the *Philadelphia Inquirer* that he found "literally pages of information dealing with the mind — the thoughts of a very profound man." This seemed to tie in with Lefty's fascination with metaphysics, a subject that caught his attention as a 14-year-old when his uncles introduced him to it. He was so intrigued by the topic that he read anything he could find dealing with the subject. Lefty was also intrigued by Briggs, and over time as more letters arrived, Lefty couldn't wait to read more about Briggs' thoughts. Lefty and his wife, Beverly, actually knew his first name, but they simply called him Briggs, and although they saved his letters, they were not interested in sharing them with others. They were clearly sold on Briggs, especially when Lefty lost just one more game in 1970 after receiving his first letter. Carlton acknowledged that his outlook not only on life, but pitching as well, was changed by Briggs, who quoted philosophers and the Bible in his writings.

But as much as Briggs affected Carlton, Chris Wheeler believes that the biggest impact came from Gus Hoefling, one of America's leading gurus in martial arts. The two of them connected in 1975. "That type of focus came from Gus Hoefling, as opposed to this guy (Briggs)," Wheeler said. "Lefty was always amenable to suggestions like that because he was always trying to find a higher power, of something that could make him pitch better. He liked to have that tunnel vision. I think Lefty kinda enjoyed that aura of mystique around him, even though he was one of the guys when he went out. I think he was OK with that. How much that guy had to do with it, I don't remember. But to me, the biggest influence on him and channeling him toward the martial arts and all those things, it was Gus Hoefling."[32]

It was no coincidence that Lefty's work with Hoefling was paying off when he posted a .652 winning percentage from 1976 to 1984 with 165 wins and four of his six 20-win seasons. He had a stretch of 18 straight seasons with 161 or more K's en route to finishing his career second all-time in strikeouts (4,136), behind only Nolan Ryan. "Back then, Gus Hoefling was the strength and conditioning guy with the Phillies, and there were a lot of things that Carlton did between starts that no one else could even attempt to do because they were so strenuous and demanded so much strength in arms and hands and so forth," Tommy Herr said. "So I think he kinda set the standard back at that time for a guy who really worked hard between starts."[33]

Those strenuous workouts were part of his "strength and flexibility" conditioning program, which he did with Hoefling. According to Joe Flower's article in his 1983 *SPORT* magazine article, there were 80 routines in the program, including sitting on the edge of a table and doing sit-ups while bent backward from the waist, putting his hands and one foot on buckets and performing one-legged push-ups, and twisting a stick horizontally into a tub of rice time after time. According to Larry Bowa, Carlton and Hoefling did their workout routine for at least an hour and a half the day after Lefty pitched, and then gradually backed off as he approached his next start. "Everyone says pitchers have to run. Well, he proved that wrong because he was one guy that didn't run," Bowa said. "I think if guys watched him, they would much rather run than try to go through that routine. It wasn't like a 20-minute routine. He'd punish himself the day after he pitched. It was pretty devastating."[34]

Chris Wheeler added, Gus Hoefling "totally changed Lefty's conditioning, because Lefty was a guy who hated to run. He looked like a giraffe when he ran and he hated it — he hated it with a passion. Pitchers all had to run, and he was always last in the group and he would just fight it. He didn't want to be out there. So when Gus came along and got him into martial arts, and then he was so successful, they equated that with what Gus was doing for him and he didn't have to run anymore. He loved that. He loved never having to run anymore."[35]

The other thing Lefty did not do too often was shag balls during batting practice. That was the case even when Mike Krukow pitched for a Phillies team managed by Pat Corrales during the 1982 season. "Carlton was kinda on a same [workout] program and it may have pissed a few people off," Krukow said. "But Corrales said at a team meeting, 'Everybody's going to take batting practice. There will be no exceptions.' And he was talking to Carlton because Carlton never shagged. He went in, did his workout with Gus Hoefling, he worked his ass off for an hour and a half, and he came in and got ready for a game. So Carlton goes out to center field and every ball that got hit to him, he would throw over the backstop from center field. He could throw a bomb.... He didn't want to be out there. So he got his point across and he was going to keep throwing them out there until he won his point. Corrales said, 'Alright, go ahead, see you later.' And we didn't see him on the field the rest of the year. We thought it was pretty comical. But I think if there's a guy that ever deserved his own program, it was him. And his whole program wasn't sitting around with his feet up on a table reading *Playboy* magazine blowing farts at the clubhouse kids. He outworked everybody and he had his own program."[36]

When the Phillies traveled to the Windy City, there was no place inside of Wrigley Field for Lefty to do his program. As a result, he went through his workouts in broad daylight on the diamond, where others watched in awe. "You watched everything that this guy did because he was the prototype that everyone wanted to be like," Krukow said. "I mean, this guy was a machine and he had this invincibility about him, playing against him. And I think everybody who played against him experienced the same things.... [His workout] was incredibly intense, incredibly difficult. It was an incredibly long arduous workout that when you got done, you were spent. You were spent."[37]

Carlton's routine in which he drove his hands and arms into a bucket of rice was one of legendary stuff. "It helps your forearms and your wrists and he would go right to the bottom of those things," Bowa said. "Most guys would maybe get through a third of it. He'd go all the way to the bottom."[38] Larry Shenk also got a first-hand look at Carlton's workout and could only shake his head. "Usually pitchers did a lot of running for the conditioning thing," Shenk said. "He didn't do that. But he had Gus Hoefling and the Martial Arts thing and that rice pit. It was almost impossible for a human being to do what Lefty did in there."[39] Chris Wheeler noted that Carlton made himself the exception to the rule because of the incredible career that he was carving out for himself. "He was so good and so successful, and normally you don't want to have 24 guys [on a program] and then one guy on his own, but this case was different," Wheeler said. "Totally different."[40]

Lefty also showed his strength in a workout in which he put a bar that was about six feet in length on his shoulders as if he was doing twists. Hoefling would then hold one end of it for resistance, and although the Phillies' strength coach was a very strong man himself, he had trouble holding it. "Once Gus put his hands up there, you couldn't move it," Bowa said. "But Lefty could move it. He would just whip it around. And he'd do all these things with his legs, kicks and squats with weights on his ankles. It was a gruesome workout."[41] Jerry Martin, too, remembered that resistance exercise with the bar on Lefty's shoulders and said that it was similar to a guillotine with the way Carlton rested his hands on it. "Gus could kill you in a matter of minutes with that because when you start doing that, you can't hardly breathe. That's the kind of stuff he did with him — and also the Kung Fu moves. He just did a lot of stretching with Gus. Lefty was in pretty doggone good shape. He was a strong man — big and strong — and that's the type of starting pitcher you want to have on your staff."[42]

After Danny Ozark took over as the Phillies' manager in 1973, he found out just how gruesome Lefty's workout was during an occasion in the mid-seventies. "I remember Larry Christenson went in and I think Danny Ozark said, 'I could do Steve's program,'" Bowa recalled. Christenson "said, 'Go ahead.' I think he tried it one day and that was the end of that. It was that gruesome and it was a tough workout. And Carlton worked out in the winter and he was extremely strong. He was a guy that loved what he was doing and he knew he was as good as anybody in baseball when he went out on the mound."[43]

Sparky Lyle, admittedly, was another one of those who couldn't do the workouts that Carlton performed. Lyle had his own description of those workouts, calling them very, very rigorous. "You heard all the stuff about the rice barrels and bins and all that. There wasn't anybody that could put their hands down in that rice up to their shoulders except him," Lyle said. "I tried it. I got to about there [end of the palm]. It's just the blindfolding, when Hoefling would try to hit him with that big pole and stuff. Some of the stuff was pretty far out. But the whole thing about him was that's what he did in place of what everybody else did to prepare to pitch. If he didn't want to do the other stuff, he could do that. But I don't know of anybody that can do it except him."[44]

Gary Matthews said that Lefty got to the ballpark early to do his workout routine. Although Sarge didn't know everything that Carlton and Hoefling did in their workouts, he knew that it helped him become an ace. "The fact is, you know he was there early and doing it," Matthews said. "A lot had to do with self-defense and some other things he came up with Taekwondo or whatever it was. It worked for him and it didn't necessarily work for some of the other guys."[45]

Those intense workouts with Hoefling were all Lefty needed for his preparation. Whereas other pitchers threw bullpen sessions between starts or played long toss or had a game of catch, Mike Krukow remembers from their days as teammates that Lefty never even touched a ball on a day that he wasn't pitching. Carlton's preparation consisted only of his intense workouts with Hoefling. "The only time he picked up a ball was every five days when it was his turn to start," Krukow said. "It was one of the most remarkable things I've ever seen. That's how intense that workout was that he did. He was one of the most incredible athletes that I've ever been around. Mentally, he was a stud. It blew my mind because my approach was 'Get a feel of the ball, keep the release point, get on the mound, do a lot of throwing.' With him, you threw when you pitched. And I've never seen anybody do that since."[46] Chris Wheeler, when asked about Krukow's comments, added, "He was stronger than any human being you ever wanted to see. But he didn't throw."[47]

Legendary New York Yankees manager Casey Stengel surely would have loved to have Lefty on his pitching staff. It was 1966 when Stengel and Ted Williams were being inducted into the National Baseball Hall of Fame that Jim Kaat got his first look at Lefty; Carlton, then just 21 years old, was summoned by the Cardinals from Tulsa in the Pacific Coast League to pitch against the Twins in an exhibition game at Doubleday Field. Kaat left Cooperstown that day impressed with the young lefty. "He struck out a bunch of us in, like, seven innings. But that was the first I'd ever heard of him. They said the Cardinals were bringing this young left-hander up that has a lot of promise."[48] Years later, Carlton was fulfilling that promise by the time Kaat arrived in Philadelphia in 1976. While they were together, Kaat learned a lot about Carlton's mental discipline. He believed that Lefty, with his strong mind, might have had a mental picture of his motion and how to repeat it every time. And not throwing between starts could have been his strategy to avoid disturbing that rhythm. "It's an advantage to a pitcher when you're pitching every four days and you're pitching for seven or eight innings," Kaat said. "If you have a couple of short starts and then it's awhile before you go back to the mound, sometimes you almost have to go to the bullpen and have a little side session to try to find it. He never had to do that, fortunately for him."[49]

Even in 1972, Lefty acknowledged that he did not pick up a baseball to do any throwing over the winter. Instead, his routine consisted of walking five to six miles each day in addition to going quail hunting. Bullpen sessions have evolved in the game since the early seventies, but prior to Lefty getting together with Hoefling, he and the other pitchers did play catch in the outfield between starts. "I don't remember bullpens the way they do now," Wheeler said. "Would they go throw between starts? Yes, I guess. It was playing catch because those guys threw a lot. It was stretching your arms and all. So I'd imagine he did that."[50]

Lefty's mental toughness was another by-product of his intense workout routine. Mike Krukow said that Lefty's workout habits were his "backbone" and that they gave him a shield of invincibility. "I really believe that," Krukow said. "It insulated him against a lot of distraction. If there was something around the clubhouse or whatnot that was a distraction, he could always leave, separate himself, get into his workout, and for two hours, he could be alone with his thoughts, with his prep. But it would build. That was Monday and if he pitched on Saturday, he would get more quiet as the pitch day got closer."[51] Tim Flannery was never a teammate of Carlton, but was well aware that Lefty was a very strong individual. "We knew that the workouts that he did not only were physical workouts," Flannery said. "They were mental workouts as well, and that every fifth day was the day you knew what he was going to come at you with."[52]

Krukow remarked that Lefty was as mentally prepared a pitcher as he has ever seen. "I think a lot of his deal was he felt that if he worked as hard as he did, he outworked his opponent, and therefore he deserved it more," Krukow said. "Working out as hard as he did enabled him to be able to throw at the level which he pitched at. And like I said, there was no pitch count to him. If he threw 160 pitches, 90 of them would be breaking balls. He was incredibly strong, he was incredibly athletic. Just as far as mentally tough, I think he felt of himself as kind of a robot on pitch day. It was unbelievable."[53]

He was a robot who never let his opponent see him sweat. That was one of the many lessons that Krukow learned from Carlton during the 1982 season, when the two of them lockered next to each other. Krukow was 45–50 in six seasons with the Cubs before being dealt to Philadelphia, but Lefty taught him to become a better pitcher. "I was 30 years old at the time, and he taught me a lot of things that I thought were invaluable in the way that I grew as a professional," Krukow said. "He taught me about preparation, about mental prep going into a game, about being able to maintain composure. Emotionally, you pretty much knew what my emotions were when I was on the field because I would get excited over a good play. I would stomp over a bad call. And he kinda calmed all that down and I really saw the wisdom in that. You just don't let your opponent feel like he has any edge on you at all. Just get the ball, go back and make another pitch. It was invaluable information for me because I tried to apply it. He definitely made me a better pro, no question."[54]

Overall, Lefty's preparation produced unquestioned results. Consider the following mind-boggling statistic: Carlton pitched at least 229 innings all but one time over a 17-year stretch from 1968 to 1984. The only season in which he did not was the strike-shortened 1981 campaign, in which Lefty tossed 190 innings. For comparison's sake, in the 26 seasons between 1985 and 2010, Phillies' pitchers reached at least 229 innings only nine times. They were Kevin Gross in 1986 (241.2) and 1988 (231.2), Shane Rawley in 1987 (229.2), Terry Mulholland in 1991 (232) and 1992 (229), Curt Schilling in 1993 (235.1), 1997 (254.1), and 1998 (268.2), and Roy Halladay (250.2) in 2010.

In 1972, Lefty failed to complete only 11 of his 41 starts. Furthermore, there were only three games in which he turned the game over to the bullpen in the middle of an inning. Every other time, his stuff was good enough that he was at least able to save manager Frank Lucchesi a trip to the mound.

Obviously, Lefty still had tremendous ability during the 1980 season, when he won the third of his four Cy Young awards. During that particular campaign, teammate Bob Walk recalled only one occasion that Lefty was forced from the game in the middle of an inning. That came on a July 2 game in Montreal when Lefty handed the ball over to reliever Dan Larson with one out in the eighth inning of a 6–1 loss to the Expos. "That's how solid he was," Walk said. "That's pretty impressive. You certainly don't see that nowadays."[55]

Bill Lyon and Wayne Twitchell agreed that Carlton was a pioneer with the workout routine that he employed to keep his body in fantastic shape. "Without question, he was ahead of his time," Bill Lyon said. "The whole thing, when he convinced the Phillies to bring Gus Hoefling on board, he was just his personal trainer. And the whole thing with sticking your arm in a bucket of rice ... I think privately, *privately*, a lot of his teammates were rolling their eyes. Anything like that was seen as eccentric in those days. Of course now, it wouldn't seem weird at all. I don't recall that anyone else was doing it."[56]

Twitchell remembers going to his first spring training with the Houston Astros in 1967 or '68 and seeing three or four pitchers doing their running workouts wearing rubber suits to sweat off the extra weight that they had gained in the off-season. "They either drank so much beer or ate so much food and drank beer and whatever else in the winter and they'd report to spring training and be 30 pounds over their playing weight," Twitchell said. "So they had to go sweat it off. During the time I played, that era kinda ended. Players didn't let their bodies go over the winter. I'd work out with [Atlanta Braves star] Dale Murphy. And Lefty, I'm sure he had a far more rigorous workout schedule than I did. He'd come to spring training and look like he's ready to play. If we'd start playing the next day, he could start opening day and pitch nine innings."[57]

In 1972, Carlton tossed 30 of the Phillies' 43 total complete games. He threw seven more than the next two closest pitchers, Hall of Famers Bob Gibson and Fergie Jenkins, who tied with 23 apiece. That year, Lefty equaled the number of complete games that Jenkins threw in '71 and Juan Marichal threw in 1968; the total was the most in the NL since Robin Roberts' 33 in 1953. With the evolution of today's set-up men and closers, the 2008 season saw AL leader Roy Halladay finish with nine complete games and NL leader C.C. Sabathia with seven. "The game has evolved to that point where six innings is considered a quality start and pitchers in the minor leagues are kinda brain-washed into looking at the sixth inning and shutting it down after that," Tommy Herr said. "Back in the day when Carlton pitched, the mentality was you get handed the ball, go nine. And that's what the goal was every start, was to go nine. It has changed."[58]

Ray Burris threw 47 complete games with seven clubs over a 15-season career, beginning with the Chicago Cubs in 1973. In the same season that the big six-foot-five righty made his major league debut, guys like Lefty and Nolan Ryan each threw 300-plus innings, but that has become a bygone era. "Guys back in those days pitched for a long time," Burris said. "You think about Nolan Ryan pitching for 26 seasons and the amount of innings that he pitched — 300 and some innings a year — that's a lot of innings. And guys took care of themselves back then. But they also had a mental toughness, and that's what Steve had. He had a mental toughness. 'Give me the ball. It's my time to pitch.' To go out and win 27 games in 1972, and that was pretty much half of your team's wins, that says a lot right there."[59]

Bill Lyon, when asked what Lefty would have thought of set-up men and closers, remarked, "I would say two words — sneering disdain. That reminds me of Ed Wade's comment about Curt Schilling, 'Every fifth day, he's a horse and the other days he's a horse's ass.' I think Carlton would have just really pooh-poohed the whole notion [of specialty roles]. It's one of those 'Just give me the ball and get the hell behind the plate.' I think that's the attitude he took with him. I don't know that they even had pitch counts in those days. How about Nolan Ryan? What do you think he thinks of pitch counts?"[60]

Larry Bowa recalls times when Danny Ozark had the bullpen ready to go and would come out to get the ball from Lefty, only to be rebuffed. "He wouldn't do it," Bowa said of turning the game over to set-up relievers and closers. "The longer he was there (in Philadelphia), and as we started getting real good, there were a couple of times that Danny came out and Carlton goes, 'This is my game. You're not going to the bullpen. This is my game.' His philosophy was 'If I'm going to give it up, I'm going to give it up. I'm not letting somebody else give it up.'"[61]

With all of his complete games, it was easy to see how Lefty finished the season with 346 innings. Ken Reynolds was second on the Phillies' staff with 154 and one-third innings pitched. "A generation or so back, 300 innings wasn't all that rare," Lyon said. "I'd have to look it up, but just thinking of Koufax in those five years who was maybe the best pitcher in the history of the game, he challenged 400 innings. And Lord knows what Cy Young [pitched]. And guys like Walter Johnson would pitch both ends of a doubleheader. You can think yourself into trouble by relying on all these things like pitch counts and long toss. They never did any of that. You can outsmart yourself sometimes."[62]

♦ 12 ♦

THE STREAK MARCHES ON

Beginning in 2003 and going forward, the winning league in the Mid-Summer Classic was awarded home-field advantage in that year's World Series. Thirty-one years earlier, that idea was not even a twinkle in Commissioner Bowie Kent Kuhn's eyes. Suffice it to say, however, that Carlton and the rest of the National League all-stars were to happy pull out a 4–3 win over the American League, as Joe Morgan's base hit drove in Nate Colbert with the game-winning run in the 10th inning. Hank Aaron delighted the hometown fans in Atlanta with a two-run blast over the left-field fence in the bottom of the sixth against Gaylord Perry.

But with Carlton playing for the cellar-dwelling Phillies, the only way he was getting to the World Series in '72 was by purchasing a ticket. He continued to pitch like a champ, however, picking up where he left off after the break with another shutout, this time a 2–0 conquest of the Chicago Cubs at Veterans Stadium. "All I know is that as a player, I knew full well when we came into Philadelphia if Carlton was going to be pitching in that series," Rick Monday said. "You knew ahead of time. Truly to this day, I did not enjoy going to home plate to hit against him."[1]

While extending his streak of scoreless innings to 27 straight over his past three starts, Lefty also notched his tenth win in a row and improved his record to 15–6. Lefty yielded just four hits, all singles, and benefitted from a two-run homer by Willie Montanez in the bottom of the ninth inning that broke up a duel between Carlton and Chicago's Milt Pappas. "Carlton was a machine and he just seemed invincible," Mike Krukow said. "Everything was off a hard release. He was kind of a two-pitch guy — a big slider and a fastball away. His fastball was low nineties, but he had exceptional command with it and he'd just sit on the outside corner and just hit that knee-high location all day long. He never pitched inside. But from the very first pitch of the game to the very last pitch of the game, he was locked in and he could go 160 pitches. He was a machine."[2]

Among the 12,453 in attendance that night was Phillies legend Robin Roberts, whose streak of nine consecutive wins was broken that night by Lefty. After the game, Roberts jokingly said to reporters, "I came down here to root against him, but he won anyway." Chris Wheeler said that anybody who knew Roberts knows that he actually would have been one of Carlton's biggest supporters that night. "That's the classiest man that walked the face of the earth," Wheeler said. "Robin Roberts? To this day, he's still one of the best human beings you'd ever want to meet. Robin Roberts wouldn't root against anybody. If anything, Robin Roberts would have been in awe of watching Lefty do what he was doing, as great of a baseball fan that he is to this day. Robin loves the game so much and the people that can do the things that Lefty did."[3]

Carlton's seven K's against the Cubs extended his major league-leading strikeout total to 208, which was 38 in front of AL leader Nolan Ryan of the California Angels. His 10th consecutive win left him just two shy of the Phillies' record of 12, set by Charlie Ferguson while pitching for a fourth-place Philadelphia squad in 1886. "When you're in that kind of rhythm, you're just looking for him every fourth or fifth day," Don Money said. "Just go out there, let's go about our business, and score him two runs, and we've got a heck of a chance of winning this ball game. And you know when a guy is only giving up two runs or less, he's dealing. It didn't matter if it was the Dodgers or the Giants or Montreal or whoever. He went out there on a roll, and players behind him knew that. We knew it. Like I said, we didn't play any harder for him than we did for anybody else. It was just, he gave up two runs and maybe the other starters gave up five. It was a great feeling. It was a great experience. Today, you don't see pitchers dominate like he did. You'll see pitchers win the Cy Young and they'll be 18–6 or 18–4 or whatever it is. But he was 27–10 and flat out dealing. [Tim] Lincecum with the Giants, he's a young pitcher. He's unorthodox ... the way he pitches. Carlton pitched the way he pitched. He threw hard, he had a good breaking ball."[4]

Tommy Herr, who was a teammate of Carlton's in Minnesota in 1988, said that Lefty's long winning streak showed a level of consistency in which he was throwing the ball with great quality in every start. "It also shows how a pitcher of his stature can elevate his team," Herr said. "Even though they were a bad team, when he was pitching they felt unbeatable. So that's huge. That's why teams go out and find aces because aces elevate their teammates and they try to create a level of confidence that's not ordinarily there."[5]

That confidence was there again on August 1, as Lefty beat Jerry Koosman and the New York Mets, 4–1, in the nightcap of a doubleheader to give the Phillies a split. Carlton's victory, along with the solid work of rookie reliever

Mac Scarce, helped to give the Phillies their first series win in New York in nearly four years. They took three of four in Queens, marking the first time they had accomplished that feat since September of 1968. Scarce, a seventh-round selection in the June 1971 free-agent draft, proved to have a rubber arm by pitching in six of seven games during a stretch in late July and early August. The 23-year-old lefty, who was 1–2 with a 3.44 ERA in 1972, notched his first career win and a save in that series against the Mets, and he struck out six and did not allow a single hit in 3 two-thirds innings of relief while pitching in three of the four games. Scarce struck out both batters he faced in the opening game of the Phillies' twinbill with the Mets, but unfortunately it wasn't enough, as New York won, 3–2, in 18 innings. The nightcap looked like it, too, might go extra innings, with Lefty and Koosman taking a 1–1 tie into the eighth inning. But Bill Robinson's two-out, bases-clearing double was the difference and it kept Carlton's win streak intact at 11 straight. The only thing that stood between Lefty tossing a fourth straight shutout was Cleon Jones' fourth-inning one-out RBI single to right field that drove in Willie Mays for an unearned run, snapping Carlton's scoreless innings streak at 30 and one-third innings.

Outside of Carlton, Phillies pitchers combined for only five other shutouts during the 1972 season, with Wayne Twitchell, Dave Downs (a sixth-round draft choice of the Phillies in 1970) and Barry Lersch each throwing one after the All-Star break. But with the Phillies playing ten doubleheaders from July through September, including three in less than three weeks in late July and early August, Philadelphia had more games than it did starting pitchers. Even Woodie Fryman, who had been demoted to the bullpen, made his last start for the Phils in late July prior to being claimed off waivers by the Detroit Tigers on August 2. The doubleheaders certainly didn't help matters for a Phillies staff that did not have a lot of depth. Overall, Philadelphia used 11 different starting pitchers in '72.

"That's a lot for any era," Chris Wheeler said. "Downs was in Atlanta that night, he had a great start in Atlanta. In September, you can bring your call-ups, so they probably brought some guys up like Dave Downs that year. He was a big blonde guy from Utah. Good guy. Twitch, you could see he had some ability. I think they used so many pitchers because they were just trying to make something work. There were probably some injuries in there too."[6]

Overall, those who made at least one start for the Phillies in 1972 included Steve Carlton, Dick Selma, Woodie Fryman, Bill Champion, Barry Lersch, Ken Reynolds, Jim Nash, Gary Neibauer, Bucky Brandon, Wayne Twitchell, and Dave Downs, whom some considered at the time to be the Phillies' best young prospect since Fergie Jenkins. "Listen to some of those names we're throwing out," Wheeler said. "What are you going to do? [Rick] Wise's last year was '71 because we traded him. You replace one good pitcher for another who turned out to be fabulous. It was a bad team. I don't even think about closers back in those days. You really didn't have a closer. So it was just up and down the staff. Other than Lefty, it was just a team that was going to lose a heck of a lot more than it won."[7]

Beginning with his solid effort against the Cubs in the nightcap of a doubleheader on July 27, in which he pitched six and one-third innings (his longest stint at the major league level), Twitchell ended up taking a regular turn in the rotation every four or five days after the break and finished with 15 starts. "If I would have had a choice at the time, I would have preferred to have started," Twitchell remarked. "Although relieving, I was able to warm up quickly and I could pitch multiple days in a row. So I knew that was a benefit also. In fact, I think every year with the exception of one maybe, I did both things sometime during the season, both started and relieved."[8]

Although he was 3–8 with four no-decisions in his 15 starts, Twitchell proved capable of throwing a quality performance from time to time. In his seven starts that he either earned a win or no-decision, Twitchell had a 1.64 ERA in 44 innings. In his eight losses, his ERA ballooned to 5.32. Including 34 relief appearances, the 24-year-old Twitchell was 5–9 with a 4.06 ERA, 112 strikeouts and 56 free passes in 139 two-thirds innings. But this was the opportunity Twitchell envisioned when he rejected an athletic grant-in-aid to play quarterback for the Oregon State University Beavers. Wayne's father, Ralph, was an All-Coast tailback at Oregon State in the 1930s, and OSU coach Demosthenes Adrecopoulos offered to change the Beavers' entire offense to capitalize on the younger Twitchell's abilities as a drop-back passer. "Had I gone to college out of high school, that's probably where I would have wound up," Twitchell said. "Even though, honestly, I went down to the University of Arizona in Tucson, and boy, that's a nice campus and atmosphere."[9]

In all, Twitchell received more than 40 scholarship offers from college coaches to bring his golden right arm to their program. Some of the big-time universities that were trying to land his talents included Oregon, Oregon State, Southern Cal, Stanford, UCLA, the University of Washington, Washington State, Notre Dame, and Penn State. There was interest "all over the country," Twitchell acknowledged.[10] Arizona and Oregon State were even willing to give Twitchell a 50–50 scholarship to play football and baseball, so they would not have required him to play spring football or fall baseball. Looking back, he doesn't regret not playing football at the collegiate level. In fact, if Twitchell had opted to go the college route, it would have been to play baseball. "I regretted at times not going to college right out of high school," Twitchell said. "I would come home in the winter for the eight, nine years that I played baseball and take a semester of classes — there's a college here in downtown Portland, Oregon — but it wasn't the same as being a full-time student at a Division-I school."[11]

Citing a six-hour knee operation from playing baseball in 1973, Twitchell figures he made the right decision to not continue his football career. "Even though regretting missing the [college] experience, probably the best thing I did was not go to college to play football," he said. "I probably would have experienced that [injury] earlier in life."[12] Twitchell ended up signing with the Astros after being selected with the third pick of the first round in 1966. He was later purchased by the Milwaukee Brewers in November of 1969 and then traded to the Phillies in April of 1971.

The Houston organization was also one of eight stops in the big leagues for Bucky Brandon. Philadelphia eventually acquired Brandon in a trade with the Chicago White Sox in January of 1971: he became one of the Phillies' top relief pitchers during the '72 season. But even Brandon was called upon to make six starts that season. His first one came on July 9 in a 5–4 loss to the Padres, marking his first start since June of 1969 while with the Seattle Pilots. In that particular game, he failed to make it out of the second inning.

Carlton, though, did not have that problem when he registered his sixth and seventh shutouts of the season in his next two starts, throwing back-to-back whitewashings against St. Louis and Pittsburgh. "He did it all on his own," Bill Lyon said. "The rest of them together only won five more games than he did. It was really a bad team, a really bad team, and yet every start they had a better-than-even chance at winning."[13] Lefty faced his former team on August 5 and hurled a complete-game five-hit gem in a 5–0 victory over the Redbirds. Bill Robinson and Greg Luzinski each slugged a two-run homer against losing pitcher Reggie Cleveland, and Lefty took care of the rest. He registered seven more K's and walked just one. His conquest of the Cardinals also gave the Phillies their fifth straight win, their longest streak of the season. "Why was he so dominating? Was there motivation there because of being traded by the Cardinals? I don't know that," Larry Shenk said. "But I guess there may be something to that."[14]

The Phillies scored 26 runs in their five-game win streak, but their offense came to a screeching halt in their next two contests, one a 6–0 loss to St. Louis' Al Santorini, who faced Wayne Twitchell, and the other a 7–2 defeat to the Pittsburgh Pirates' Dock Ellis, who beat Bill Champion. "A lot of times, it seemed like when I did start toward the end of the year, I would start the next night (after Carlton), and he pitched some fabulous games that year, particularly in that 15-game consecutive win streak," Twitchell said. "He also pitched some games that he could have lost and the Phillies for some reason scored six, seven runs and I'd pitch the next night and we'd score one. I thought, 'Save some.' It was an amazing thing to watch."[15]

The fact that Lefty held Hall of Famer Lou Brock to an 0-for-4 night atop the Cardinals' lineup certainly had a lot to do with Lefty's win as well. Brock, who was batting .315 at the time, was one of the players still left from the Cardinals' World Series teams in 1967 and '68, and although the Redbirds stumbled to a fourth-place finish in the NL East with a 75–81 record in 1972, Brock was still a major threat at the top of the lineup, playing in the ninth of his 16 seasons in St. Louis. He finished that season with a .311 batting average and 63 stolen bases. "It was great (having Brock at the top of the lineup) because you knew that not only was he a good hitter and a base stealer, but he was also a power guy," Joe Torre said. "He could hit some home runs. He was definitely a table setter and an RBI guy."[16] Brock was certainly making things happen during a stretch of games from June 4 until July 8, when the Redbirds won 24 of 30 games.

Tim Raines, who was cut out of Brock's mold as a leadoff hitter and a base-stealing threat (808 career stolen bases), said it's invaluable to keep those guys off the bases, and it was no different for Carlton in his latest win. "It was probably the most important thing because when you have guys like that, speed is the difference," Raines said. "If you lead off, get on base, steal second, bunt him over and get a fly ball — or a ground ball works sometimes — you can score a run without even getting a hit. I've always felt, even in those Cardinals days, if they kept speed off the bases, you've got a chance to win. If you don't keep them off the bases, you don't even have to get a hit for them to score runs. So a good pitching performance can go null and void because maybe you don't give up many hits, but you end up losing 1–0 or 2–1 or something like that. And that can be the difference. The keys I think to any pitching staff are two top pitchers keeping the first two guys, especially the guys that can run, off the bases. Normally, you can neutralize the power hitters, but a lot of times those little guys are the ones that get you in trouble."[17]

Even in '72, Lefty was frustrating batters with his nasty slider. But the lineups he faced that year might have been glad that he wasn't throwing it as often as he would after becoming reunited with Tim McCarver in 1975. "Do I think that all helped him with Gus Hoefling? Yes, I think that all helped him," Chris Wheeler said. "He became physically stronger. I think when Timmy came around with him later on too, Timmy made him throw the slider more. Timmy insisted he throw the slider. He threw it a lot before then, but McCarver just insisted he throw the slider. That was the thing about

Timmy. He knew how to handle him and he knew that was his best pitch, and he made him throw it. He made him use his fastball and other things too, but he really had him throw the slider."[18]

His slider certainly helped him in his next start against a Pirate team that would win the National League East in '72 with a 96–59 record before losing to the Cincinnati Reds, three games to two, in a best-of-five League Championship Series. This was the same Pittsburgh team that won the World Series in 1971, and they were just three outs from returning to the Fall Classic in '72. With the Bucs leading 3–2 going into the bottom of the ninth of the fifth and deciding game, Johnny Bench slugged a game-tying home run, and then George Foster scored the winning run when Bob Moose threw a wild pitch to pinch-hitter Hal McRae. "Our team was just as good as the team that won in '71," Richie Hebner said. "But the ball didn't bounce the right way. That was an ugly way to lose. I lost a lot of games in the big leagues— I won more than I lost—but that loss right there was probably one of the ugliest losses I ever had. A wild pitch. [Foster] was on third base and he just walked home and the playoffs ended."[19]

It was indeed a tough way to lose for a Pittsburgh team that won its third straight NL East Division title in '72. Team chemistry was arguably a reason that the Pirates were enjoying a lot of success. The '72 Bucs lost six games in a row in late April and early May to fall to 5–9, but they never lost more than four straight the rest of the season. The team had good chemistry "because we won," Steve Blass said. "I preach that all the time. Chemistry is a result, not a cause. If you win, you have good chemistry. Nobody wants good chemistry if you're losing. You're having fun and losing? Chemistry is fun. It's a mix of personalities. You win a lot of games, you get a lot of guys having a lot of fun and you get close to each other."[20]

Plus, it didn't hurt to have a lot of talented players, such as right fielder Roberto Clemente, first baseman Willie Stargell, catcher Manny Sanguillen, center fielder Al Oliver, second baseman Dave Cash, third baseman Richie Hebner, and Rennie Stennett. No one would argue that the Bucs fielded a formidable lineup. "I would rank it as fun (having that batting lineup)," Blass said. "Manager Bill Virdon said about those early seventies teams, 'I'm driving to the ball park figuring I'm going to get five or six runs every night.' Obviously, it was fun to pitch in front of that group. I was pitching in front of Stargell, Clemente and Mazeroski—three Hall of Famers. So it was all good."[21]

Amazingly, however, Carlton was 2–1 that year against the best-hitting team in baseball; he had a 1.44 ERA, against the Pirates including his 2–0 blanking against Pirate ace Blass on August 9. That was Lefty's 13th straight win, breaking Charlie Ferguson's club record, and it raised his record to 18–

6. While racking up his fourth shutout in five games, Lefty also stretched his streak of consecutive innings without allowing an earned run to 54. Carlton repeatedly pounded the strike zone against a Pittsburgh team that entered the game hitting .278 as a team and had five players in the lineup that night batting over .300. In the process, Lefty made the Pirates' vaunted lineup look mortal while striking out 12 and allowing only three hits. Lefty was so dominant that when the Phillies took a 2–0 lead with single runs in the second and third innings, it must have seemed like climbing a mountain from the Pirates' dugout. Philadelphia scored its first run when Willie Montanez singled and circled the bases on Greg Luzinski's base hit that was misplayed in the outfield. Lefty added an insurance run with a round-tripper — the fourth of his career — against Blass in the third by connecting on a hanging breaking ball.

Steve Carlton helped himself with the bat during his career, slugging 13 home runs and adding 130 RBIs. His long ball against Pittsburgh Pirates ace Steve Blass on August 9, 1972, proved pivotal in a 2–0 victory, his 13th straight win.

"I can see the ball going over the right-center field fence," Blass said. "I can remember that. I have good memories of games like that because that's a good ball game. I was good and he was better. But I always liked him because that was his office out there. You enjoyed competing against a guy like that because you knew you were going against the best. And if you win every once in awhile, it's really good. And even if you come up a little short, you had the opportunity to go against the best and that's why you play. That's why they call it the big leagues."[22]

Carlton was definitely "big league" on the mound that night, as he retired the first ten batters he faced, with 12 strikeouts, before Stennett stroked a one-out double to right field in the bottom of the fourth inning. Sanguillen added a single to center field leading off the fifth inning, but then Lefty struck out the next five batters he faced. Going into the bottom of the ninth inning, Carlton was still in control with a two-run lead. Overall, "Super Steve" registered all 12 of his strikeouts in the first six innings. The Pirates had six right-handed batters in their starting lineup, which played right into Carlton's strength. "When he threw that slider down and in, you had no chance," Larry Shenk said.[23]

Looking to finally break through against Carlton in their last at-bat, the Pirates sent up one of the game's most feared hitters in Clemente. Lefty did not run 3–2 counts to a lot of hitters, but against Clemente, he did. Then Pittsburgh's superstar fouled off six pitches and eventually worked a free pass. And when Gene Clines, batting a lusty .332, stroked a single to center field, sending pinch runner Dock Ellis to second base, the Bucs had something brewing. It didn't take long, however, for Pittsburgh's rally to hit a major speed bump. The Pirates' next batter, Ronnie Stennett, popped weakly to the mound trying to bunt the runners over; Lefty caught the ball just above the turf, spun and nailed Ellis, who was running on the play, to complete the twin-killing. Oliver followed and gave Philadelphia a brief scare when he launched a 2–2 pitch from Lefty to deep right field, but Roger Freed grabbed it in front of the fence and that was the ball game.

"Carlton had good stuff. He could beat anybody," said Hebner, who played on ten playoff teams in his career, including six with the Pirates. "He won a lot of games like that. When he pitched, the Phillies didn't have to score many runs. You just didn't want to give up four-out innings. Just make the plays, get a few runs and with Carlton on the mound, there was a real good chance when you were taking a shower that you had a win.... Blass was a good pitcher. He was consistent throwing strikes, he didn't walk many batters, and he kept the ball down. He was just outpitched that night."[24]

Blass, who was the winning pitcher for the Pirates in game seven of the 1971 World Series, finished the '72 campaign with a 19–8 record and a 2.49 ERA. Overall, he was one of four starting pitchers with 13 or more wins for Pittsburgh that season, including Dock Ellis (15–7, 2.70 ERA), Nelson Briles (14–11, 3.08 ERA), and Bob Moose (13–10, 2.91 ERA). "The pitching staff was underrated," Blass said. "We had a good pitching staff. I was having good years and I was winning 15, 18 games. Dock Ellis was great. Briles, Bob Moose [were great]. Dave Giusti was saving a bunch of games. Without having superior dominant stuff, I don't know of anybody that was more mentally tough than Giusti in the ninth inning. He just didn't want people to beat him. And we had Ramon Hernandez, who had as big a curve as you'd see. So we had a very balanced team. We had a good bench and we had [Jose] Pagan and [Vic] Davalillo and [Gene] Clines and Milt May. So those are rock solid baseball teams."[25]

Ellis, in fact, had a long winning streak of his own during the 1971 season. And with a good offense supporting him and the other pitchers, the Pirates proved to be a tough team to beat. "We had good hitting, but not many people talked about our pitching," Hebner said. "But our pitching was good and our defense was good enough."[26]

Carlton was more than good enough, and in the next day's papers, manager Paul Owens was quoted after the game as saying, "I just can't believe anyone can pitch better than he has. And he's a competitor. You give him a run or two early and he really gets tough." Larry Bowa saw just how tough Lefty was while playing shortstop behind him for many years. "The one thing about Steve was his fastball was overpowering, his slider was overpowering, and he had a good curve ball," Bowa said. "He just had great stuff. Guys like that don't come along too often."[27]

Combined against the National League's two best clubs in 1972, the Pirates and Reds, Lefty finished 4–2 with a 2.75 earned run average. Asked if that was a statement as to just how good Carlton was in 1972, Larry Shenk said, "I think it was. I mean, he could just dominate, no matter who you were."[28] Although it was the Reds who represented the National League in the '72 Fall Classic, Shenk thought that the Pirates were actually the better team. "I always give the edge to the Pirates. In '76, there was no doubt about the Reds," Shenk said. But the Pirates "were tough. We had some great battles with them."[29]

"Those two teams were known for their hitting, the 'Big Red Machine' and the 'Lumber Company,'" Bowa said. "and you very seldom saw a pitcher just shut them down, but Steve did. I think everybody knew how good Steve was. I don't think he had to make a statement. But when you do shut those teams down, or you're 4–1 against those teams, you've got pretty good stuff."[30]

Willie Stargell summed up the frustration that many hitters experienced with his famous remark about Lefty. "I hit him like I used to hit Koufax, which is like drinking coffee with a fork." Dave Parker could definitely sympathize with the '72 Pirates when he joined the Bucs the following year. Although the Pittsburgh slugger finished his fine career with 339 home runs, he didn't hit many of those against Lefty. Carlton owned Parker and often had him swinging at sliders that dropped into the dirt. For his career, Parker hit just .258 against Carlton with 35 strikeouts in 120 at-bats. "He wore out

Dave Parker," Bowa said. "Dave Parker had no chance. And in all fairness to Parker, he played every time. He didn't ask out or anything. He just kept trying to battle. I can honestly tell you this, as long as I played, and I played a long time, I've never seen as many hitters swing at balls in the dirt off a pitcher in my life as they did against Carlton because of that slider. It was so devastating. It looked like a fastball and the bottom would just fall out, especially against right-handed hitters — he'd throw it at their back leg. If I've seen one guy do it, I've seen 20 guys swing at pitches that literally hit their back foot. I eventually got traded and I had to face him when he was in Philly and I was with the Cubs, and he was tough."[31]

Carlton being on top of his game was one thing. But opponents also had to deal with the fact that the Phillies' defense took their game to another level with Lefty on the hill. In 1972, the Phillies committed 116 errors in the field. But in 21 of Lefty's 41 starts, Philadelphia played error-free ball behind him. When Mike Schmidt and Larry Bowa patrolled their positions in Phillies pinstripes, Philadelphia had one of its best combinations on the left side of the infield. Although Schmidt started his career at the end of the '72 season, Bowa was the Phillies' regular shortstop that season and finished with a solid .987 fielding percentage and just nine errors in 715 total chances.

"Guys are on their toes all the time to try to make plays for those types of guys," Tim Raines said. "When you have someone out there who takes their time and walks a lot of people, guys get on their heels on defense. All of a sudden you walk two or three guys and the next thing you know, the ball is hit in the gap and the guy's not ready. They're just not ready to make plays. A Carlton game will probably last an hour and maybe 30 minutes. When you have a pitcher who gets the ball and throws it, you know you're going to be out on defense for a short period

Against the National League's two best teams in 1972, the power-packed Pittsburgh Pirates and Cincinnati Reds, Lefty combined to post a 4–2 record with a solid 2.75 ERA.

of time and then you're going to be hitting. You're going to hit and most of the guys want to hit. For any pitcher, not just the top pitchers, I think when you have those guys that want to get it and throw it, you're on your toes because they're going to pitch every time. When Carlton pitched, it was going to be in his rhythm."[32]

On the same night that Lefty shut out the Bucs, former Phillie Woodie Fryman threw a 6–0 whitewashing at Thurman Munson, Bobby Murcer and the New York Yankees while pitching for the Detroit Tigers. After taking the decision in a 5–4 loss to the Expos on June 24 to fall to 2–8 with the Phillies, Fryman was beginning to wonder if he was a starter or a reliever for Philadelphia. During a span of five weeks, he made three starts and also pitched six times in relief. Finally, on August 2, the Tigers claimed the Kentucky tobacco farmer off waivers. So in that quick of a span, Fryman went from a team floundering in last place to a team leading the American League East standings. And for awhile, it looked like Deron Johnson might be joining Fryman in the Motor City. The Tigers and the Boston Red Sox both expressed interest in the man nicknamed "Big D," but the Tigers were the only club who claimed the power-hitting first baseman when Paul Owens placed him on waivers. Initially, it seemed to be a good thing that the Tigers were the only team that claimed Johnson. If the Red Sox or other teams had also done so, Owens either would have had to say good-bye to Johnson for the $20,000 waiver price or he would have needed to recall him on waivers and freeze him on the roster for the balance of the season. As it was, since only one club claimed Johnson, the Phillies and Tigers had the league's blessing to negotiate a deal. But the deadline of Wednesday, August 8, to make a deal came and went, and Johnson, as it turned out, never switched zip codes. The Phillies eventually traded Johnson to the Oakland Athletics in May of 1973 for minor league infielder Jack Bastable. Asked if Philadelphia was looking for too much from Detroit for Johnson, Lyon said, "Yeah, they might have overvalued him, at least in Detroit's mind."[33]

By this time in the season, there was little reason for the fans to go to Phillies' games except when Lefty pitched. As Bill Lyon noted, the Phillies might have broken the 76'ers' record for futility when they went just 9–73 during the 1972–73 season, if it had not been for Carlton's dream season. Over 79 home dates at the Vet that summer, the Phils drew just 1,343,329 fans, an average of 17,000 per game. But on Sunday, August 13, there was an added bonus for fans to come out to the Vet for a doubleheader between the Phillies and Expos. Not only was Lefty pitching the first game of the twinbill while going for his 14th straight win and his 19th victory of the season, but the 67-year-old Karl Wallenda, of the famed Flying Wallenda Circus act, was scheduled to walk across a tightrope stretched from one side of the stadium to the other. In the end, neither one disappointed the fans. Carlton took care of business first, shutting the Expos down on just three hits in a 2–1 Phillies win. Then in between games, Wallenda navigated his way across the Vet high above the turf, even stopping to stand on his head at one point. Earlier, Lefty had stood on his head while dominating the Expos' lineup and raising his season-high strikeout total to 240 with eight more K's in another complete-game gem. He did so without having his best stuff. Afterward, Lefty was quoted as saying, "I didn't have good stuff and I couldn't get the slider over. I was lucky to get away with it."

There was nothing lucky about the Phillies' first-inning rally against Montreal pitcher Ernie McAnally, when they scored both of their runs on Willie Montanez's RBI double and Greg Luzinski's run-scoring single. Carlton, meanwhile, had a no-hitter for three and two-thirds innings before Montreal third baseman Bob Bailey launched a solo home run in the top of the fourth. That was all the Expos mustered against Lefty, however, as he moved within five wins of the major league record of 19 consecutive victories, set by the New York Giants' Rube Marquard in 1912. "I'm not thinking about records or strikeouts," Carlton said in the following day's papers. "I want the win. Those other things take care of themselves."

Carlton brought that same mentality to the ballpark when the National League West-leading Cincinnati Reds visited Philadelphia on Thursday, August 17, with the Phillies riding another three-game losing skid, and a total of 42,635 fans turned out at the Vet to see Lefty beat Ross Grimsley by a 9–4 score. That win was Carlton's 20th of the season, giving him back-to-back 20-win campaigns for the first time in his career, and it extended his win streak to a remarkable 15 in a row. Grimsley figured that he might have won about five in a row at the start of a season, but he never approached what Lefty accomplished. "I was a completely different pitcher than him," Grimsley said. "He struck guys out, he had above-average stuff, breaking ball, fastball. He had above-average stuff most of his career, wherein he was the same type of pitcher. So that made it even more amazing. They knew what they were getting and they still didn't do much with it, so that's a testament to him right there. The more you think about it, 15 in a row for anybody ... if you won ten in a row, that's amazing. But 15 games on a poor team? It's almost unheard of. And you'll probably never hear it again."[34]

Besides winning his 15th straight, Carlton also earned the distinction of being Philadelphia's first 20-game winner since left-hander Chris Short achieved the feat while going 20–10 for the fourth-place Phils in 1966. Short was on the disabled list while recovering from surgery to his back at the time

Lefty won his 20th, but he did not miss the opportunity to congratulate Lefty on his gem. "It was loud," Chris Wheeler said of the atmosphere at the Vet that night. "He beat Ross Grimsley and we scored a bunch of runs and it was loud. I don't know that it was loud because it was 15 in a row as opposed to 14 or 13 or 16. It was just that there were a lot more people in the ballpark when he would pitch. I mean, he was selling tickets, there's no doubt about it. When Lefty would pitch, you would have a big crowd. And then when Lefty wouldn't pitch, the attendance would go back to being whatever it was. And it was electric. We weren't going anywhere, but everybody was recognizing there was some greatness going on. Maybe this was a Cy Young Award winner on a bad team like that. I wasn't a broadcaster in those days, but I know we felt it

Steve Carlton was known to tip his cap to the fans following big wins during his playing days with the Phillies. One such occasion happened on August 17, 1972, when he defeated Ross Grimsley and the Cincinnati Reds by a 9–4 score to win his 20th game of the season.

was 'win night.' And he used to call it: 'OK, boys, this is win day. OK, boys, this is win night.' He would will it."[35]

Up to that point, Carlton had not beaten the Reds since the 1967 season when he was with the Cardinals. But Lefty had some added incentive to beat the Reds in that start. The win was a birthday present for his wife, Beverly. As the story goes, Beverly looked at the calendar after Carlton won his 15th game of the season on July 28 against the Cubs and figured that Steve would be going for win number 20 on August 17 against Cincinnati. For Carlton to achieve that milestone, however, he would have to do it against a formidable Reds lineup that included Pete Rose, Joe Morgan, Johnny Bench, Dave Concepcion, and George Foster. It was the beginning of Cincinnati's vaunted Big Red Machine, which would win back-to-back World Series championships in 1975 and 1976. The Reds would win the National League pennant in 1972 by defeating the Pittsburgh Pirates in the League Championship Series, and then lose to the Oakland Athletics four games to three in the Fall Classic, but their time was coming.

In the Reds' match-up against Lefty, Deron Johnson ripped his seventh home run of the season in the bottom of the first inning against Grimsley to give the Phillies an early 2–0 advantage. But the Reds answered with three in the top of the third on Concepcion's single, Bill Plummer's RBI double, Rose's RBI single, and Morgan's run-scoring double to take a 3–2 lead. But in the fifth inning, Don Money's sac fly tied the game and then Willie Montanez smashed a two-run homer to put the Phils on top for good, 5–3. They added two more in the sixth and two in the seventh, as Bill Robinson finished a perfect 3-for-3 at the plate, Greg Luzinski went 3-for-4, and Terry Harmon, Larry Bowa, Montanez, and John Bateman all had two hits in Philadelphia's 16-hit onslaught against three Reds pitchers. Looking over the box score again years later, Grimsley could only shake his head. "Yeah, I got the shit kicked out of me," Grimsley laughed. "That would figure against the Phillies. I didn't fare real well against them."[36]

Overall, Luzinski batted .357 against Grimsley in his career, going 10-for-28 with two home runs. A self-described soft-tossing left-hander, Grimsley learned a changeup in Cincinnati, but admittedly became a better pitcher after he went to Baltimore starting in the 1974 season. The Phillies "obviously liked to hit against me," Grimsley said. "Luzinski, I had trouble with him. Just by the way I pitched and the way he hit, it was just hard for me. I had to really be on to do well against them. It was one of those teams. I beat the Giants, the Cardinals, and the Yankees. I beat Cleveland and a lot of teams that had a lot of left-handed hitters. It was just one of those teams that give you a hard time, that you didn't fare well against."[37]

Carlton only struck out two, while walking four and scattering four hits, but he was good enough, as he held the Reds to just one run over the final six innings. The Reds' top four hitters in the lineup — Pete Rose, Joe Morgan, Bobby Tolan, and Johnny Bench — batted only a combined 3-for-14 against Lefty in the game. "Pittsburgh and Cincinnati were powerhouse teams, but Lefty could equalize lefty and righty bats with that devastating slider," Tommy Hutton said.[38] The fact that he beat that powerhouse Reds team for his 20th win of the season — and his 15th in succession — had to make it at least a little bit satisfying. As Bill Lyon said, "That just made it all the sweeter, I would think."[39]

At game's end, after Carlton had gone back to the clubhouse, the fans chanted, "We want Steve! We want Steve!" Lefty acknowledged the crowd by returning to the field to tip his hat to the crowd. "He was good at tipping his

On a Phillies pitching staff that threw 43 total complete games in 1972, ten-time All-Star pitcher Steve Carlton accounted for 30 of those by himself. Lefty had nine straight complete games to help him win 15 straight decisions that year.

cap. Lefty would do that," Chris Wheeler said. "Lefty would come off and do that. He would acknowledge the crowd. I don't remember exactly what it was like, but if you would see the old tape and film of him as he's going toward the dugout after a special game, he would tip his cap to the crowd. He was not a bad guy or anything. He didn't hate the fans or anything. He was just focused. There was nothing else. I mean, the game was all that mattered. He was flat-out focused."[40]

That occasion marked the first time in Philadelphia sports history that an athlete was called back to the field by Philly fans since the Eagles' Chuck Bednarik was summoned at Franklin Field after his final football game with the team. Afterward, when describing his 20th victory and the ensuing curtain call, Lefty was quoted telling reporters that it was "the greatest thing that's ever happened to me in baseball. There's been nothing even close." Asked about that comment that Lefty made to reporters, Wheeler said, "If you go back and look at the attendances for those games and how they would increase when he would pitch … that place that night was electric. The noise (was

Steve Carlton was selling tickets all by himself for the 1972 Phillies. With Lefty on the hill that season, the team attracted five crowds of more than 40,000 people to Veterans Stadium.

incredible). We started to play playoff games in this town a few years later, but that was the closest we ever came in my early years with the Phillies to being in a playoff atmosphere. He had experienced that in St. Louis. But I think he truly appreciated the way fans reacted to him, because it was a love-in. We used to draw 30 or 40,000 for when he would pitch and draw 15 or 20 thousand, if that, for the other games, unless there was a giveaway or unless Bill [Giles] was trying to shoot somebody into the stadium on a kite or whatever the hell he was trying to do back in those days."[41]

The crowd that turned out that night for Philadelphia's game against the Reds was the fifth largest of the season at Veterans Stadium. Overall, the team attracted six crowds of 40,000 fans or more in Philadelphia in 1972, and Lefty started five of those games, so it was more than coincidence. On one occasion, with a traffic jam snaking along outside of the Vet, Lefty's start was delayed by nearly one hour as the fans filed into the stadium. And on the night that Lefty won his 20th of the season, the Walt Whitman Bridge and Schuylkill

Expressway were so jam-packed with cars that police estimated that 5,000 fans did a U-turn, unable to reach the Vet.

"Nothing less than extraordinary," current Phillies general manager Ruben Amaro Jr. said of Lefty's '72 season. "I think more than anything else, what I remember about Lefty was that it was like a holiday every time he pitched. Literally, the whole team geared up, the whole city geared up to watch him pitch. It was that special. And very, very few times in our organization's history do you find that happening. You found that happen a little bit with Curt Schilling at one point and now a little with [Roy] Halladay. But for years, this city used to stop and drop every time he pitched, and certainly in that '72 season as well."[42]

Dan Baker, of course, was soaking everything up in his first year as the Phillies' PA announcer. He wasn't far removed from teaching fifth and sixth grades and coaching the basketball team at Landreth Elementary School on 23rd and Federal streets, not far from the Philadelphia sports complex. But nothing compared to this dream job that he had with the Phillies and seeing the adrenaline in the stands when Lefty had the ball. "Every time he pitched, it was an event," Baker said. "The fans really responded to him. On a team that struggled mightily, every time Steve pitched, we were at least a pretty tough opponent for whomever we played when Carlton was on the mound."[43]

No doubt about it, when Lefty pitched in '72, the Phillies' faithful came through the turnstiles in force, excited to see their hero while wearing T-shirts emblazoned with the words "Super Steve." And when Lefty beat the Reds, the Phillies flashed "Super Steve 20–6" in big script across Phanavision. Carlton "was phenomenal," Larry Shenk said. "It was electric when he pitched at the Vet. It was a different atmosphere, and players played better because they knew they had a chance to win. 'Super Steve' people called him. He was unbelievable that year. He got into a groove and he was our hero. And I guess he fed off of that. You felt you were going to win — the players and the fans and all of us in the front office. It became an event."[44]

The attendance numbers, in fact, bear that out. In 20 starts by Lefty at the Vet that season, there were a total of 484,595 fans that came out to see him pitch, an average of 24,230 per night. But during a stretch of five games that Carlton pitched at the Vet in July and August, that number climbed to an average of 33,510 fans. And on the 12 dates that Lefty did not throw in that span, attendance dropped to an average of 18,710. The difference was about 14,800 paying customers, for a total of 74,000 extra tickets in those starts. On the road, Lefty attracted three crowds of 30,000 or more fans during the '72 season, all after the All-Star break as he was chasing history. That included a turnout of 41,644 in New York in late September, when Lefty pitched against Tom Seaver.

"He was worth extra tickets, especially as the year went along," Bill Lyon said. "There was no other reason to buy them. And the thing is, at the time, they didn't really have any competition. I've often remarked, when I was lured away from the heartland to the grit and grime of the northeast, I had told my wife and two sons — we'd moved like three times in 16 years previously and I said, 'This is it. I'm not going to uproot us again. We're going to the big time. Bright lights, big city, this is great. Winners everywhere you look.'"[45] Unfortunately for the Lyons, however, that's not exactly how it worked out — at least initially anyway. "Well, we knew what the Phillies were," Lyon said. "The Eagles were 2–11–1. The Flyers missed the playoffs in the last minute of the last game of the regular season. And the 76ers had nine wins and 73 losses, and I told my wife, 'Good God, what have I gotten us into?' Carlton was it. He was the show in this whole town. The 76ers didn't have Doc [Julius Erving] yet. But the renaissance was just around the corner because the Flyers won back-to-back Cups in '74 and '75. The Eagles got a little better, the Phillies got better quicker. And then we segue all the way up to 1980 when all four teams played for the world championship."[46]

By that mid–August game against the Reds, Lyon had already gone to the Philadelphia Eagles' training camp at Albright College in Reading. After a long, dismal summer of Phillies baseball, people's thoughts were beginning to turn to the Birds and whether they could improve on their 6-7-1 finish in 1971 with Po James leading the rushing game and quarterbacks John Reaves and Pete Liske throwing passes to Harold Jackson. "By then, outside of Carlton, there was nothing to be gained from watching" the Phillies, Lyon said.[47]

Still, Lefty's 15-game winning streak was a feat that was admired by a lot of people. "It's difficult for a number of reasons," Jim Kaat said. "You have to get a lot of good fortune because there's going to be a lot of games where you might end up winning a 6–5 game and you might not pitch that well. I think in that case, the year that Lefty had, he was just so consistent start after start. And that's another difficult thing, for 15 starts in a row to be able to repeat your motion and throw strikes and be consistent. Baseball or pitching is the same as any other game at the top level. You can never own it. You can only rent it for periods of time. And it will leave you for a little while and then you get it back. But the year Carlton had that year was probably an indication of how unusual it is for someone to keep it together for 41 starts."[48]

Sparky Lyle added, "For one thing, you've got to have them score runs for you. You're not going to pitch a shutout every time and all that. But I think that was one of the reasons he was so great. The team was never out of a game too much when he pitched. Everybody is going to have one of those days, but he always had the team in the game. That's probably why he won 15 in a row. He had four pitches that he could get over the plate and he threw hard. That in itself is reason to have a 15-game winning streak."[49]

13

Lum Breaks It Up

Lancaster's Gene Garber, while pitching for the Atlanta Braves, will forever hold the distinction of breaking up Pete Rose's hitting streak at 44 games on a humid night in Atlanta on August 2, 1978, at Atlanta–Fulton County Stadium. Rose was hitless in his first four at-bats before facing Garber in his final trip to the plate in the top of the ninth inning. After running the count to 2–1, Garber threw a change-up that Rose fouled off. Then with a screaming crowd on its feet, Rose went down swinging on another change-up.

It was another Atlanta Brave who snapped Carlton's 15-game winning streak during the 1972 season. Mike Lum was the first American of Japanese ancestry to play in the major leagues and was the only player to ever pinch-hit for Hall of Famer Hank Aaron. Lum, though, was not pinch-hitting when he dug in at the plate in the top of the 11th inning on August 21 on a rainy night in Philadelphia. The stage was set, however, by Dusty Baker, who stroked a two-out double to center field after Lefty had retired Felix Millan on a pop out and Hank Aaron on strikes looking. As it turned out, Aaron's advice to Baker a couple of hours earlier proved to be very valuable.

"I remember that it was raining big time and it didn't look like we were going to play. We ended up playing cards with everybody (in the clubhouse) and then Hank Aaron told me, 'Let's go sit outside in the elements in the dugout. Imagine yourself playing because you can always turn it off, but it's hard to turn it on.' I tell my guys that right now when it's raining ... 'Go sit out in the dugout,'" said Baker, who is currently the Cincinnati Reds' skipper. "Especially in Philly in those days with the Astroturf and that Zamboni machine, Carlton was a great pitcher on a bad team and they were going to try to play that game."[1]

Baker, who batted .321 during the 1972 season, doubled to left in the third inning off of Carlton, in addition to going down on strikes in the first, grounding out to third in the fifth, and popping out to third base in foul territory in the eighth inning. But he got a pitch that he could handle from Lefty in the top of the 11th inning and didn't waste it. "Hank Aaron used to give us a theory and a philosophy as young hitters how to approach Steve Carlton and Tom Seaver or Bob Gibson and some of those guys," Baker said. "If you don't have a theory and a philosophy, you have very little chance of hitting those guys. And when you get your pitch, you can't miss it because you ain't going to get it again."[2]

With the score tied 1–1, Baker was the potential go-ahead run, and Lefty intentionally walked catcher Earl Williams to get to Lum. Unfortunately for the Phillies, though, the strategy backfired as Lum reached for a slider low and away and flared a broken bat single over shortstop Larry Bowa's head into center field to drive in Baker with the tie-breaking run. "All I know is I was trying to haul ass because at that time, we were a bad team too," Baker said. "So you try to make up things to get you motivated for that game — like playing the Dodgers or playing the Reds or trying to break up Carlton's winning streak. These are things that you try to do when you're on a team that's not winning. We took some pride in trying to beat him."[3] In the end, Baker's tie-breaking run left the Phillies' faithful stunned, with Carlton on his way to losing for the first time in nearly three months. His previous was a 7–0 defeat to the New York Mets on May 30. There was "a lot of electricity in the air, a lot of excitement," Larry Shenk said. "You almost didn't believe that he had lost because you were just so accustomed to him dominating and winning. But Mike Lum was not a great player. He was an average major leaguer."[4]

Lum played for the Atlanta Braves, Cincinnati Reds, and Chicago Cubs in his 15-year big league career. But as Twitchell noted, Lum was somebody that could find a way to get the job done. "As I remember, Mike Lum put the bat on the ball," Twitchell said. "He wasn't the best hitter in the lineup, but he was still somebody that you considered when pitching against him. He could hurt you if you threw the ball in the wrong spot. Dale Murphy is somebody that I've become very close friends with, and I remember the first time I faced him when Atlanta called him up. He walked up to home plate and he had a big smile on his face and stuff, and he had one of those darn Louisville Sluggers with him. Those things cause pitchers problems. So I always thought it didn't matter what kind of stuff you had — if they come up to the plate and they're willing to swing that thing two or three times in the strike zone and you happen to throw the ball in the strike zone, they've got a chance of making contact."[5]

In the next day's papers, Carlton said that he thought initially when the ball left Lum's bat that Bowa might have a chance for it. But when he looked again, he knew there was no way. "It was a broken bat single," Chris Wheeler said. "I can still hear it shatter. Mike Lum was a left-handed hitter from Hawaii. Mike Kenwaii Lum they used to call him."[6] Even as solid as Bowa was with the glove, he had no shot at grabbing Lum's base hit. "If I remember, it was a clean hit," Wheeler said. "It was one of those little floaters that broke his bat."[7]

From there, Hall of Famer Phil Niekro retired the Phillies in the bottom of the 11th to preserve the one-run win. Right fielder Bill Robinson, batting seventh in the order, reached first base on a strikeout-passed ball and then advanced into scoring position on John Bateman's sacrifice bunt. Terry Harmon then grabbed a bat to pinch hit for Lefty, but the Braves' crafty knuckleballer got him on a ground out to third baseman Darrell Evans. Niekro then retired leadoff batter Denny Doyle on a grounder to second baseman Felix Millan to end it. "The game was back and forth," Twitchell said, "and my only thought was if the game goes much longer and if Steve continues to want to pitch, Niekro actually has an advantage because he's probably not tired. Steve pitched a different kind of baseball game than Phil Niekro did, certainly. Niekro never got real tired, I don't think."[8]

Niekro finished his complete-game gem with ten strikeouts, while allowing just one earned run on nine hits and three walks. "Niekro was unbelievable that night with the knuckle ball," Wheeler said. "That was when he was in his prime. He was another Hall of Famer. That was a pretty good game."[9] Certainly, the Phillies have seen their share of knuckleball pitchers over the years, with the likes of Niekro, Tim Wakefield, R.A. Dickey and Charlie Hough. But Niekro was one in particular who gave the Phils a lot of nightmares. "Niekro used to give us fits," Bowa said. "Not the singles hitters, but the big hitters like Schmitty and Luzinski and guys like that. He was tough on the Phillies. Even before those guys got there, he was always tough on the Phillies. When you take batting practice and everything in spring training, you can ask for curveballs and sliders and changeups, but very seldom do you ask for a knuckle ball."[10] Twitchell echoed Bowa's comments, saying, "We had a terrible time trying to hit Niekro. It's such an odd pitch to what hitters see every day. I can remember pitching against Niekro a couple of times and going up there trying to hit—it was ridiculous."[11]

It was not uncommon for Carlton and Niekro to be matched up against one another; Bruce Keidan said that the Braves' knuckleballer was a nemesis of Lefty's. "Not directly, but they pitched head-to-head so often and they both pitched so well when they pitched head-to-head and they both rose to the occasion," Keidan said. Carlton "wasn't with a great offensive club, he had very little margin for error, but he wasn't pitching defensively. That sort of

Here is the 1980 Cy Young Award presented to Steve Carlton after he finished the 1972 season with a 24–9 record and a 2.34 ERA. Having also taken home the honor in 1972, 1977 and 1982, he became the first player ever to win four Cy Youngs.

defensive mindset just wasn't part of him, which by the way is why he had such a tough time retiring. His mindset was always, 'If he's mortal, I've got him.' That's not the exact words he used, but I'll just leave it at that."[12]

With the extra-inning loss to the Braves, Lefty's 15-game winning streak was history, but Keidan suggested that Carlton probably did not think much about the streak anyway. "I don't think he thought in terms of streaks," Keidan said. "That was just a media thing. He went out there to win every night."[13] That sentiment was supported by Marty Bystrom, who was a teammate of Carlton's when Lefty notched his 3,000th strikeout on April 29, 1981, in a 6–2 win over the Montreal Expos at Veterans Stadium. By striking out Tim Raines, Jerry Manuel, and Tim Wallach in the first inning, Carlton became the first left-hander in major league history—and 6th overall—to record 3,000 strikeouts. "He needs three strikeouts and he goes out in the first inning and strikes out the side," Bystrom said. "There's 60-some thousand people at Veterans Stadium, Carlton gets a standing O, he's tipping his cap, and he comes off the field, puts his hat and his glove down in the same spot where he sat all the time in the dugout. He looks around at everybody that's congratulating him and he goes, 'Alright, now that shit is over. Let's win the ball game.'"[14]

At the end of the 1982 season, Lefty captured his fourth and final Cy Young Award, making him the first pitcher to win that many in a career. But instead of putting the awards on his mantle, Carlton talked to Larry Shenk about putting them someplace where others could see them. "We lent them to the Hall of Fame so they could be on display up there," Shenk said. "He didn't want them. He wanted the Cy Youngs to be seen by somebody, and the Hall of Fame was more than happy to take them and put them on display. He wasn't materialistic. He wasn't interested in records and all that. He just wanted to win. There wasn't anything (record-wise) that he cared about. One time, he took over the lead for strikeouts over Nolan Ryan briefly. And then Ryan came back and kept punching them out. That was a big deal as far as us and the media, but it didn't faze him. Winning was the whole thing he wanted to do."[15]

With that mentality, Carlton still had an outside chance to reach the 30-win mark. With a little more than a month remaining in the season, Lefty had a 20–7 record. "You didn't think he was ever going to lose when he went out there," Wheeler said. "And he pitched, what, 330 innings that year or something? He didn't come out of the game. He almost always took it right to a decision. So we all thought he had a chance (at 30 wins), sure. Every time he went out there, you thought he was going to win. And he'd help himself too. He could hit a little bit, he hit some home runs. He didn't like to run. But he could help himself. He could bunt. He had a move to first base that was a little bit in between and held runners on pretty good. So he was the total package this guy."[16]

Carlton returned to the win column five days later with another victory over the Reds, outdueling Jim McGlothlin, 4–3 in Cincinnati. Actually, Carlton received a little bit of help from reliever Mac Scarce in notching his 21st victory. Lefty was knocked out of a game for the first time in ten outings, but he still achieved a career-high victory total. Scarce preserved the victory by pitching the ninth inning and stranding the potential tying run on third base while working against the heart of the Reds' lineup. Six pitchers earned at least one save for the Phillies in 1972, led by Scarce's team-best four. Others were Dick Selma (3), Joe Hoerner (3), Bucky Brandon (2), Woodie Fryman (1), Chris Short (1) and Wayne Twitchell (1). Scarce tossed two innings in two of his four saves, and although he only went only one frame in relief of Lefty in Philadelphia's win over the Reds, it was significant because the Phils finished just 2–8 against the National League champion Reds that year. Not surprisingly, Lefty picked up both of those victories.

"Naturally," Ross Grimsley said when told of that stat. "Your outstanding pitchers are going to win against anybody they pitch against. He was heads above everybody else. No wonder he won that many games. Like I said, he threw strikes, he had a great breaking ball, the hitters didn't like to hit against him — left-handers hated it — and he was just an intimidating figure on the mound, being as big as he was and throwing as hard as he threw. And then he'd let you know he was out there occasionally by buzzing one up and in. He just did everything you could possibly do."[17]

On the second to last day of August, the same day that Roberto Clemente tied Hall of Famer Honus Wagner for the Pittsburgh Pirates' club mark of 2,970 hits, Lefty went out against Jerry Reuss and the Houston Astros to try for win number 22. In the early innings, Carlton was pitching well; Jim Wynn's two-out walk in the first inning was Houston's only base runner through 4 and one-third frames. Terry Harmon's one-out home run in the top of the fifth gave the Phillies a 1–0 lead, and Lefty retired 11 straight batters until Doug Rader worked a one-out free pass in the bottom of the fifth. Then, unfortunately for Lefty, Tommy Helms broke up his no-hitter with a single to left to spark a two-run rally, and the Astros dealt Carlton a 5–3 loss to drop him to 21–8 on the season. The Astros capitalized on a couple of unearned runs in the seventh inning, as second baseman Denny Doyle failed to cover the bag on a throw from catcher John Bateman on Cesar Cedeno's stolen base.

Doyle's double play partner Larry Bowa was back in the lineup after a war of words with Paul Owens a few days earlier. It started when Owens benched Bowa and two other regulars in the sixth inning of a game in which the Braves had piled up a 7–0 lead against Wayne Twitchell, explaining to reporters that he thought Bowa was tired and needed a rest. With the frustrations from a losing season boiling over, the fiery Bowa responded harshly, telling reporters afterward, "If the man doesn't think I can play, he might as well trade me. If I'm not good enough to play the whole game when there's an off-day the next day, he should get rid of me." The Phillies' shortstop added that he thought Owens did not appreciate his defensive efforts, which represented the strength of his game, and that despite the fact he was hitting near .300, Owens wasn't doing him any favors with his lack of confidence in him at the plate.

Owens responded with some pretty harsh words in his own right. The Phillies' manager/general manager described Bowa's outburst as "dumb," explained that he lifted two other regulars at the same time, and pointed out that he used 19 players in the lopsided loss. In the next day's newspapers, Owens was quoted as saying, "Some people aren't smart enough to understand anything. I wanted to get some of those guys off the bench, and being down 7–0 seemed like a good time to do it." Years later, however, Bowa indicated that the incident had absolutely no lasting effect on the relationship he enjoyed with the Pope. "Pope and I, we might have had our differences during my career there, but we got along as good as anybody," Bowa said. "And then the owner of our team, Ruly Carpenter, who is the best owner anybody could ever have in sports, was great."[18]

Ken Reynolds, however, was not great. He lost his first 12 decisions of the season while fashioning an ERA of 4.43. Finally, on September 1, he entered the win column with an 11–1 victory over the Braves, supported by a 15-hit attack; Joe Lis hit a home run and Bowa went 4-for-6 with three RBIs against Atlanta's Ron Reed. Braves left fielder Rico Carty hit a solo home run in the second inning to spoil the shutout. It proved to be a rare offensive outburst for the Phillies, who had just four batters hitting over .250 on the final day of August. Terry Harmon, a platoon player at second base, had a team-best .294 average, followed by Greg Luzinski (.278), Tommy Hutton (.257) and Doyle (.255). For Reynolds, the win prevented him from setting a dubious club record all to himself. With 12 straight losses, Reynolds joined Russ Miller (1928) and Hugh Mulcahy (1940) in having the longest streak in team history. Asked what he remembered about pitchers like Reynolds and Bill Champion, Bill Lyon said, "Journeymen at best. I don't think they're a threat for the Hall of Fame."[19]

Lefty, though, was having a Hall of Fame season, and beginning with his start against the Atlanta Braves on September 3, he reeled off back-to-back wins. And Carlton proved that there was more to his repertoire than just a nasty slider. Despite having nearly 300 innings under his belt to that point, Lefty was still bringing the heat in the late innings of yet another complete-game gem en route to an 8–0 shutout. His fastball, combined with his slider and curve, handcuffed Hank Aaron, Dusty Baker and the rest of the Braves' lineup, and limited Atlanta to just five hits. Afterward, Lefty told reporters, "I think the fact that I'm pitching every four days has helped more than anything else. It has caused me to be more consistent. I went back to my slider this year, and pitching every four days helps the slider. I didn't use the slider last year and won 20, so it was not an easy decision to go back to it. But I'm glad I did, for I'm a better pitcher with the slider."

Joe Torre thought that it was in the late 1960s or early seventies that clubs started adding a fifth pitcher to the rotation. But he suggested that it was simply common sense for the Phillies to pitch Carlton every four days with him mowing down the competition in dominant fashion. "When you have a pitcher like him, you're going to really conform your rotation to what's good for him," Torre said. "I mean, he's going to pitch every four days. What everybody else does is inconsequential. He's your best guy, and if you know physically he's going to be able to handle that, you do it."[20] While with St. Louis in 1971, Carlton and Bob Gibson headlined a five-man rotation. Those two, along with Jerry Reuss and Reggie Cleveland, all had 31 or more starts, and Mike Torrez, Chris Zachary, and Al Santorini combined for 23 more. Lefty made eight starts on just four days rest that season and went 4–2 in those outings. But he pitched every fourth day on a regular basis in 1972, when his 41 starts that season represented a career-high.

"I think that is a fact," Larry Shenk said, talking about Carlton's success pitching every fourth day. "There's a lot written by today's media, 'Oh geez, Cliff Lee is starting a World Series game on three days rest.' That wasn't the focus back then. Lefty went every four days. With the team we had in '72, we wanted him to pitch every other day."[21] Shenk was not alone in those thoughts. Larry Bowa also believes that the pitchers' focus was different in that era. "I think the more you throw, the better your arm is, the stronger your arm is," Bowa said. "I think pitchers today don't understand the difference between aches and severe pain."[22]

Carlton and Jim Kaat were two pitchers who certainly believed in that theory. Bowa remembers the two of them would throw a complete game and then go out to left field and center field the next day to throw long toss and stretch their arms out. "Jim Kaat's theory was 'If you don't use it, you lose it.'" Bowa said. "I think too many guys are babied now. I don't think it's the players' fault. I think it's the organizations' philosophies' fault. Who sets the bar at 100 pitches and that's it? Now, as soon as a guy hits 100 pitches, bells and whistles go off, like 'OK, get him out of there.' I don't understand it. I remember a lot of times, Carlton would be out of his rhythm the first couple innings and then finally get into a groove and in the seventh inning, he probably had 125, 135 pitches and he would keep going. I'm not saying everybody's like that, but major league baseball ... they're creating this problem, believe me." Today's game pushes "five-man rotations, don't throw more than 100 pitches, get them out after a quality start, specialists in the seventh inning, a left-handed situation pitcher in the eighth, your closer in the ninth. Owners wonder why payrolls are so high. It's because they have all these specialists. It used to be, when I first came up, if you were in the bullpen, you weren't good enough to start. Now they have all these specialties."[23]

Ross Grimsley acknowledged that there are different thoughts behind the theory that your arm gets stronger as you pitch more. But more than that, the former Reds pitcher suggested that with the kind of season that Carlton was having, he just wanted to go the mound as much as he could. "You always want to play, so the sooner you get out there the better. Obviously, if you're doing well, you want to get out there as quick as you can," Grimsley said. "When you're not doing so good, you don't really want to go out there. 'I don't want to go out there against this team.' It's a kids' game, it's fun to play, and if it's fun to play, you want to go out and do it as often as you can. It's just fun to go out and compete, and I'm pretty sure that's the type of guy Carlton was."[24]

Greg Luzinski was certainly having a lot of fun hitting long balls in '72 as the Bull slugged his 13th homer of the season in Carlton's 8–0 whitewashing of the Braves on September 3. Joe Lis added his fifth of the year as the Phillies pounded out 12 hits against Jim Hardin and three Braves relievers. Over the final 36 games of the season, Lis made 18 starts at first base, but Willie Montanez received the lion's share of work at first over the last two-plus weeks, making 14 starts there. Despite reports that the Bull was souring on playing left field and looking to get back to first base, it did not happen. In fact, Montanez went on to become the Phils' regular first baseman in 1973. But years later, the Bull indicated that it was a non-issue. "Actually, I led in fielding that year in left field, so the Pope, Paul Owens, at that time just obviously said, 'That's where you're going to stay,'" Luzinski recalled. "It was a good situation for me because people probably forget, at that time Deron Johnson was a Phillie and I think he had, if I'm not mistaken, three consecutive years with 30 home runs, which was a big number then. And he was in the twilight of his career, so it was easier for me to move than him. And once I was out there, I just stayed there.... Then obviously [Richie] Hebner came in [to play first] and Dick Allen, so there was no room."[25]

Bill Lyon said that both Montanez and Luzinski were fan favorites, but Montanez was better suited to be a first baseman. "I don't know that Montanez could have played the outfield," Lyon said. "He didn't have much of an arm.... But Willie Montanez was a real fan favorite. And so was Luzinski because his home runs tended to be tape-measure shots. So that endeared him. And Montanez, the way he flipped the ball when he caught it and everything, it was the old saying, 'There's not enough mustard in the world to cover that hot dog,' that kind of thing. Probably in the long run, maybe Luzinski's power would have won out over Montanez's showboating. He was pretty flamboyant and Bull was just the opposite. He was stoic, especially compared to Montanez."[26]

The Bull also hit another shot in Carlton's next start against the Cardinals, as Lefty's focus was put to the test following a fifth-inning confrontation between his battery-mate John Bateman and home plate umpire Shag Crawford. The two exchanged words following a pitch by Carlton that was called a ball, and Crawford allegedly used a profanity as the incident became heated. Not even that exchange could throw Lefty off his game, however, as Carlton went on to strike out nine St. Louis hitters to boost his season total to 272 and break Jim Bunning's single-season club record of 268. Lefty also reached a milestone against his former teammates with the 100th win of his career, defeating Al Santorini and the Cardinals, 2–1.

"Steve would be the first to tell you that when he pitched, he had such a focus," Larry Bowa said. "He honestly said this one day to a bunch of us guys that he didn't know who was hitting. He saw himself delivering the pitch and he saw the catcher and where the catcher was set up. There were some guys, as we got a little bit older, we would go up to him and say, 'Where do you want me to play this guy?' Because of that devastating slider, especially me and Mike Schmidt, we got a lot of ground balls when he didn't strike guys out. So we would play right-handers a little bit to pull. It was pretty simple with him. He just got the ball and he threw it. There was no indecision on his part, and his infielders and outfielders knew as soon as he got the ball, he was going to throw it. He didn't shake off, step off, throw ball one, ball two, ball three. He attacked the hitters, and as players behind him, you're on your toes and you're alert. You're waiting for the ball to come to you. Not only was he a great pitcher, but he made people around him better because of his demeanor on the mound and his ability to get the ball and throw it."[27]

The Redbirds scored their only run of that game in the top of the seventh inning, as Ken Reitz stroked a leadoff single, Joe Torre delivered a two-out base hit while pinch hitting for Santorini, and Bill Stein followed with an RBI single to center field. For his career, Torre batted .271 against Carlton (16-for-59) with three home runs, while working nine walks and striking out just eight times. "He was more uncomfortable facing me than I was facing him — maybe because he was left-handed and I was right-handed," Torre said. "But I think he gave me more credit than I deserved, thinking I was smarter than I really was and had to hit him. I had a couple of hits off of him. I think I hit my 200th home run off of him, if I'm not mistaken, in Philly. But he was no fun to hit against. As I say, it was a little easier because he was coming from the left side and I was a right-handed batter. And the one thing that was good is he worked fast, so he didn't leave you waiting there very long."[28]

With 23 wins at that point, and only six more starts remaining for Carlton in the season, Paul Owens brought up the idea of perhaps using Lefty for an inning or two in relief in a tie game to try to get him to 30 wins. "Anything to get to 30," Bill Lyon said. "From a PR standpoint, it would have been a good thing because it wasn't like the infamous juggling of the rotation in the collapse of 1964. This Phillies' team was dreadful and they weren't in contention for anything. So if you were at least trying to keep people interested, that was really their only option. As I said, they weren't going anywhere."[29]

Lefty, though, wasn't crazy about that suggestion of pitching in relief and was quoted telling reporters, "I'll do whatever they want me to do, but it's a pretty tight schedule and I've already worked, what, close to 300 innings this year." Joe Torre was not surprised in the least to hear of Carlton's comments. "He was very low maintenance and he wasn't wrapped up in numbers," Torre said. "He was wrapped up in winning. And certainly, 30 instead of 27 would not have changed what he meant to that club because his responsibility was going out there and giving his team a chance to win, and when he got a lead, to take them to the finish line. And as far as his own numbers, they weren't as important as the team. He learned that in St. Louis too."[30]

Knowing Lefty to be a team player, Chris Wheeler, too, would have foreseen Carlton being reluctant to put that milestone of 30 wins at the front of his mind. "Knowing Lefty the way I know him, personal goals were nothing to him," Wheeler remarked. "First of all, you weren't on salary drives the way you're on today. You weren't out there to become a free agent your walk year, or maybe if you had two more wins, it would make you another $50 million. It wasn't like that then. Whether if he had gotten to 29 and he'd have pitched in relief to get to 30, I don't know. That's another hypothetical that would be kinda tough for me to say. But knowing him the way I knew him, and I did know him very well, he was great with us.... To Lefty, it was win for the team. It was win day when he went out there, you played as a team, you won as a team, you lost as a team, and you never heard him talking about how many wins (he had). If he pitched well, yeah, he was happy. If he pitched bad, he was mad at himself. But it didn't carry over. That guy was so focused the day of a game. This guy we have now, [Roy] Halladay, reminds me of him. He walks in with that same look. Ooh, boy. Don't go near him."[31]

Carlton's chances for 30 wins, however, sustained a blow in his next start against Jerry Koosman and the Mets. Although he went the distance in a 4–2 loss, he didn't have sharp command and walked four batters, including back-to-back free passes in the fourth inning to Bud Harrelson and John Milner—the first time he allowed consecutive free passes since May 30. That allowed New York to tie the game at 2–2, with one run scoring on Jim Beauchamp's bloop RBI double to right field. Then Mets catcher Duffy Dyer hit a solo home run in the sixth inning and added an RBI triple in the eighth inning.

Although Lefty was not crazy about the idea of pitching in relief to get to 30 wins, he certainly would have loved to reach that figure by taking his regular turn in the rotation. According to a newspaper report, Lefty admitted after his loss to the Mets that he'd been thinking of 30 wins. "I feel 30 is mathematically eliminated now," a dejected Carlton reportedly said. "Too many things have to happen to win 30."

Unfortunately for Lefty, those things did not happen and his bid to become the first major leaguer to win 30 games in a season since the Detroit Tigers' Denny McLain in 1968 fell short. No National League pitcher has won 30 games in a season since Dizzy Dean accomplished the feat in 1934, going 30–7 with the St. Louis Cardinals. "If he was pitching that way with our '80 team.... He was a great pitcher all the way through I was with him," Larry Bowa said, "but if he'd have had a good team, he would have won well over 30. No question. We didn't really score that many runs for him that year. There were a lot of 3–2 games, 2–1."[32]

Don Money added, "Oh shoot, man, he had a crack at 30. To win 30, you've got to go out there and be very lucky and fortunate and have the ability [and not] miss any starts due to injuries. And then if you gave up five runs, maybe your team scores five for you, like Detroit did for McLain over there. We just didn't have that kind of offensive team. Carlton was outstanding. He was just dominating from day one, even though he lost the five or six in a row. He gets a little out of sync and then all of a sudden, boom, you get back in sync. Sometimes, just a small tweak gets you back on the track, the same thing with hitters. Just a tweak. They tweaked him, then things started going right for him, and he ended up having a great year."[33]

In Carlton's ten losses and four no-decisions in 1972, the Phillies mustered two runs or fewer in eight of those games. Overall, the Phillies scored a total of just 18 runs in Lefty's ten losses that year. "I don't know what we would have won if he wasn't there," Larry Shenk said. "Twenty-seven out of 59 ... I don't know. He never came close to 27 wins again. What, 23 was his high after that. You just don't win 27 games."[34] Yet it was not just for Lefty that the Phillies failed to score runs. Amazingly, in 66 of Philadelphia's 156 games in 1972 (42 percent), Philadelphia scored two or fewer runs. Opposing pitchers shut the weak-hitting Phillies' team out 13 times and held them to just one run on 29 other occasions. "Without a doubt, he could have been a 30-game winner," Tommy Hutton said. "It's amazing that he lost ten games that year. That alone is an indication of how bad a team we were in 1972."[35]

Besides Carlton's quest for 30 wins, the September call-ups of Bob Boone and Mike Schmidt were about the only other developments that were newsworthy in Philadelphia. The night following Lefty's 4–2 loss to Koosman and the Mets, Hall of Famer Schmidt collected his first major league hit against Mets righty Jim McAndrew, a two-out single in the hole between shortstop and third base. Boone batted next against McAndrew and picked up his first big league hit with a single to center field. The Phillies' catcher went 2-for-4 in that game, including a ninth-inning RBI single, but it was not enough as the Phillies lost 5–3. Incidentally, it was also McAndrew who gave up Boone's first big league spring training hit. "It was a pretty nervous time. It's a goal everybody wants to achieve [to reach the major leagues]. I got a hit in my first game and hit pretty good for most of the month," said Boone, who went 14-for-51 (.275) with one homer and four RBIs in 1972. "That was an incredible time for me, a young player that finally gets to the big leagues, which is your goal from the time you start playing baseball."[36]

As Bill Lyon related, that was the start of Schmidt and Boone becoming part of the nucleus that would win won the Phillies' first World Series in 1980, a time similar to when young homegrown players like Jimmy Rollins, Chase Utley, and Ryan Howard were developing before helping Philadelphia win it all in 2008. "I think it was much like what is going on now with these Phillies, with their core — Utley and [Jayson] Werth and Ryan and maybe [Cole] Hamels," Lyon said. "And I think how could they not help but be in awe of Carlton. First of all, physically he was imposing. And then what he was doing in that season, I'm sure they were a little bit in awe. I think they were probably all saying, 'Glad we don't have to hit against him.'"[37]

Mets pitcher Jon Matlack probably couldn't wait to pitch to a Phillies lineup that had all of ten combined years of major league experience for its game on September 13. Dubbed the "Sesame Street Gang" by the *Philadelphia Inquirer*, a handful of starters — pitcher Dave Downs, Boone, Schmidt, and shortstop Craig Robinson — were still learning their way around the big league clubhouse. Second baseman Terry Harmon, at 28 years old and in his fourth major league season, was the oldest player in the Phils lineup. Left fielder Greg Luzinski and first baseman Joe Lis each had one year of experience, while center fielder Willie Montanez and right fielder Roger Freed were in their sophomore seasons.

Boone was back on the bench and John Bateman was behind the plate on September 15 when Lefty matched up against the Montreal Expos and 16-game winner Mike Torrez, who was traded in 1971 from the Cardinals. Going into that start, the Phillies had dropped six straight games and were seemingly headed for a 100-loss season. Philadelphia's record was 49–89 at that point, with 18 games left in the season, so the Phillies had to win at least eight more to avoid that dubious distinction. Chris Wheeler, when asked if 100 losses were in the back of the players' minds, said, "It probably was. That team was just terrible. We had no pitching other than Carlton. When you look at the pitching, it was awful. You did have some stars starting to come, like Bowa was here and Luzinski. Schmidt came in September. Booney too. So you could see there was some light at the end of the tunnel, you thought. But not that year."[38] Luzinski, like Wheeler, could see some hope for the future, but there were no immediate results for the Phillies in 1972. "You kinda get depressed," Luzinski said. "Nobody wants to lose, obviously. But again, we weren't very good. Everybody leaves spring training with the idea that you're going to win and it comes pretty quick after that if you're not good enough to compete, and we weren't good enough to compete. Obviously, you don't want to be embarrassed, but we weren't a very good club."[39]

As bad as the Phillies were, however, they did not come close to the 1962 New York Mets' record of 120 losses in one season. "I don't remember thinking about breaking the Mets' record of 120," Wheeler said. "Of course, you weren't that far removed from it at the time. You were ten years removed from it. Look, that Phillies team was so bad, there wasn't much they could do about it. Except, it was funny, when Carlton would pitch, they'd play like a good team. They'd catch the ball, and of course, he didn't give up anything. They knew that all they had to do was get a couple of runs. Whereas, with the other guys that were out there, they thought they'd have to score a lot every night to win. But I don't remember them consciously going, 'We don't want to be as bad as the Mets,' or something like that. They were what they were. They just weren't very good."[40]

The Phillies had to score more than a couple of runs in Lefty's start against the Expos, but they rallied from behind to defeat Montreal, 5–3, and on "Steve Carlton Night" at Veterans Stadium in front of 20, 120 fans, Lefty improved his record to 24–9. In a pre-game ceremony featuring Robin Roberts as master of ceremonies, Carlton received a new 1973 Chrysler Imperial and a standing ovation from the Phillies' faithful. The club flew his wife, Beverly, in from St. Louis, along with his parents, Joe and Anne from Miami. The Phillie also brought in city representative Harry Belinger to join Lefty on the field. Plus, all fans received a color picture of Lefty while kids received an iron-on decal emblazoned with "Carlton 32." When the festivities finally ended, Lefty needed just under two hours to justify the generosity, pitching his team past the Expos.

Down the stretch, the Phillies did avoid reaching the 100-loss mark, in large part due to Lefty, who won four of his final five starts to help Philadelphia go 10–8 over the final three weeks. But Carlton was not sharp in his 37th start of the year, yielding 10 hits and three walks in his outing against Montreal's Torrez. Part of that could have been due to his appearance on the Mike Douglas television show a couple of days earlier, when he threw 50 to 60 pitches at a dunk tank.

Coco Laboy's second-inning home run on a fastball that Lefty did not get far enough inside (one of just three home run that Laboy hit that year) gave the Expos a 1–0 lead. But the Phils answered right away in the bottom of the frame on Don Money's sac fly, which drove in Luzinski, who was hit by a pitch. After Montreal went back in front, 3–1, in the third, Montanez's two-run single pulled Philadelphia even again. Luzinski's towering home run in the sixth inning then gave Carlton and the Phillies a lead they never relinquished. Second baseman Denny Doyle's double play in the seventh inning, on a hard-hit ball by Bob Bailey, thwarted a potential rally by the Expos and helped Lefty preserve the victory.

Having an ace like Carlton on the mound "elevates all aspects of their game — certainly defense is a part of that," Tommy Herr said.[41]

14

A WISE ENCOUNTER

In today's world, there would be a lot of media attention if Steve Carlton were pitching against the player for whom he was traded. The ESPN trucks would be parked in front of the stadium, Comcast SportsNet would be covering the story, and print, radio, and television reporters would be crowding into the press box. Nearly 40 years after the Carlton-for-Wise trade, the Phillies made national headlines by trading for a former Cy Young Award winner in Roy Halladay. Although Philadelphia's 2009 World Series hero, Cliff Lee, was not dealt in that trade, the acquisition of Halladay led to the departure of Lee. Although Philadelphia fans were excited to get Halladay, Lee, like Wise, was a popular figure in Philly, and many were upset to see him go to the Seattle Mariners. Those circumstances would lead media and fans alike to compare the stats of Halladay and Lee from that point forward. Neither Carlton nor Wise had won a Cy Young award prior to 1972, but if there had been a similar level of media coverage that year, the comparisons no doubt would have been running rampant between Carlton and Wise as well.

"Sure, absolutely," Chris Wheeler said. "Everybody would be second-guessing. The Halladay-Lee thing is different because of the year the Phillies were coming off of with Lee ... I mean, Wise was coming off of a great year, but not like in a World Series, and [Halladay and Lee] weren't traded for each other. But that's a good analogy. There's something to that. I just think in my opinion, the deal would have been deemed unpopular. A bad trade. I really do. And I felt that in 1972 when it was made, that that's where it was going to be made. Did I think Lefty would be that good? No. I didn't know as much about the game as I thought I did, but I was a fan. I remember thinking Carlton was pretty good, but was he better than Wise? I don't know."[1]

Carlton removed those doubts during the 1972 season, one in which he beat Cardinal pitchers Bob Gibson, Reggie Cleveland and Al Santorini through their first four series of the year. Wise, meanwhile, still followed the Phillies by reading the box scores in the newspapers, but remarkably, he still hadn't faced his former squad up through mid–September. That finally changed on September 20, when Lefty took the ball against Wise in St. Louis, and although it was a good story, there was not an overwhelming degree of media attention. Yet, that the match-up likely meant a lot to both Carlton and Wise. Asked if players get a little more excited when pitching against players that they were traded for, Wheeler said, "Totally with guys like him. Lefty was intensely competitive. We kid about 'win day,' but it was 'win day' when he went out there. He wanted to win. He was totally focused on it. He cared every time he went out there. I keep comparing [Roy] Halladay to him because Halladay is like him. He's got that look, tunnel vision, like 'Do not bother me. This is my day, I prepared for this and I want to get them today.' That's the way Lefty was."[2]

Surprisingly, only 5,569 people came through the turnstiles at Busch Stadium for the Carlton-Wise matchup, the second smallest crowd in the history of the stadium at that point. Given that it was a marquee pitching matchup, combined with St. Louis being a great baseball town, the attendance figure was surprising. But hot and humid conditions in the Midwest that day no doubt contributed to the sparse crowd. The weather did not seem to affect Carlton and Wise, however, as they hooked up in what Bruce Keidan described as a classic pitcher's duel. In the end, Lefty came away with the complete-game win, as Tommy Hutton led off the top of the sixth with a double and scored the game-winning run on Bill Robinson's RBI ground out to second in a 2–1 win. With three starts left, Carlton's record was 25–9, making him the first 25-game winner in the big leagues that season. It also enabled him to reach the goal he had set for himself at the start of the season. A couple of months later, when Lefty won the first of his four Cy Young awards, he told reporters from his home in St. Louis that he was already targeting 30 wins as a goal for the 1973 season. Friends said that it was unrealistic for him to think about 30 wins — and equaling Denny McLain's 1968 feat — while pitching for such a poor team in '72. "It's not even what you set your goals for," Joe Torre said. "You don't always control [your fate]. You can only control so much."[3]

As Torre noted, however, Lefty's mental makeup involved pushing himself. "If Lefty had said, 'I want to win 15,' it wouldn't have stopped him at 15," Torre said. "So even though 27 was it, he constantly challenged himself. And again, you had to love that about him. He's a very special guy."[4] Greg Luzinski also said that it was unrealistic for Carlton to set a goal for 30 wins with the '72 team that surrounded him. "I guess he probably looked at what was around him," Luzinski said. "I mean, he can control so much, but if you get beat 1–0, you pitched a pretty damn good game. And you may leave with no-decisions pitching a great game. So there's different things obviously, but like I said, his ability to concentrate and his physical strength obviously made him a great pitcher."[5]

Carlton had full concentration against Wise and the Cardinals on September 20, although his two strikeouts against the Redbirds matched his season-low for a single game in 1972. But as he told reporters afterward, "I just wanted to survive the nine innings, to throw as few pitches as possible. I was bearing down on every pitch, but I wasn't trying for strikeouts." In the first inning, Lou Brock chopped the first pitch he saw from Lefty over the head of Larry Bowa, who was charging on the play. As the ball rolled slowly into left field, Brock sprinted to second base, and then after stealing third, he scored on Ted Sizemore's RBI single to center. Brock's run pulled the Redbirds even after the Phillies had taken a 1–0 lead in the top of the first inning.

Denny Doyle also delivered a first-pitch blow, lacing a double to the right-field corner, taking third on Bowa's perfect bunt, and scoring on Tommy Hutton's RBI single to right. It remained that way through four scoreless innings, as Lefty retired 13 straight before issuing a one-out free pass in the fifth, while Wise was perfect in the second and third innings before Luzinski stroked a leadoff hit in the fourth. In the top of the sixth, Hutton lined a double to right and went to third on Willie Montanez's ground out. Hutton did not score when Luzinski reached on an infield single, following a lunging dive by first baseman Joe Torre to knock down a hard grounder, but Robinson's RBI fielder's choice eventually sent Hutton home with what proved to be the game-winner.

Lefty, who scattered just six hits in the game, pitched out of a two-out bases loaded jam in the bottom of the sixth following Brock's leadoff single, Torre's two-out single, and an intentional walk to Ted Simmons; Carlton then retired Ken Reitz on a fly out to right field. He then retired the final five batters of the game, including a game-ending foul pop out by center fielder Jorge Roque, to preserve the one-run victory.

For Wise, it was yet another one-run loss on his way to a 16–16 record with the Cardinals in 1972. "I had an inordinate amount of one-run losses that year — it was just one of those things," Wise said. "I was involved in 19 one-run games. I lost 12 of them, I won four and I had three no-decisions by one run. Everyone said the Cardinals got robbed. I won 16, I think I had 20 complete games which was third in the league, which is unheard of now. Whole leagues don't even get 20 anymore. But anyway, Carlton goes 27–10, I go 16–

16, they said it was a robbery. Well, I was involved in 19 one-run games. No one saved a game for me that year, so I was there until the end and got the decisions, 12 of them were by one run and losses. But the very next year, I represented the Cardinals (in the All-Star Game) and I was the starting and winning pitcher in the All-Star Game, and Carlton lost 23 games in '73. And all that got me is getting traded to Boston. Both times I bought a home and made the All-Star team in my career, I got traded. So much for security."[6]

Lefty, however, was building himself security in Philadelphia, despite a 2–1 loss to Tom Seaver and the Mets at Shea Stadium on September 24 in his next start. Tommie Agee hit a home run against Carlton in the first and then Robinson returned the favor with a solo shot against Seaver. The Mets then broke the tie on Lute Barnes' sac fly in the eighth inning. Willie Montanez led off the Phils' ninth with a hot smash that Seaver grabbed. Then Tug McGraw entered and picked up his 24th save of the season to help Seaver improve to 19–12.

A crowd of 41,644 came out to Shea to see the late–September matchup between Carlton and Seaver. "By the time I got here halfway through the year, Carlton was on such an incredible streak that he could have just been pitching against himself and there would have been build-up," Bill Lyon said. "Those marquee matchups were nice. I guess basically what they did was validate what an incredible season he was having."[7] Asked if he thought that Carlton's opponents faced extra pressure not to give up a lot of runs against him, Lyon said, "Yeah, I think if you were them, you went out saying, 'I better well pitch a shutout. One run may be too many.'"[8]

Pirate pitcher Bob Moose gave up one run too many in his start against Carlton on September 28 at the Vet. Denny Doyle's throwing error led to an unearned run for the Bucs in the second inning. But that was all the Pirates could muster against Lefty. Philadelphia, meanwhile, scored both of its runs against Moose in the fifth. Don Money led off with a single, took second when John Bateman reached on a fielder's choice, and scored on Lefty's double to the right field corner. Doyle then singled home Bateman with the game-winning run. From there, Carlton rode one of his best fastballs of the season, in addition to a nasty curve, en route to his 26th win of the year. He was still throwing darts in the ninth when he struck out Willie Stargell and Bob Robertson to start the inning. Manny Sanguillen connected for a two-out hit, but then Carlton retired Rennie Stennett to end the game. His nine K's against the Pirates pushed his season total to 303, putting him in an elite class with only seven other pitchers at that point in history who had 300 or more strikeouts in a single season — Bob Feller, Sandy Koufax, Rube Waddell, Mickey Lolich, Sam McDowell, and Nolan Ryan.

14 ♦ A Wise Encounter

A crowd of 12,216 turned out at the Vet for Lefty's final home start of the '72 season. Back in those days, when the Vet still had its orange and yellow and brown seats, the stadium also had a pitcher's mound in front of the Phillies' dugout. So for those fans that arrived at the park early, they could have been treated to seeing Philadelphia's starting pitcher warming up for the game. If it happened to be on a day that Lefty was pitching, it was particularly special for the fans. "His stuff was really special," Bob Boone said. "In Philly, they put the bullpen mound right by the dugout, and it was really for him. He warmed up in front of the fans. His stuff was phenomenal. When he warmed up, it was something special for the fans."[9] For a period of time, Lefty wanted Bill Robinson or John Vukovich to pose as a batter beside the plate every time he warmed up on that mound. "I don't know if it was a superstition, but it was close to it," Bill Lyon said. "And every time he warmed up, after the last pitch, he would take the ball and flip it to a fan. Every time."[10]

As Chris Wheeler remembered, it was always a little kid that received that special souvenir. "I could still see him, when he would warm up, the last thing he would do every time is he'd walk back (toward the other end of the dugout) and he'd look for a little kid behind the dugout and flip the ball to him," Wheeler said. "He always would flip the ball to a little kid. Even if the adults were there or not, he'd find a kid and he'd flip the ball to him. I can still see him as he'd walk there, people would be roaring, and they could watch him warm up, just like old Connie Mack Stadium

Early in his career with the Phillies, Steve Carlton warmed up for his starts at Veterans Stadium on a mound in front of the team's dugout. When he finished, a lucky young fan always received the baseball as a souvenir.

was at one time. You could see him right in front of the dugout. The mound was right there, which was not good. They finally had to kick that mound out of there because guys were tripping over it and everything. It was bad, it was not a good spot for the mound."[11]

Fans were also afforded an up-close view of the bullpen mound at Wrigley Field, where Lefty made his final start of the year. For Carlton, he finished the '72 season where he began it, and with the same result — a victory over the Cubs. This time, it was not Fergie Jenkins on the mound for Chicago, but rather Dan McGinn, whom the Phillies battered in a dominant 11–1 win to give Carlton his 27th victory. That tied Lefty with Sandy Koufax for the modern National League win total for a left-hander. Greg Luzinski and Don Money slammed two home runs apiece, while Bill Robinson and Terry Harmon each slugged one, as the Phils took a 6–0 lead after three and never looked back. It was the first time that an NL club homered six times in one game in '72.

At season's end, Lefty was named the starting pitcher on the Newspaper Enterprise Association's All-Major League Team, as chosen in a poll by the 600 players in both leagues. It was a fitting honor for Lefty, who led the National League in wins (27), complete games (30), starts (41), innings (346 and one-third), strikeouts (310), and earned run average (1.98). Eighty-one percent of the players' ballots named Lefty, who finished well ahead of the White Sox's Wilbur Wood (24–17 in '72 in 376 and two-thirds innings), who was named on 12 percent of the ballots. Joining Carlton on the NEA All-Major League Team were White Sox first baseman Dick Allen, Cincinnati Reds second baseman Joe Morgan, Chicago Cubs shortstop Don Kessinger, St. Louis Cardinals third baseman Joe Torre, Pittsburgh Pirates left fielder Willie Stargell, Houston Astros center fielder Cesar Cedeno, Cubs right fielder Billy Williams, Reds' catcher Johnny Bench, and New York Yankees relief pitcher Sparky Lyle. "1972 is probably a dream year (for Carlton), obviously winning 27 games with the team that we had that wasn't very good," Greg Luzinski said. "He was obviously the big bright spot in it and continued on to Hall of Fame success. When you're talking about Steve Carlton, I think you're talking about one of the greatest left-handers ever."[12]

In the off-season, as Paul Owens had promised, the Phillies began to reshuffle their lineup around Lefty. Although the Phils made a minor deal on October 25, 1972, purchasing Tom Haller and Don Leshnock from the Detroit Tigers, they pulled off a blockbuster just six days later, sending Don Money, Bill Champion, and John Vukovich to Milwaukee for Jim Lonborg, Ken Brett, Ken Sanders, and Earl Stephenson. That was just the start. Sanders, Joe Lis, and Ken Reynolds were the next ones to go, as they packed their bags for

Minnesota in exchange for Cesar Tovar in a deal on November 30, 1972. Then the next day, Owens shipped Oscar Gamble and Roger Freed to the Cleveland Indians for Del Unser and Terry Wedgewood.

Coming off of a wretched season, the Phillies' players certainly had to be concerned that they might be playing in a different city in 1973. "I would have thought they'd been worried if they were going to get traded," Bill Lyon acknowledged. "I can't believe that anybody — I'd say Luzinski and Carlton, obviously — I don't know if anybody else could have considered themselves untouchable. On the other hand, if you look at it from their standpoint, maybe they were hoping though, 'Well, if I do get traded, I'll get sent to a decent team.'"[13]

Not all of Philadelphia's big news happened on the transaction wire, however. Prior to the start of the 1973 season, Lefty received from Philadelphia what he was unable to receive from St. Louis. He earned a huge payday. On January 16, 1973, Carlton signed a one-year contract worth $167,000. In addition to becoming the first Phillies player to break the $100,000 barrier, Lefty also became professional baseball's highest-paid pitcher.

The Phillies' current general manager, Ruben Amaro Jr., was only seven years old at the time, but he was not far from Philadelphia's wheelings and dealings. His father, Ruben Amaro Sr., worked in the front office with Owens and Dallas Green. Ruben Jr. was still too young to remember the Carlton contract, but he was able to lend some perspective, nonetheless. "I was around, at least around in existence, during that era," Amaro said. "But clearly, I mean, anybody's who is winning 27 games in this day and age would be making more than C.C. Sabathia." Carlton's '72 season was "very, very extraordinary [it was] and hard to believe that he would have that kind of impact on the club."[14] Amaro left no doubt that the contract for Lefty was well deserved. "It's hard to deny what he did, when he was playing for a team that was relatively weak, I mean, a very weak club, and to be able to have that kind of impact, to impact half the games, that's pretty amazing," Amaro said. "It was a pretty special year for him, a pretty special year especially when you think about how pitching has transformed now. Especially now."[15]

Bill Lyon, too, said that Carlton was worth every penny. Prior to Lefty receiving his contract, Bob Gibson was believed to be the highest-paid pitcher with an annual salary of $150,000. "Blessed with 20–20 hindsight, $167,000 is what they tip a clubhouse attendant at the end of the season, isn't it?" Lyon said. "It's just unbelievable. There wasn't any risk involved because obviously, physically, there turned out to be no problem at all. In retrospect, it seems silly to even think ... I mean, he routinely churned out 300 strikeouts and 300 innings. He was a horse."[16]

Undoubtedly Lefty had a very merry Christmas in December of 1972, as he and Paul Owens had worked out the agreement during that month. But Carlton did not actually sign the deal until later in January because some details needed to be ironed out with Lefty's financial advisor. Owens acknowledged to reporters that the Phillies considered Gibson's salary when determining how much they would offer Lefty. Philadelphia's general manager noted that he and Lefty weren't that far apart when they sat down to talk about his salary in '73. "We know Steve is now above Gibson," Owens was quoted as saying. "We did some research and we feel we are justified in saying Steve is the highest paid pitcher ... I took a lot of things into consideration. Not only the things he could do for us in '73, but also what he could do for us in the future."

Don Money was earning a salary of just $26,000 in 1972, so Carlton's contract was worth more than six times that. "That was a lot — darn right that was a lot," Money said years later of Carlton's $167,000 salary. "Probably back in those days, I bet you the minimum was only 20 [thousand], maybe. He deserved it, of course. He won 27 ball games. Today, if he were on the free agent market, where would he be? In the same role. Everybody was happy. Everybody said, 'Hey, if he can do it, I can do it'.... Everybody thought, '$167,000, holy me oh my.'"[17]

Money pointed out that, unlike today's game where players are signing multi-year, multi-million dollar contracts, players basically received one-year deals. And at that time, the number of players earning six-figure salaries was still a rarity. Unlike in the 21st century, where many players are earning $100,000 per game, there were roughly only 20 players going into 1972 who pulled down that kind of salary over an entire season. Hank Aaron topped everyone when he signed with the Atlanta Braves for $200,000 that season. "It was all based on your performance and sometimes you did well, but the team did bad," Money said. "Hopefully, you would do your job and then the other 24 players, if they do their job, that's when you usually win. But two or three guys can't go out there and make a team win."[18]

Money, of course, was no longer a member of the team when it finally did begin to win later in the 1970s. But the players that Money helped to net the Phils in their trade with the Brewers, combined with those from other deals, gave Lefty hope that their fortunes would improve. "They were definitely good trades," Lefty told reporters, "because we kept the nucleus of a club that can compete. But we're gonna have to work on scoring more runs than the other teams this spring." Carlton was so excited, in fact, that he asked Owens not to trade him. "I like it here and I think we have the nucleus of a good club," Owens said that Lefty told him.

Conclusion
How Does '72 Rank?

In the annals of baseball history, there are pitchers who have had better single-season statistics than Steve Carlton compiled in '72. Like Lefty, the list is a Who's Who of National Baseball Hall of Fame inductees. Carlton's onetime teammate Bob Gibson fashioned a 1.12 earned run average in 1968 while going 22–9 in 34 starts for the Cardinals. Los Angeles Dodgers right-hander Don Drysdale set a record in 1968 with 58 consecutive scoreless innings. Drysdale teamed up with Sandy Koufax in the Sixties to form one of the most dominant pitching duos in history, and together they combined to win 49 games in 1965, with Drysdale finishing 23–12 and Koufax going 26–8. Speaking of Koufax, he won the Cy Young Award in 1963, 1965, and 1966 while winning the pitcher's triple crown each of those seasons, finishing tops in wins, strikeouts, and earned run average. Bob "Rapid Robert" Feller certainly had his share of single-season masterpieces with three no-hitters and 12 one-hitters, for which he shares the major league record, accomplished during an 18-year career with the Cleveland Indians. Walter Johnson, who won 417 games in his career and tossed an all-time career record 110 shutouts, went 33–12 with a 1.39 ERA in 1912 and 36–7 with a 1.14 ERA in 1913. Overall, he won 23 or more games on 10 different occasions in his career.

"Koufax and Drysdale together were worth about 60 wins," Bill Lyon said. "And then if you go all the way back to around the first two decades of the 1900s, Walter Johnson's statistics are just incredible. Bob Feller threw 12 one-hitters. That's just amazing."[1]

Plus, Denny McClain won 31 games in 1968 and remains the only modern-day pitcher with more than 30 wins during a single season. But what none of them accomplished was winning 46 percent of his team's games in one season, as Carlton did for a bad Phillies team in 1972. "They were one team when anybody else pitched and they were another team when Carlton pitched," Bruce Keidan said. "They played with more confidence. Sometimes your star pitcher goes out there and everybody sits around and watches. That wasn't the case with the Phillies that season. Winning wasn't that easy for them, and when they sent Carlton out, they knew they had a chance to win and they played so. He was just a dominating pitcher. The trade was a little bit controversial and I saw him that year in spring training and I remember being behind the batting cage somewhere or behind the catcher and he threw a slider and I went, 'My God, how does anybody hit that?' So I said to Ted Simmons, 'You caught him. How does anybody hit that slider?' He said, 'Well, it forms this little red dot.' I said, 'What are you talking about?' He said, 'The slider, as it comes in, it forms a little red dot.' I said, 'I have a hard enough time seeing the ball, let alone a little red dot.' He said, 'Yeah, but you're not a major league hitter.' Well, Major League hitters couldn't hit it."[2]

The MLB Network ranked Lefty's 1972 season ninth on its list of baseball's greatest pitching seasons in a "Prime Nine" feature. Pedro Martinez's season with the Boston Red Sox in 2000 in which he went 18–6, with a 1.74 ERA and 284 strikeouts in 217 innings, was ranked number one, followed by Walter Johnson's 1913 season (36–7, 1.14 ERA), Bob Gibson's 1968 season, Dwight Gooden's 1985 season (24–4, 1.53), Christy Mathewson's 1908 season (37–11, 1.43), Sandy Koufax's 1965 season (26–8, 2.04), Greg Maddux's 1995 season (19–2, 1.63), Ron Guidry's 1978 season (25–3, 1.74) and finally Lefty's 1972 campaign. But the popular Jayson Stark, a senior baseball writer for ESPN.com since 2000, noted that, depending on the criteria, you would be hard-pressed to find a better season than Lefty had in 1972. "The sheer power of the numbers in a vacuum is not what makes it a great season," Stark said. "It's the sheer power of the numbers combined with the context of the disaster that was going on around him that makes it a great season. I mean, on the degree of difficulty scale, then it's got to be number one on this ("Prime Nine") list, doesn't it?"[3]

Stark added that Johnson and Mathewson put up the numbers that they did in what was considered the dead ball era, a period of time leading up to 1920, when the live ball era was considered to have started. "Walter Johnson was freakin' amazing, but it was the dead ball era," Stark said. "If you really look at pitching and pitching feats and pitching numbers, before Babe Ruth came along, it was almost like a different sport. The great thing about baseball is you can connect the dots from this generation to that generation to that generation, but once you get into 1908, it's pretty rough."[4] Stark, who earned a newspaper journalism degree from Syracuse University and then covered the Phillies for the *Philadelphia Inquirer*, said that what Lefty did in 1972 just defies logic. "It's before my time, but if you listen to guys like Larry Bowa, who played with him, that was a different team when he took the mound because that was their chance to win a game, their chance to play like a real team," he said. "You wouldn't think it would be possible for a team that bad to elevate its game that much, but he was so good. I mean, he didn't need a lot of help. They just had to be there to keep from losing. He would do the rest. I know it happened. I still have no comprehension how it happened or of how that's possible."[5]

Lyon admitted that he would put Carlton's '72 season among the top-ever performances in baseball history, but he hesitated in terms of where exactly he would rank it. "I don't know where I would put it. I wouldn't put it in the top five probably, or maybe even the top 10 if you're talking about in the entire history of baseball," Lyon said. "But it would be there somewhere because he had to do most of it on his own, which refers me back to Walter Johnson and the number of times he lost 1–0. I don't know numerically where I'd rank it, but it had to be (among the best ever)."[6]

Steve Blass argued too that Carlton's 1972 season has to rank right at the top of the all-time best single-season performances because of the ratio of games that he won for a bad Phillies team. "You win almost half of your team's games? C'mon. Who else did that?" Blass asked. "Are there any other comparisons? There's that and then there's other good years. The Gibson year, 1968, was phenomenal ... I mean, he had a 1.12 ERA and he lost nine games. How does that happen? But the ratio of his 22 wins to the total team wins — that's the dazzling part to me. Maybe research would show there are closer ratios, but I don't know of any."[7] Blass said that Hall of Fame lefty Sandy Koufax has always been his hero, but he acknowledges that Lefty belongs in the same conversation when discussing the top left-handed pitchers of all time. "He's right in that neighborhood. I wouldn't mind running either one of them out there for the seventh game of the World Series."[8]

But in addition to Carlton and Koufax, there's another left-hander that many would put among the top left-handers of all time — Randy Johnson. At the end of the 2009 season, Carlton ranked fourth all-time with 4,136 strikeouts, and 11th alltime with 329 wins. Johnson was second and 22nd, respectively, with 4,869 and 303. Both have World Series rings. One (Carlton) was a first-ballot Hall of Famer and the other (Johnson) is a future fixture in Cooperstown. But who would get the ball with one game to win in Game Seven of the Fall Classic? Tim "Rock" Raines, a seven-time All-Star during a 23-year big-league career, has a unique perspective on that question. After coming up with the Montreal Expos in 1979, he dug into the batter's box to face Carlton in his prime for quite a few battles against the Phillies. He was also a teammate of Johnson's in Montreal when "The Big Unit" was just starting out, and later, Raines batted against him when Johnson had developed into a big-time star. But Raines barely hesitated when considering whom he would send to the mound in a Game Seven. "Carlton because I faced him, even when he was older, and he was still dominant," Raines said in the visiting manager's office at Lancaster's Clipper Magazine Stadium while serving as skipper of the Newark Bears. "It took Randy awhile to become the pitcher that he became. Carlton was like an instant good pitcher. Randy threw much harder, but Carlton was a better pitcher. Randy just started becoming a pitcher right around '92, '93, maybe '94, and now he's learned how to pitch. To me right now, he's pitching like Carlton pitched his whole career."[9]

"Randy was a teammate of mine in Montreal and if he found the plate, that was a good thing," Raines quipped. "But I remember Randy throwing a no-hitter and losing. You'd never see Carlton do that. I don't know if Carlton threw many no-hitters, but he definitely was a pitcher that always kept you in a game. He kept the ball down and he had an excellent slider. Probably one of the best sliders I've ever seen. Randy was more of a power pitcher. Steve Carlton was a finesse pitcher who had some good pop. I mean, I think he threw 92–93 miles an hour. I just remember facing him and facing Randy, and I was much more comfortable facing Randy than I was facing Carlton, even when he was much older."[10] Raines said that Carlton was much more seasoned than Johnson when he became a major league pitcher, noting that it took The Big Unit awhile to perfect his slider. He "is a power pitcher and a lot of people like power pitchers," Raines said. "I'm not taking anything away from Randy. Randy was, and still is, a great pitcher. But in their primes, Carlton was better."[11]

Tommy Herr also faced Carlton when Lefty was in his prime and he too would have gone with the Phillies' ace. "You can't go wrong with either one of them, but I would probably say since Carlton came more out of my era, I would go with him," Herr said. "But that's certainly not any slight against Randy Johnson because he's truly great in his own right."[12] Herr said Carlton's devastating slider was not unlike facing the split-fingered pitch of Bruce Sutter, the Hall of Fame closer for the Chicago Cubs, St. Louis Cardinals, and Atlanta Braves. "I would say Sutter's split-finger fastball in his prime was as close to an unhittable pitch as I've seen," Herr remarked. "That would be your best comparison. Maybe [Fernando] Valenzuela's screwball when he was in his prime."[13]

Raines, too, compared Carlton's slider to the nasty repertoires of other big-name pitchers. "There's probably tons of guys now that have nasty stuff, but consistently.... Roger Clemens was a fastball-splitter guy. He had a curve ball, but it wasn't like Carlton's slider. Nolan Ryan even had a good curve ball. But there weren't too many guys who had sliders like [Carlton]. Curve balls and sliders were different pitches, and the slider is much harder. I would say the only guy who comes closest to him right now is Mariano Rivera and he's a closer. And you're talking about a guy who pitched nine innings instead of one or two. And you only see him once. You see Carlton three times. So he's like a Mariano from the first inning to the ninth. I mean, that's tough."[14]

Certainly, Lefty's 1972 season will be tough to duplicate. Even 40 years later, it stands up as one of the most incredible single-season performances ever. "Nobody ever wins 20 anymore," Bill Lyon said. "Now, if you win 18, you're probably going to win the Cy Young. He won nine more than that — and as I said, on a really bad team. That holds up in any era."[15]

Chapter Notes

Chapter 1

1. Steve Blass, interviewed by the author, July 24, 2011 at PNC Park in Pittsburgh, PA.
2. Marty Brennaman, interviewed by the author, May 23, 2011 at Citizens Bank Park in Philadelphia, PA.
3. Larry Bowa, interviewed by the author, February 3, 2010 by telephone.
4. Johnny Bench, interviewed by the author, September 26, 2009 at Valley Forge Convention Center in King of Prussia, PA.
5. Jayson Stark, interviewed by the author, September 25, 2010 at Citizens Bank Park in Philadelphia, PA.
6. Greg Luzinski, interviewed by the author, July 26, 2009 at Citizens Bank Park in Philadelphia, PA.
7. Ibid.
8. Dan Baker, interviewed by the author, June 8, 2010 at Citizens Bank Park in Philadelphia, PA.
9. Bob Boone, interviewed by the author, September 27, 2009 at Valley Forge Convention Center in King of Prussia, PA.
10. Ibid.
11. Tim Raines, interviewed by the author, July 29, 2009 at Clipper Magazine Stadium in Lancaster, PA.
12. Tommy Herr, interviewed by the author, July 29, 2009 at Clipper Magazine Stadium in Lancaster, PA.
13. Larry Shenk, interviewed by the author, January 7, 2010 at Citizens Bank Park in Philadelphia, PA.
14. Tim Raines, interviewed by the author, July 29, 2009 at Clipper Magazine Stadium in Lancaster, PA.
15. Ibid.
16. Jerry Martin, interviewed by the author, June 20, 2011 at FirstEnergy Stadium in Reading, PA.
17. Tommy Herr, interviewed by the author, July 29, 2009 at Clipper Magazine Stadium in Lancaster, PA.
18. Bill Lyon, interviewed by the author, October 11, 2009 by telephone.

Chapter 2

1. Rick Wise, interviewed by the author, August 22, 2009 by telephone.
2. Ibid.
3. Ibid.

4. Chris Wheeler, interviewed by the author, August 19, 2009 at Citizens Bank Park in Philadelphia, PA.
5. Rick Wise, interviewed by the author, August 22, 2009 by telephone.
6. Larry Shenk, interviewed by the author, January 7, 2010 at Citizens Bank Park in Philadelphia, PA.
7. Chris Wheeler, interviewed by the author, August 19, 2009 at Citizens Bank Park in Philadelphia, PA.
8. Larry Shenk, interviewed by the author, January 7, 2010 at Citizens Bank Park in Philadelphia, PA.
9. Ibid.
10. Ibid.
11. Chris Wheeler, interviewed by the author, August 19, 2009 at Citizens Bank Park in Philadelphia, PA.
12. Joe Torre, interviewed by the author, August 11, 2010 at Citizens Bank Park in Philadelphia, PA.
13. Ibid.
14. Chris Wheeler, interviewed by the author, August 19, 2009 at Citizens Bank Park in Philadelphia, PA.
15. Larry Shenk, interviewed by the author, January 7, 2010 at Citizens Bank Park in Philadelphia, PA.
16. Ibid.
17. Scott Palmer, interviewed by the author, January 25, 2010 at Sheraton Reading Hotel in Reading, PA.

Chapter 3

1. Don Money, interviewed by the author, January 27, 2010 by telephone.
2. Ibid.
3. Ibid.
4. Larry Bowa, interviewed by the author, February 3, 2010 by telephone.
5. Ibid.
6. Tommy Hutton, interviewed by the author, July 15, 2010 by email.
7. Larry Shenk, interviewed by the author, January 7, 2010 at Citizens Bank Park in Philadelphia, PA.

Chapter 4

1. Chris Wheeler, interviewed by the author, April 14, 2010 at Citizens Bank Park in Philadelphia, PA.
2. Ibid.
3. Ibid.
4. Larry Bowa, interviewed by the author, February 3, 2010 by telephone.
5. Ibid.
6. Greg Luzinski, interviewed by the author, July 26, 2009 at Citizens Bank Park in Philadelphia, PA.
7. Mike Krukow, interviewed by the author, July 27, 2011 at Citizens Bank Park in Philadelphia, PA.
8. Bruce Keidan, interviewed by the author, November 1, 2009 by telephone.
9. Tommy Hutton, interviewed by the author, July 15, 2010 by email.
10. Ferguson Jenkins, interviewed by the author, Saturday, March 27 at the Ephrata Rec Center in Ephrata, PA.
11. Rick Monday, interviewed by the author, August 11, 2010 at Cititzens Bank Park in Philadelphia, PA.
12. Joe Torre, interviewed by the author, August 11, 2010 at Citizens Bank Park in Philadelphia, PA.

13. Chris Wheeler, interviewed by the author, September 25, 2010 at Cititzens Bank Park in Philadelphia, PA.
14. Dan Baker, interviewed by the author, June 8, 2011 at Citizens Bank Park in Philadelphia, PA.
15. Chris Wheeler, interviewed by the author, August 19, 2009 at Citizens Bank Park in Philadelphia, PA.
16. Greg Luzinski, interviewed by the author, July 26, 2009 at Citizens Bank Park in Philadelphia, PA.
17. Chris Wheeler, interviewed by the author, August 19, 2009 at Cititzens Bank Park in Philadelphia, PA.
18. Bill Lyon, interviewed by the author, June 16, 2010 by telephone.
19. Ibid.
20. Don Money, interviewed by the author, January 27, 2010 by telephone.
21. Marty Bystrom, interviewed by the author, January 25, 2010 at the Sheraton Reading Hotel in Reading, PA.
22. Larry Bowa, interviewed by the author, February 3, 2010 by telephone.
23. Larry Shenk, interviewed by the author, January 7, 2010 at Citizens Bank Park in Philadelphia, PA.
24. Ibid.
25. Rich Hebner, interviewed by the author, March 6, 2010 by telephone.
26. Chris Wheeler, interviewed by the author, April 14, 2010 at Citizens Bank Park in Philadelphia, PA.
27. Ibid.
28. Ibid.
29. Ibid.
30. Ibid.
31. Chris Wheeler, interviewed by the author, August 19, 2009 at Cititzens Bank Park in Philadelphia, PA.
32. Tito Fuentes, interviewed by the author, September 18, 2010 by telephone.
33. Wayne Twitchell, interviewed by the author, June 25, 2010 by telephone.
34. Chris Speier, interviewed by the author, July 9, 2010 at Citizens Bank Park in Philadelphia, PA.
35. Ibid.
36. Ibid.
37. Larry Bowa, interviewed by the author, February 3, 2010 by telephone.
38. Larry Shenk, interviewed by the author, January 7, 2010 at Citizens Bank Park in Philadelphia, PA.
39. Wayne Twitchell, interviewed by the author, June 25, 2010 by telephone.
40. Bruce Keidan, interviewed by the author, November 1, 2009 by telephone.
41. Ibid.

Chapter 5

1. Chris Wheeler, interviewed by the author, July 27, 2011 at Citizens Bank Park in Philadelphia, PA.
2. Tim Flannery, interviewed by the author, August 18, 2010 at Citizens Bank Park in Philadelphia, PA.
3. Ibid.
4. Tito Fuentes, interviewed by the author, September 18, 2010 by telephone.
5. Chris Speier, interviewed by the author, July 9, 2010 at Citizens Bank Park in Philadelphia, PA.
6. Bill Lyon, interviewed by the author, October 11, 2009 by telephone.
7. Ferguson Jenkins, interviewed by the author, March 27, 2010 at the Ephrata Rec Center in Ephrata, PA.
8. Greg Luzinski, interviewed by the author, August 4, 2010 at FirstEnergy Stadium in Reading, PA.

Chapter 6

1. Larry Bowa, interviewed by the author, February 3, 2010 by telephone.
2. Tommy Hutton, interviewed by the author, July 15, 2010 by email.
3. Ibid.
4. Bill Lyon, interviewed by the author, June 16, 2010 by telephone.
5. Tommy Hutton, interviewed by the author, July 15, 2010 by email.
6. Chris Wheeler, interviewed by the author, April 14, 2010 at Citizens Bank Park in Philadelphia, PA.
7. Willie Montanez, interviewed by the author, March 25, 2010 by telephone.
8. Tommy Hutton, interviewed by the author, July 15, 2010 by email.
9. Ibid.
10. Don Money, interviewed by the author, January 27, 2010 by telephone.
11. Larry Shenk, interviewed by the author, January 7, 2010 at Citizens Bank Park in Philadelphia, PA.
12. Wayne Twitchell, interviewed by the author, June 25, 2010 by telephone.
13. Chris Wheeler, interviewed by the author, September 25, 2010 at Citizens Bank Park in Philadelphia, PA.
14. Ibid.
15. Don Money, interviewed by the author, January 27, 2010 by telephone.
16. Chris Wheeler, interviewed by the author, September 25, 2010 at Citizens Bank Park in Philadelphia, PA.
17. Rich Hebner, interviewed by the author, March 6, 2010 by telephone.
18. See Don Money, interviewed by the author, January 27, 2010 by telephone.
19. Larry Shenk, interviewed by the author, January 7, 2010 at Citizens Bank Park in Philadelphia, PA.
20. Don Money, interviewed by the author, January 27, 2010 by telephone.
21. Larry Shenk, interviewed by the author, January 7, 2010 at Citizens Bank Park in Philadelphia, PA.
22. Ibid.
23. Dan Baker, interviewed by the author, June 8, 2011 at Citizens Bank Park in Philadelphia, PA.
24. Bruce Keidan, interviewed by the author, November 1, 2009 by telephone.
25. Bill Lyon, interviewed by the author, October 11, 2009 by telephone.
26. Greg Luzinski, interviewed by the author, July 26, 2009 at Citizens Bank Park in Philadelphia, PA.
27. Don Money, interviewed by the author, January 27, 2010 by telephone.
28. Larry Bowa, interviewed by the author, February 3, 2010 by telephone.
29. Chris Wheeler, interviewed by the author, August 19, 2010 at Citizens Bank Park in Philadelphia, PA.
30. Greg Luzinski, interviewed by the author, July 26, 2009 at Citizens Bank Park in Philadelphia, PA.
31. Bob Boone, interviewed by the author, September 27, 2009 at Valley Forge Convention Center in King of Prussia, PA.
32. Larry Bowa, interviewed by the author, February 3, 2010 by telephone.
33. Chris Wheeler, interviewed by the author, August 19, 2010 at Citizens Bank Park in Philadelphia, PA.

Chapter 7

1. Sparky Lyle, interviewed by the author, August 17, 2009 at Clipper Magazine Stadium in Lancaster, PA.
2. Rick Monday, interviewed by the author, August 11, 2010 at Citizens Bank Park in Philadelphia, PA.
3. Ray Burris, interviewed by the author, June 20, 2011 at FirstEnergy Stadium in Reading, PA.

4. Johnny Bench, interviewed by the author, September 26, 2009 at Valley Forge Convention Center in King of Prussia, PA.
5. Bill Lyon, interviewed by the author, June 16, 2010 by telephone.
6. Chris Wheeler, interviewed by the author, April 14, 2010 at Citizens Park in Philadelphia, PA.
7. Greg Luzinski, interviewed by the author, July 26, 2009 at Citizens Bank Park in Philadelphia, PA.
8. Marty Bystrom, interviewed by the author, January 25, 2010 at the Sheraton Reading Hotel in Reading, PA.
9. Larry Shenk, interviewed by the author, January 7, 2010 at Citizens Bank Park in Philadelphia, PA.
10. Marty Bystrom, interviewed by the author, January 25, 2010 at the Sheraton Reading Hotel in Reading, PA.
11. Wayne Twitchell, interviewed by the author, June 25, 2010 by telephone.
12. Johnny Bench, interviewed by the author, September 26, 2009 at Valley Forge Convention Center in King of Prussia, PA.
13. Larry Shenk, interviewed by the author, January 7, 2010 at Citizens Bank Park in Philadelphia, PA.
14. Larry Bowa, interviewed by the author, February 3, 2010 by telephone.
15. Ross Grimsley, interviewed by the author, June 11, 2010 at FirstEnergy Stadium in Reading, PA.
16. Larry Shenk, interviewed by the author, January 7, 2010 at Citizens Bank Park in Philadelphia, PA.

Chapter 8

1. Larry Bowa, interviewed by the author, February 3, 2010 by telephone.
2. Ibid.
3. Ibid.
4. Greg Luzinski, interviewed by the author, July 26, 2009 at Citizens Bank Park in Philadelphia, PA.
5. Willie Montanez, interviewed by the author, March 25, 2010 by telephone.
6. Ibid.
7. Larry Shenk, interviewed by the author, January 7, 2010 at Citizens Bank Park in Philadelphia, PA.
8. Larry Bowa, interviewed by the author, February 3, 2010 by telephone.
9. Willie Montanez, interviewed by the author, March 25, 2010 by telephone.
10. Larry Shenk, interviewed by the author, January 7, 2010 at Citizens Bank Park in Philadelphia, PA.
11. Ibid.
12. Bill Lyon, interviewed by the author, June 16, 2010 by telephone.
13. Larry Shenk, interviewed by the author, January 7, 2010 at Citizens Bank Park in Philadelphia, PA.
14. Willie Montanez, interviewed by the author, March 25, 2010 by telephone.
15. Bruce Keidan, interviewed by the author, November 1, 2009 by telephone.
16. Willie Montanez, interviewed by the author, March 25, 2010 by telephone.
17. Jerry Martin, interviewed by the author, June 20, 2011 at FirstEnergy Stadium in Reading, PA.
18. Chris Wheeler, interviewed by the author, August 19, 2009 at Citizens Bank Park in Philadelphia, PA.
19. Larry Bowa, interviewed by the author, February 3, 2010 by telephone.
20. Gary Matthews, interviewed by the author, August 19, 2009 at Citizens Bank Park in Philadelphia, PA.
21. Bob Boone, interviewed by the author, September 27, 2009 at Valley Forge Convention Center in King of Prussia, PA.
22. Wayne Twitchell, interviewed by the author, June 25, 2010 by telephone.

23. Greg Luzinski, interviewed by the author, August 4, 2010 at FirstEnergy Stadium in Reading, PA.
24. Larry Bowa, interviewed by the author, August 11, 2010 at Citizens Bank Park in Philadelphia, PA.
25. Larry Bowa, interviewed by the author, February 3, 2010 by telephone.
26. Chris Wheeler, interviewed by the author, August 19, 2009 at Citizens Bank Park in Philadelphia, PA.
27. Rick Monday, interviewed by the author, August 19, 2009 at Citizens Bank Park in Philadelphia, PA.
28. Tim Raines, interviewed by the author, July 29, 2009 at Clipper Magazine Stadium in Lancaster, PA.
29. Larry Bowa, interviewed by the author, February 3, 2010 by telephone.
30. Ibid.
31. Larry Shenk, interviewed by the author, January 7, 2010 at Citizens Bank Park in Philadelphia, PA.
32. Bruce Keidan, interviewed by the author, November 1, 2009 by telephone.
33. Bill Lyon, interviewed by the author, October 11, 2009 by telephone.

Chapter 9

1. Don Money, interviewed by the author, January 27, 2010 by telephone.
2. Ibid.
3. Larry Bowa, interviewed by the author, February 3, 2010 by telephone.
4. Ibid.
5. Ibid.
6. Ibid.
7. Chris Wheeler, interviewed by the author, April 14, 2010 at Citizens Bank Park in Philadelphia, PA.
8. Ibid.
9. Gary Matthews, interviewed by the author, August 19, 2009 at Citizens Bank Park in Philadelphia, PA.
10. Ibid.
11. Wayne Twitchell, interviewed by the author, June 25, 2010 by telephone.
12. Ibid.
13. Sparky Lyle, interviewed by the author, August 17, 2009 at Clipper Magazine Stadium in Lancaster, PA.
14. Ibid.
15. Rich Hebner, interviewed by the author, March 6, 2010 by telephone.
16. Tommy Hutton, interviewed by the author, July 15, 2010 by email.
17. Wayne Twitchell, interviewed by the author, June 25, 2010 by telephone.
18. Ibid.
19. Ibid.
20. Chris Wheeler, interviewed by the author, April 14, 2010 at Citizens Bank Park in Philadelphia, PA.
21. Larry Shenk, interviewed by the author, January 7, 2010 at Citizens Bank Park in Philadelphia, PA.
22. Ibid.
23. Greg Luzinski, interviewed by the author, August 4, 2010 at FirstEnergy Stadium in Reading, PA.
24. Jerry Martin, interviewed by the author, June 20, 2011 at FirstEnergy Stadium in Reading, PA.
25. Ibid.
26. Bruce Keidan, interviewed by the author, November 1, 2009 by telephone.
27. Ibid.
28. Scott Palmer, interviewed by the author, January 25, 2010 at the Sheraton Reading Hotel in Reading, PA.

29. Larry Shenk, interviewed by the author, January 7, 2010 at Citizens Bank Park in Philadelphia, PA.
30. Ibid.
31. Ibid.
32. Ibid.
33. Ibid
34. Ibid.
35. Ibid.
36. Ibid.
37. Bob Boone, interviewed by the author, September 27, 2009 at Valley Forge Convention Center in King of Prussia, PA.
38. Ibid.
39. Larry Shenk, interviewed by the author, January 7, 2010 at Citizens Bank Park in Philadelphia, PA.
40. Ibid.
41. Ibid.
42. Ibid.
43. Chris Wheeler, interviewed by the author, September 25, 2010 at Citizens Bank Park in Philadelphia, PA.
44. Ibid.
45. Mike Krukow, interviewed by the author, August 18, 2010 at Citizens Bank Park in Philadelphia, PA.
46. Tito Fuentes, interviewed by the author, September 18, 2010 by telephone.
47. Bob Walk, interviewed by the author, July 24, 2011 at PNC Park in Pittsburgh, PA.
48. Tim Flannery, interviewed by the author, August 18, 2010 at Citizens Bank Park in Philadelphia, PA.
49. Gary Matthews, interviewed by the author, August 19, 2009 at Citizens Bank Park in Philadelphia, PA.
50. Wayne Twitchell, interviewed by the author, June 25, 2010 by telephone.
51. Jerry Martin, interviewed by the author, June 20, 2011 at FirstEnergy Stadium in Reading, PA.
52. Jim Kaat, interviewed by the author, July 23, 2011 in Cooperstown, N.Y.
53. Chris Wheeler, interviewed by the author, September 25, 2010 at Citizens Bank Park in Philadelphia, PA.
54. Larry Shenk, interviewed by the author, January 7, 2010 at Citizens Bank Park in Philadelphia, PA.
55. Chris Wheeler, interviewed by the author, September 25, 2010 at Citizens Bank Park in Philadelphia, PA.
56. Larry Shenk, interviewed by the author, January 7, 2010 at Citizens Bank Park in Philadelphia, PA.
57. Chris Wheeler, interviewed by the author, August 19, 2009 at Citizens Bank Park in Philadelphia, PA.
58. Bob Boone, interviewed by the author, September 27, 2009 at Valley Forge Convention Center in King of Prussia, PA.
59. Steve Blass, interviewed by the author, July 24, 2011 at PNC Park in Pittsburgh, PA.

Chapter 10

1. Sparky Lyle, interviewed by the author, August 17, 2009 at Clipper Magazine Stadium in Lancaster, PA.
2. Jerry Martin, interviewed by the author, June 20, 2011 at FirstEnergy Stadium in Reading, PA.
3. Bob Walk, interviewed by the author, July 24, 2011 at PNC Park in Pittsburgh, PA.
4. Steve Blass, interviewed by the author, July 24, 2011 at PNC Park in Pittsburgh, PA.
5. Bill Lyon, interviewed by the author, October 11, 2009 by telephone.

6. Chris Wheeler, interviewed by the author, July 27, 2011 at Citizens Bank Park in Philadelphia, PA.
7. Tito Fuentes, interviewed by the author, September 18, 2010 by telephone.
8. Gary Matthews, interviewed by the author, August 19, 2009 at Citizens Bank Park in Philadelphia, PA.
9. Dusty Baker, interviewed by the author, May 23, 2011 at Citizens Bank Park in Philadelphia, PA.
10. Tim Flannery, interviewed by the author, August 18, 2010 at Citizens Bank Park in Philadelphia, PA.
11. Chris Wheeler, interviewed by the author, August 19, 2009 at Citizens Bank Park in Philadelphia, PA.
12. Larry Shenk, interviewed by the author, January 7, 2010 at Citizens Bank Park in Philadelphia, PA.
13. Chris Wheeler, interviewed by the author, April 14, 2010 at Citizens Bank Park in Philadelphia, PA.
14. Ibid.
15. Larry Shenk, interviewed by the author, January 7, 2010 at Citizens Bank Park in Philadelphia, PA.
16. Bill Lyon, interviewed by the author, October 11, 2009 by telephone.
17. Larry Shenk, interviewed by the author, January 7, 2010 at Citizens Bank Park in Philadelphia, PA.
18. Ibid.
19. Ibid.
20. Ibid.

Chapter 11

1. Chris Wheeler, interviewed by the author, September 25, 2010 at Citizens Bank Park in Philadelphia, PA.
2. Chris Wheeler, interviewed by the author, April 14, 2010 at Citizens Bank Park in Philadelphia, PA.
3. Ibid.
4. Ibid.
5. Ibid.
6. Bill Lyon, interviewed by the author, June 16, 2010 by telephone.
7. Ibid.
8. Larry Shenk, interviewed by the author, January 7, 2010 at Citizens Bank Park in Philadelphia, PA.
9. Don Money, interviewed by the author, January 27, 2010 by telephone.
10. Ibid.
11. Bob Boone, interviewed by the author, September 27, 2009 at Valley Forge Convention Center in King of Prussia, PA.
12. Gary Matthews, interviewed by the author, August 19, 2009 at Citizens Bank Park in Philadelphia, PA.
13. Greg Luzinski, interviewed by the author, July 26, 2009 at Citizens Bank Park in Philadelphia, PA.
14. Ferguson Jenkins, interviewed by the author, March 27, 2010 at the Ephrata Rec Center in Ephrata, PA.
15. Larry Bowa, interviewed by the author, February 3, 2010 by telephone.
16. Ibid.
17. Bill Lyon, interviewed by the author, October 11, 2009 by telephone.
18. Sparky Lyle, interviewed by the author, August 17, 2009 at Clipper Magazine Stadium in Lancaster, PA.
19. Joe Torre, interviewed by the author, August 11, 2010 at Citizens Bank Park in Philadelphia, PA.
20. Bill Lyon, interviewed by the author, October 11, 2009 by telephone.

Notes — Chapter 11

21. Ferguson Jenkins, interviewed by the author, March 27, 2010 at the Ephrata Rec Center in Ephrata, PA.
22. Bruce Keidan, interviewed by the author, November 1, 2009 by telephone.
23. Tommy Hutton, interviewed by the author, July 15, 2010 by email.
24. Rich Hebner, interviewed by the author, March 6, 2010 by telephone.
25. Larry Shenk, interviewed by the author, January 7, 2010 at Citizens Bank Park in Philadelphia, PA.
26. Joe Torre, interviewed by the author, August 11, 2010 at Citizens Bank Park in Philadelphia, PA.
27. Ibid.
28. Steve Blass, interviewed by the author, July 24, 2011 at PNC Park in Pittsburgh, PA.
29. Joe Torre, interviewed by the author, August 11, 2010 at Citizens Bank Park in Philadelphia, PA.
30. Larry Shenk, interviewed by the author, January 7, 2010 at Citizens Bank Park in Philadelphia, PA.
31. Steve Blass, interviewed by the author, July 24, 2011 at PNC Park in Pittsburgh, PA.
32. Chris Wheeler, interviewed by the author, April 14, 2010 at Citizens Bank Park in Philadelphia, PA.
33. Tommy Herr, interviewed by the author, July 29, 2009 at Clipper Magazine Stadium in Lancaster, PA.
34. Larry Bowa, interviewed by the author, February 3, 2010 by telephone.
35. Chris Wheeler, interviewed by the author, April 14, 2010 at Citizens Bank Park in Philadelphia, PA.
36. Mike Krukow, interviewed by the author, August 18, 2010 at Citizens Bank Park in Philadelphia, PA.
37. Ibid.
38. Larry Bowa, interviewed by the author, February 3, 2010 by telephone.
39. Larry Shenk, interviewed by the author, January 7, 2010 at Citizens Bank Park in Philadelphia, PA.
40. Chris Wheeler, interviewed by the author, September 25, 2010 at Citizens Bank Park in Philadelphia, PA.
41. Larry Bowa, interviewed by the author, February 3, 2010 by telephone.
42. Jerry Martin, interviewed by the author, June 20, 2011 at FirstEnergy Stadium in Reading, PA.
43. Larry Bowa, interviewed by the author, February 3, 2010 by telephone.
44. Sparky Lyle, interviewed by the author, August 17, 2009 at Clipper Magazine Stadium in Lancaster, PA.
45. Gary Matthews, interviewed by the author, August 19, 2009 at Citizens Bank Park in Philadelphia, PA.
46. Mike Krukow, interviewed by the author, August 18, 2010 at Citizens Bank Park in Philadelphia, PA.
47. Chris Wheeler, interviewed by the author, September 25, 2010 at Citizens Bank Park in Philadelphia, PA.
48. Jim Kaat, interviewed by the author, July 23, 2011 in Cooperstown, N.Y.
49. Ibid.
50. Chris Wheeler, interviewed by the author, September 25, 2010 at Citizens Bank Park in Philadelphia, PA.
51. Mike Krukow, interviewed by the author, August 18, 2010 at Citizens Bank Park in Philadelphia, PA.
52. Tim Flannery, interviewed by the author, August 18, 2010 at Citizens Bank Park in Philadelphia, PA.
53. Mike Krukow, interviewed by the author, August 18, 2010 at Citizens Bank Park in Philadelphia, PA.
54. Ibid.
55. Bob Walk, interviewed by the author, July 24, 2011 at PNC Park in Pittsburgh, PA.
56. Bill Lyon, interviewed by the author, June 16, 2010 by telephone.

57. Wayne Twitchell, interviewed by the author, June 25, 2010 by telephone.
58. Tommy Herr, interviewed by the author, July 29, 2009 at Clipper Magazine Stadium in Lancaster, PA.
59. Ray Burris, interviewed by the author, June 20, 2011 at FirstEnergy Stadium in Reading, PA.
60. Bill Lyon, interviewed by the author, June 16, 2010 by telephone.
61. Larry Bowa, interviewed by the author, February 3, 2010 by telephone.
62. Bill Lyon, interviewed by the author, June 16, 2010 by telephone.

Chapter 12

1. Rick Monday, interviewed by the author, August 11, 2010 at Citizens Bank Park in Philadelphia, PA.
2. Mike Krukow, interviewed by the author, August 18, 2010 at Citizens Bank Park in Philadelphia, PA.
3. Chris Wheeler, interviewed by the author, April 14, 2010 at Citizens Bank Park in Philadelphia, PA.
4. Don Money, interviewed by the author, January 27, 2010 by telephone.
5. Tommy Herr, interviewed by the author, July 29, 2009 at Clipper Magazine Stadium in Lancaster, PA.
6. Chris Wheeler, interviewed by the author, April 14, 2010 at Citizens Bank Park in Philadelphia, PA.
7. Ibid.
8. Wayne Twitchell, interviewed by the author, June 25, 2010 by telephone.
9. Ibid.
10. Ibid.
11. Ibid.
12. Ibid.
13. Bill Lyon, interviewed by the author, October 11, 2009 by telephone.
14. Larry Shenk, interviewed by the author, January 7, 2010 at Citizens Bank Park in Philadelphia, PA.
15. Wayne Twitchell, interviewed by the author, June 25, 2010 by telephone.
16. Joe Torre, interviewed by the author, August 11, 2010 at Citizens Bank Park in Philadelphia, PA.
17. Tim Raines, interviewed by the author, July 29, 2009 at Clipper Magazine Stadium in Lancaster, PA.
18. Chris Wheeler, interviewed by the author, August 19, 2009 at Citizens Bank Park in Philadelphia, PA.
19. Rich Hebner, interviewed by the author, March 6, 2010 by telephone.
20. Steve Blass, interviewed by the author, July 24, 2011 at PNC Park in Pittsburgh, PA.
21. Ibid.
22. Ibid.
23. Larry Shenk, interviewed by the author, January 7, 2010 at Citizens Bank Park in Philadelphia, PA.
24. Rich Hebner, interviewed by the author, March 6, 2010 by telephone.
25. Steve Blass, interviewed by the author, July 24, 2011 at PNC Park in Pittsburgh, PA.
26. Rich Hebner, interviewed by the author, March 6, 2010 by telephone.
27. Larry Bowa, interviewed by the author, February 3, 2010 by telephone.
28. Larry Shenk, interviewed by the author, January 7, 2010 at Citizens Bank Park in Philadelphia, PA.
29. Ibid.
30. Larry Bowa, interviewed by the author, February 3, 2010 by telephone.
31. Ibid.
32. Tim Raines, interviewed by the author, July 29, 2009 at Clipper Magazine Stadium in Lancaster, PA.
33. Bill Lyon, interviewed by the author, June 16, 2010 by telephone.

34. Ross Grimsley, interviewed by the author, June 11, 2010 at FirstEnergy Stadium in Reading, PA.
35. Chris Wheeler, interviewed by the author, August 19, 2009 at Citizens Bank Park in Philadelphia, PA.
36. Ross Grimsley, interviewed by the author, June 11, 2010 at FirstEnergy Stadium in Reading, PA.
37. Ibid.
38. Tommy Hutton, interviewed by the author, July 15, 2010 by email.
39. Bill Lyon, interviewed by the author, October 11, 2009 by telephone.
40. Chris Wheeler, interviewed by the author, August 19, 2009 at Citizens Bank Park in Philadelphia, PA.
41. Chris Wheeler, interviewed by the author, April 14, 2010 at Citizens Bank Park in Philadelphia, PA.
42. Ruben Amaro Jr., interviewed by the author, June 11, 2010 at FirstEnergy Stadium in Reading, PA.
43. Dan Baker, interviewed by the author, June 8, 2011 at Citizens Bank Park in Philadelphia, PA.
44. Larry Shenk, interviewed by the author, January 7, 2010 at Citizens Bank Park in Philadelphia, PA.
45. Bill Lyon, interviewed by the author, October 11, 2009 by telephone.
46. Ibid.
47. Ibid.
48. Jim Kaat, interviewed by the author, July 23, 2011 in Cooperstown, N.Y.
49. Sparky Lyle, interviewed by the author, August 17, 2009 at Clipper Magazine Stadium in Lancaster, PA.

Chapter 13

1. Dusty Baker, interviewed by the author, May 23, 2011 at Citizens Bank Park in Philadelphia, PA.
2. Ibid.
3. Ibid.
4. Larry Shenk, interviewed by the author, January 7, 2010 at Citizens Bank Park in Philadelphia, PA.
5. Wayne Twitchell, interviewed by the author, June 25, 2010 by telephone.
6. Chris Wheeler, interviewed by the author, August 19, 2009 at Citizens Bank Park in Philadelphia, PA.
7. Ibid.
8. Wayne Twitchell, interviewed by the author, June 25, 2010 by telephone.
9. Chris Wheeler, interviewed by the author, August 19, 2009 at Citizens Bank Park in Philadelphia, PA.
10. Larry Bowa, interviewed by the author, February 3, 2010 by telephone.
11. Wayne Twitchell, interviewed by the author, June 25, 2010 by telephone.
12. Bruce Keidan, interviewed by the author, November 1, 2009 by telephone.
13. Ibid.
14. Marty Bystrom, interviewed by the author, January 25, 2010 at the Sheraton Reading Hotel in Reading, PA.
15. Larry Shenk, interviewed by the author, January 7, 2010 at Citizens Bank Park in Philadelphia, PA.
16. Chris Wheeler, interviewed by the author, August 19, 2009 at Citizens Bank Park in Philadelphia, PA.
17. Ross Grimsley, interviewed by the author, June 11, 2010 at FirstEnergy Stadium in Reading, PA.
18. Larry Bowa, interviewed by the author, February 3, 2010 by telephone.
19. Bill Lyon, interviewed by the author, June 16, 2010 by telephone.

20. Joe Torre, interviewed by the author, August 11, 2010 at Citizens Bank Park in Philadelphia, PA.
21. Larry Shenk, interviewed by the author, January 7, 2010 at Citizens Bank Park in Philadelphia, PA.
22. Larry Bowa, interviewed by the author, February 3, 2010 by telephone.
23. Ibid.
24. Ross Grimsley, interviewed by the author, June 11, 2010 at FirstEnergy Stadium in Reading, PA.
25. Greg Luzinski, interviewed by the author, August 4, 2010 at FirstEnergy Stadium in Reading, PA.
26. Bill Lyon, interviewed by the author, June 16, 2010 by telephone.
27. Larry Bowa, interviewed by the author, February 3, 2010 by telephone.
28. Joe Torre, interviewed by the author, August 11, 2010 at Citizens Bank Park in Philadelphia, PA.
29. Bill Lyon, interviewed by the author, June 16, 2010 by telephone.
30. Joe Torre, interviewed by the author, August 11, 2010 at Citizens Bank Park in Philadelphia, PA.
31. Chris Wheeler, interviewed by the author, April 14, 2010 at Citizens Bank Park in Philadelphia, PA.
32. Larry Bowa, interviewed by the author, February 3, 2010 by telephone.
33. Don Money, interviewed by the author, January 27, 2010 by telephone.
34. Larry Shenk, interviewed by the author, January 7, 2010 at Citizens Bank Park in Philadelphia, PA.
35. Tommy Hutton, interviewed by the author, July 15, 2010 by email.
36. Bob Boone, interviewed by the author, September 27, 2009 at Valley Forge Convention Center in King of Prussia, PA.
37. Bill Lyon, interviewed by the author, October 11, 2009 by telephone.
38. Chris Wheeler, interviewed by the author, April 14, 2010 at Citizens Bank Park in Philadelphia, PA.
39. Greg Luzinski, interviewed by the author, August 4, 2010 at FirstEnergy Stadium in Reading, PA.
40. Chris Wheeler, interviewed by the author, April 14, 2010 at Citizens Bank Park in Philadelphia, PA.
41. Tommy Herr, interviewed by the author, July 29, 2009 at Clipper Magazine Stadium in Lancaster, PA.

Chapter 14

1. Chris Wheeler, interviewed by the author, April 14, 2010 at Citizens Bank Park in Philadelphia, PA.
2. Chris Wheeler, interviewed by the author, September 25, 2010 at Citizens Bank Park in Philadelphia, PA.
3. Joe Torre, interviewed by the author, August 11, 2010 at Citizens Bank Park in Philadelphia, PA.
4. Ibid.
5. Greg Luzinski, interviewed by the author, August 4, 2010 at FirstEnergy Stadium in Reading, PA.
6. Rick Wise, interviewed by the author, August 22, 2009 by telephone.
7. Bill Lyon, interviewed by the author, October 11, 2009 by telephone.
8. Ibid.
9. Bob Boone, interviewed by the author, September 27, 2009 at Valley Forge Convention Center in King of Prussia, PA.
10. Bill Lyon, interviewed by the author, October 11, 2009 by telephone.
11. Chris Wheeler, interviewed by the author, April 14, 2010 at Citizens Bank Park in Philadelphia, PA.

12. Greg Luzinski, interviewed by the author, July 26, 2009 at Citizens Bank Park in Philadelphia, PA.
13. Bill Lyon, interviewed by the author, June 16, 2010 by telephone.
14. Ruben Amaro Jr., interviewed by the author, June 11, 2010 at FirstEnergy Stadium in Reading, PA.
15. Ibid.
16. Bill Lyon, interviewed by the author, June 16, 2010 by telephone.
17. Don Money, interviewed by the author, January 27, 2010 by telephone.
18. Ibid.

Conclusion

1. Bill Lyon, interviewed by the author, October 11, 2009 by telephone.
2. Bruce Keidan, interviewed by the author, November 1, 2009 by telephone.
3. Jayson Stark, interviewed by the author, September 25, 2010 at Citizens Bank Park in Philadelphia, PA.
4. Ibid.
5. Ibid.
6. Bill Lyon, interviewed by the author, October 11, 2009 by telephone.
7. Steve Blass, interviewed by the author, July 24, 2011 at PNC Park in Pittsburgh, PA.
8. Ibid.
9. Tim Raines, interviewed by the author, July 29, 2009 at Clipper Magazine Stadium in Lancaster, PA.
10. Ibid.
11. Ibid.
12. Tommy Herr, interviewed by the author, July 29, 2009 at Clipper Magazine Stadium in Lancaster, PA.
13. Ibid.
14. Tim Raines, interviewed by the author, July 29, 2009 at Clipper Magazine Stadium in Lancaster, PA.
15. Bill Lyon, interviewed by the author, June 16, 2010 by telephone.

BIBLIOGRAPHY

Print and Internet

Associated Press Articles
"Aaron, Bench Head NL Star Team." *Lancaster Intelligencer Journal*, July 18, 1972.
"Allen Leads AL Vote, Rojas Also Selected." *Philadelphia Inquirer*, July 18, 1972.
"Arlin Holds Phils Hitless Until Two Out in 9th Inning." *Lancaster Intelligencer Journal*, July 19, 1972.
"As Carlton Goes, So Go Phillies." *Lancaster New Era*, June 12, 1972.
"Baseball Owners Reject Players' Offer to Settle." *Philadelphia Inquirer*, April 4, 1972.
"Bateman Fumes at Crawford." *Lancaster New Era*, September 8, 1972.
"Bench's HR Ties Mark." *Lancaster Sunday News*, June 4, 1972.
"Bobby Wine Phillies Coach." *Lancaster Intelligencer Journal*, July 18, 1972.
"Booming Buc Bats Sink Phillies Twice 7–3, 4–2." *Lancaster Intelligencer Journal*, May 30, 1972.
"Bosox Tell Representatives to Vote No to Baseball Strike." *Philadelphia Inquirer*, March 31, 1972.
"Bowa Spoils Reuss No-Hitter." *Lancaster New Era*, June 19, 1972.
"Bowa Turns Slugger as Phils Win Second in Row." *Lancaster Intelligencer Journal*, June 9, 1972.
"Cardinals Problems Insoluble." *Lancaster Intelligencer Journal*, February 26, 1972.
"Cards Dump Phils Again." *Lancaster Intelligencer Journal*, July 3, 1972.
"Cards Whip Phils Twice 6–4, 1–0." *Lancaster Sunday News*, July 2, 1972.
"Carlton, Allen on All-Stars." *Philadelphia Inquirer*, October 27, 1972.
"Carlton Beats Dodgers 5–1." *Lancaster Intelligencer Journal*, May 4, 1972.
"Carlton Beats Mets for Ninth Win." *Lancaster Intelligencer Journal*, June 30, 1972.
"Carlton Blanks Cubs for 15th." *Lancaster Intelligencer Journal*, July 29, 1972.
"Carlton Blanks Dodgers." *Lancaster Intelligencer Journal*, July 24, 1972.
"Carlton Fastballs Way to 22nd Win." *Lancaster New Era*, September 4, 1972.
"Carlton Gets Runs, Wins Ninth." *Lancaster New Era*, June 30, 1972, 29.
"Carlton Gives Phils Split." *Lancaster New Era*, August 2, 1972.
"Carlton Hurls One-Hitter at San Francisco." *Lancaster Intelligencer Journal*, April 26, 1972.
"Carlton Hurls Phillies Over Atlanta by 3–1." *Lancaster Intelligencer Journal*, June 12, 1972.
"Carlton Is NL All Star." *Lancaster Intelligencer Journal*, July 19, 1972.
"Carlton Loses First, 4–0, to Padres." *Lancaster Sunday News*, April 30, 1972.
"Carlton Named All-Star Hurler." *Philadelphia Inquirer*, July 19, 1972.

(Associated Press, continued)
"Carlton Not Mad at Cards." *Lancaster New Era*, April 20, 1972.
"Carlton Notches 12th Straight with 5–0 Win." *Lancaster Sunday News*, August 6, 1972.
"Carlton Sorry He Hit Foli ... on the Head; Was Aiming for Ribs but Ball Got Away." *Lancaster New Era*, June 26, 1972.
"Carlton, Wallenda Steal the Show." *Lancaster New Era*, August 14, 1972.
"Carlton Whips Reds for 21st." *Lancaster Sunday News*, August 27, 1972.
"Carlton Wins 11th as Phils Split Twinbill with Padres." *Lancaster Intelligencer Journal*, July 8, 1972.
"Carlton Wins 12th for Phils." *Lancaster Intelligencer Journal*, July 12, 1972.
"Carlton Wins 27th Game." *Lancaster New Era*, October 4, 1972.
"Cincinnati Slays Phils Twice in Doubleheader." *Lancaster Intelligencer Journal*, June 14, 1972.
"Clemente Ties Wagner's Mark." *Lancaster New Era*, August 31, 1972.
"Cubs Beat, Praise Carlton." *Lancaster Intelligencer Journal*, May 18, 1972.
"Cubs Rookie Stops Phils in Debut." *Lancaster Intelligencer Journal*, June 27, 1972.
"Dick Allen Leads All-Star Voting." *Lancaster New Era*, June 30, 1972.
"Dodgers Beat Carlton 3–1." *Lancaster Sunday News*, May 14, 1972.
"Dodgers 4–3 Over Phillies; Robinson Hits Homer." *Lancaster Sunday News*, July 23, 1972.
"Expos Edge Phils 2–1." *Lancaster Intelligencer Journal*, June 24, 1972.
"15 Batters, 11 Runs." *Lancaster Sunday News*, July 16, 1972.
"57,267 See Mays Beat Phillies 4–3." *Lancaster Intelligencer Journal*, May 22, 1972.
"53,376 Watch Phils Carry Carlton to 20th; Rip 16 Hits, Score 9 Runs." *Lancaster New Era*, August 18, 1972.
"Finley Blasts His Fellow Owners, Says League Presidents Hid Report." *Philadelphia Inquirer*, April 11, 1972.
"Giant Rookie Silences Phils." *Lancaster Intelligencer Journal*, July 5, 1972.
"Giants Top Phils 8–1." *Lancaster Intelligencer Journal*, July 15, 1972.
"Giants Use Home Runs to Topple Philadelphia." *Lancaster Intelligencer Journal*, July 17, 1972.
"Harmon, Doyle Spark Phillies." *Lancaster New Era*, May 8, 1972, 32.
"Ho-Hum Phillies Lose Another; Reds Score 2–0 Victory." *Lancaster Intelligencer Journal*, June 5, 1972.
"Home Run Aaron's Top Thrill." *Philadelphia Inquirer*, July 27, 1972.
"Hooton No-Hits Phils; Rookie Pitches 4–0 Win." *Lancaster Intelligencer Journal*, April 17, 1972.
"'I'll Never Surrender,' Says Frank Lucchesi." *Lancaster New Era*, June 7, 1972.
"Jerry Reuss Humbles Phils by Hurling One-Hitter; Astros Win 10–0." *Lancaster Intelligencer Journal*, June 19, 1972.
"Johnson Improved but May Miss 10 Days." *Lancaster New Era*, May 2, 1972.
"Kirby Too Much for Phils." *Lancaster New Era*, May 11, 1972, 80.
"Lockman to Take Over Cubs Here." *Philadelphia Inquirer*, July 26, 1972.
"Lucchesi Ignores Talk That He." *Lancaster New Era*, June 21, 1972.
"Lucchesi May Try Hat Trick; Phils Lose 8 in Row." *Lancaster New Era*, May 24, 1972.
"Lum's Broken Bat Single Spoils Carlton's Streak." *Lancaster New Era*, August 22, 1972.
"Mauch Suspended for 1 Game." *Philadelphia Inquirer*, June 27, 1972.
"Met Rookie Blanks Phils." *Lancaster Intelligencer Journal*, May 31, 1972.
"Mets Top Carlton; 30 Wins Impossible?" *Lancaster New Era*, September 12, 1972.
"Morgan Calls Aaron the Game's 'Big Hero.'" *Lancaster New Era*, July 26, 1972.
"Nationals Win Star Tilt 4–3; Morgan Rips Winning Hit in 10th Inning." *Lancaster Intelligencer Journal*, July 26, 1972.

Bibliography

"Nixon Intervenes to Resume Talks." *Philadelphia Inquirer*, April 10, 1972.
"One-Hitter for Arlin." *Lancaster New Era*, June 24, 1972.
"Owens and Bowa Exchange Sarcasm." *Lancaster New Era*, August 24, 1972.
"Owens Says Lucchesi Will Stay." *Lancaster New Era*, June 29, 1972.
"Phillies Blow 5–0 Lead, Lose to Reds 6–5 in 10." *Lancaster Sunday News*, Jun 4, 1972.
"Phillies Divide Pair with Cubs; Jenkins Has One-Hitter." *Lancaster Intelligencer Journal*, July 28, 1972.
"Phillies End Losing Streak." *Lancaster New Era*, June 8, 1972.
"Phillies Fall 8–5 to Padres in Ninth." *Lancaster Sunday News*, July 9, 1972.
"Phillies Finally Win; Greg Luzinski's Double Keys Sixth Win for Steve Carlton." *Lancaster Intelligencer Journal*, June 8, 1972.
"Phillies Hit, Phillies Win." *Lancaster New Era*, June 9, 1972.
"Phillies Losing Streak Reaches Ten Straight." *Lancaster Intelligencer Journal*, May 27, 1972.
"Phillies Obtain Starter." *Lancaster New Era*, June 16, 1972.
"Phillies Pitching Looks Good." *Lancaster New Era*, May 1, 1972.
"Phillies Swap Catchers." *Lancaster New Era*, June 15, 1972.
"Phillies Trade Tim McCarver; for Expos' Bateman." *Lancaster Intelligencer Journal*, June 15, 1972.
"Phillies Trade Wise to Cardinals for Carlton." *Lancaster New Era*, February 25, 1972.
"Phils Defeat Cubs, 4–2, on Cardenal's 2-Run Error with Two Out in Ninth; Outfielder Drops Fly by McCarver." *New York Times*, April 16, 1972.
"Phils Lose in 10th to Giants." *Lancaster Intelligencer Journal*, July 7, 1972.
"Phils' Nash Faces His Ex-Teammates." *Lancaster New Era*, June 20, 1972.
"Phils Outfight Montreal 1–0." *Lancaster Intelligencer Journal*, June 26, 1972.
"Phils, Pirates Split Pair." *Lancaster Sunday News*, July 30, 1972.
"Phils Playing .500 Ball Under Owens; Blast Dodgers 9–1 to Split Twinbill." *Lancaster Intelligencer Journal*, July 11, 1972.
"Phils Score 11 Runs, All in One Inning!" *Lancaster Sunday News*, July 16, 1972.
"Phils Shut Out by Sutton 3–0." *Lancaster Intelligencer Journal*, July 22, 1972.
"Phils Slug Braves 9–7." *Lancaster Intelligencer Journal*, June 22, 1972.
"Phils Topple Padres." *Lancaster Intelligencer Journal*, July 20, 1972.
"Phils Trade Wise for Carlton." *Lancaster Intelligencer Journal*, February 26, 1972.
"Phils Win 7 of 10 on West Coast." *Lancaster New Era*, May 4, 1972.
"Phils Would Like Steve Arlin Back." *Lancaster New Era*, July 19, 1972.
"Pirates' Bats Impress Phillies." *Lancaster New Era*, May 30, 1972.
"Pirates Overpower Phillies." *Lancaster Intelligencer Journal*, July 31, 1972.
"Red Hot Reds Edge Phillies." *Lancaster Intelligencer Journal*, June 15, 1972.
"Rookie Beats Phillies." *Lancaster New Era*, June 27, 1972.
"Ryan Leads Phils to Split." *Lancaster Intelligencer Journal*, June 28, 1972.
"Ryan's Hitting Sends Phillies Home with Win." *Lancaster New Era*, June 28, 1972.
"San Diego Edges Sagging Phils 5–4." *Lancaster Intelligencer Journal*, July 10, 1972.
"Say Hey—Willie Provides Spark for the Mets; Mays Hits Double, Homer." *Lancaster New Era*, May 22, 1972.
"Seaver Defeats Phillies 3–2." *Lancaster Intelligencer Journal*, June 29, 1972.
"Seaver Pitches Mets to 2–1 Win." *Lancaster Intelligencer Journal*, June 19, 1972.
"Seaver Tops Carlton for 19th." *Lancaster New Era*, September 25, 1972.
"Selma Keeps Phils Streak Alive." *Lancaster New Era*, May 2, 1972.
"Short Is Out, Wilson Returns." *Lancaster Intelligencer Journal*, June 30, 1972.
"Short Wins on 1 Pitch." *Lancaster Intelligencer Journal*, June 10, 1972.
"Spinks Makes Trade Look Good as He Beats Phils for Cards." *Lancaster Intelligencer Journal*, July 1, 1972.
"Stargell's HR Leads Pirates Over Phillies." *Lancaster New Era*, August 9, 1972.

(Associated Press, continued)
"Steady Pitching Helped Carlton to Big Season." *Lancaster New Era*, October 5, 1972.
"Steve Carlton Stuns Pirates." *Lancaster New Era*, August 10, 1972.
"Sunday Beer at Veterans Stadium." *Lancaster New Era*, June 12, 1972.
"Sutton's Fifth Win Cools Phils." *Lancaster New Era*, May 13, 1972.
"Three-Base Error Helps Phillies Win." *Lancaster Sunday News*, April 16, 1972.
"Top Pick Christenson Signs One-Year Contract." *Philadelphia Inquirer*, June 8, 1972.
"Toy Cannon Shot Beats Phillies." *Lancaster New Era*, June 17, 1972.
"Tug Rescues National League." *Lancaster New Era*, July 26, 1972.
"26th Victory for Carlton." *Lancaster New Era*, September 29, 1972.
"'What Story?' Asks Murtaugh; Gibson to Start." *Philadelphia Inquirer*, July 25, 1972.
"Wynn's Home Run Beats Phils 1–0." *Lancaster Intelligencer Journal*, June 17, 1972.

Babcock, Chip. "Phils Won't Wear Blue at Home Again." *Philadelphia Inquirer*, June 14, 1972.
_____. "2 More Phil Trades with Expos, Braves Imminent — Owens." *Philadelphia Inquirer*, June 15, 1972.
Benshoff, Al. "Cards Nip Phils in Ninth." *Lancaster Intelligencer Journal*, April 18, 1972.
_____. "Owens Takeover Surprises Lucchesi." *Lancaster Intelligencer Journal*, July 11, 1972.
_____. "Paul Owens, Man on Spot." *Lancaster Intelligencer Journal*, June 8, 1972.
_____. "Trades No Help to Philadelphia." *Lancaster Intelligencer Journal*, June 20, 1972.
_____. "Which Is Best? NL Vs. AL." *Lancaster Intelligencer Journal*, July 13, 1972.
Bernstein, Ralph. "Carlton Beats Gibson by 1–0." *Lancaster Intelligencer Journal*, April 20, 1972.
_____. "Carlton Justifies Quinn's Faith." *Lancaster New Era*, August 9, 1972.
_____. "Phils Nicknamed Blitz Kids." *Lancaster New Era*, May 5, 1972.
_____. "You Can't Change the Army So You Change Generals." *Lancaster Intelligencer Journal*, July 11, 1972.
Burnes, Robert L. "Season's High, Low Spots." *Baseball Digest*, January 1973.
Carroll, Bill. "Carlton Is Phils' Stopper." *Lancaster New Era*, May 11, 1972.
_____. "Luzinski — Bull's a Super Prospect." *Lancaster New Era*, April 19, 1972.
_____. "Phillies Erred on Tony Taylor." *Lancaster New Era*, June 30, 1972.
_____. "Phillies Give Carlton a Present." *Lancaster New Era*, September 16, 1972.
_____. "Steve Carlton Greets His Fans." *Lancaster New Era*, August 24, 1972.
_____. "Unwise Trades Handicap Phils." *Lancaster New Era*, August 7, 1972.
_____. "What Players Think of Carlton." *Lancaster New Era*, September 16, 1972.
_____. "What's on Farm? Only Lis." *Lancaster New Era*, June 8, 1972.
Courtney, Gene. "Carlton Signs Record $165,000 Contract; Goal Is 30 Victories." *Philadelphia Inquirer*, January 17, 1973.

Frank Dolson Articles

"Aaron Is Still Quinn Booster; Deron? In or Out." *Philadelphia Inquirer*, June 13, 1972.
"And Now, Baseball Like Always Before." *Philadelphia Inquirer*, April 16, 1972.
"Another Mountain for Lis to Climb?" *Philadelphia Inquirer*, March 20, 1972.
"Bill Robinson Hopes for That 2d Break." *Philadelphia Inquirer*, March 21, 1972.
"Bristol Still Eager, Waiting in Wings." *Philadelphia Inquirer*, July 26, 1972.
"Cards Give Wise Financial Standing." *Philadelphia Inquirer*, March 12, 1972.
"Carpenter Sees End of 'Bloody Firings.'" *Philadelphia Inquirer*, July 14, 1972.
"Chris Short Lets Others Rap Phils." *Philadelphia Inquirer*, March 17, 1972.
"Dave Bristol Comes Highly Recommended by Man Who Fired Him at Milwaukee." *Philadelphia Inquirer*, October 13, 1972.
"Fans Given Aerial Show Biz at Opener." *Philadelphia Inquirer*, April 18, 1972.
"Fun Is Winning on the Farm." *Philadelphia Inquirer*, July 5, 1972.

Bibliography

"Great to Be Young — and a Phillie." *Philadelphia Inquirer*, March 11, 1972.
"Happy Anniversary, Ron Stone." *Philadelphia Inquirer*, May 29, 1972, 21, 22.
"He Really Did Back the Strike, Phillies' McCarver Explains." *Philadelphia Inquirer*, April 4, 1972.
"Honesty of Owens Turns Rainfall to Deluge of Rumors." *Philadelphia Inquirer*, June 21, 1972.
"Hooton's 7th No-Hitter a Breeze After Roughing Up by Buddies." *Philadelphia Inquirer*, April 17, 1972.
"If Lucchesi Is Suffering — How About Fans." *Philadelphia Inquirer*, June 19, 1972.
"It's April Fool's Day in Majors — but Players' Strike Is No Joke." *Philadelphia Inquirer*, April 2, 1972.
"Johnson: Once Dependable, Now Expendable." *Philadelphia Inquirer*, July 30, 1972.
"'Keeping Cool' Not Easy for Family of Lucchesi." *Philadelphia Inquirer*, June 25, 1972.
"Looking Back Might Put Quinn in Front of Exit Door." *Philadelphia Inquirer*, March 26, 1972.
"Losing Streak Road Bumpy Before You Reach End." *Philadelphia Inquirer*, May 28, 1972.
"Lucchesi Benches Montanez as Phils Drop Pair to Reds." *Philadelphia Inquirer*, June 14, 1972.
"Luzinski Clears Air with Lucchesi, Then Batters Bucs." *Philadelphia Inquirer*, April 24, 1972.
"Lucchesi Still in Shock, Thinking of Others." *Philadelphia Inquirer*, July 12, 1972.
"Mauch Beats Phillies Again — by Phone Call." *Philadelphia Inquirer*, June 15, 1972.
"Modest Proposal for the Phillies." *Philadelphia Inquirer*, July 17, 1972.
"New Phils Like Bristol — but They'll Play for Ozark." *Philadelphia Inquirer*, November 1, 1972.
"NL Wins in 10th on Morgan's Hit, 4–3." *Philadelphia Inquirer*, July 26, 1972.
"No Apologies but Luzinski Will Try Harder Anyway." *Philadelphia Inquirer*, October 6, 1972.
"No Carty or Cepeda but Lis Is on Way." *Philadelphia Inquirer*, June 18, 1972.
"Owens' Firm Hand Imprinted on Phila." *Philadelphia Inquirer*, July 31, 1972.
"Owens' First Edict for the Phils; Run a Tougher Ship." *Philadelphia Inquirer*, June 5, 1972.
"Ozark the Man Clears the Air." *Philadelphia Inquirer*, November 3, 1972.
"Phil Dressing Room: Portrait of a Loser." *Philadelphia Inquirer*, June 27, 1972.
"Phillies' Mike Anderson Plays a Confidence Game." *Philadelphia Inquirer*, April 21, 1972.
"Phillies' 1st Sunday: Basketball, Squash." *Philadelphia Inquirer*, April 10, 1972.
"Phillies Flop — Even in the Firing of Lucchesi." *Philadelphia Inquirer*, July 11, 1972.
"Phils' Carpenter Ready for a Fight." *Philadelphia Inquirer*, March 25, 1972.
"Phils Miss Johnson; Leader Confined to the Clubhouse." *Philadelphia Inquirer*, June 2, 1972.
"Phils Need Better Organization, Not 'Organization Man.'" *Philadelphia Inquirer*, November 2, 1972.
"Phils' 1973 Manager? Don't Rule Out Owens." *Philadelphia Inquirer*, July 13, 1972.
"Players Find Out What's Happening — After the Fact." *Philadelphia Inquirer*, April 4, 1972.
"Rippelmeyer Next as Phils' Manager?" *Philadelphia Inquirer*, October 3, 1972.
"Quinn, Carpenter in Shouting Match as Phils, Management Meet 4 Hours." *Philadelphia Inquirer*, April 3, 1972.
"Quinn Ignores Flying Darts with Another Deal in Mind." *Philadelphia Inquirer*, March 10, 1972.
"Season Still Young — but So What?" *Philadelphia Inquirer*, May 8, 1972.
"Selma May Provide More Than Humor." *Philadelphia Inquirer*, March 19, 1972.

(Frank Dolson, continued)
"17-Year Hitch Ignored as Phillies Bounce Lucchesi." *Philadelphia Inquirer*, October 15, 1972.
"Short Fly, Long Homer Beat Phillies." *Philadelphia Inquirer*, June 15, 1972.
"The Phillies Are Getting Close to a Major Trade." *Philadelphia Inquirer*, June 12, 1972.
"The Phillies' Next Full Shot Should Go to Joe Lis." *Philadelphia Inquirer*, June 8, 1972.
"The Same Man Steps Down Gracefully." *Philadelphia Inquirer*, June 4, 1972.
"What's Wrong with the Phils Isn't Lucchesi." *Philadelphia Inquirer*, June 1, 1972.
"What You Hear Is What You Get." *Philadelphia Inquirer*, May 30, 1972.
"With 125 Games to Go, It's No Time for Quinn to Panic." *Philadelphia Inquirer*, May 22, 1972.
"Young 'Can't-Miss' Pitchers Missed with the Phillies." *Philadelphia Inquirer*, March 16, 1972.

Fimrite, Ron. "Eliminator of the Variables." *Sports Illustrated*, April 9, 1973.
Flower, Joe. "In Search of Steve Carlton." *Sport Magazine*, May 1983.
Flynn, John. "Steve Carlton: A 'Bad Kid' Makes Good." *Philadelphia Inquirer*, August 6, 1972.
Forbes, Gordon, John Dell, and Chip Babcock, "Astros Scuttle Montanez-for-Wynn Deal." *Philadelphia Inquirer*, June 13, 1972.
Greybill, Larry. "Can Phillies Keep It Up?" *Lancaster New Era*, May 3, 1972.
_____. "Control, Lots of Work Make Champion Winner." *Lancaster New Era*, May 11, 1972.
_____. "Major Trade Only Way Owens Can Help Phillies." *Lancaster New Era*, June 8, 1972.
_____. "Phillies Aren't That Bad." *Lancaster New Era*, May 23, 1972.
_____. "Phillies Look for Pitchers." *Lancaster New Era*, June 8, 1972.
_____. "Scheffing's Deals Helps the Mets." *Lancaster New Era*, May 22, 1972.
_____. "What's Wrong with Money?" *Lancaster New Era*, April 19, 1972.
_____. "Young Phillies Mature Under Patient Lucchesi." *Lancaster New Era*, May 12, 1972.
Harmon, Terry. "Harmon: We Have Best Game, Why Not Best Pension?" *Philadelphia Inquirer*, April 5, 1972.
Heisler, Mark. "Christenson Willing to be 'Told, Taught.'" *Philadelphia Inquirer*, June 7, 1972.
http://baseballalmanac.com (accessed July 26, 2009–July 31, 2011).

Bruce Keidan Articles
"Aaron Slams 649th Homer as Braves Bomb Phillies, 15–3." *Philadelphia Inquirer*, June 11, 1972.
"Anderson on Way Out with Phils." *Philadelphia Inquirer*, June 1, 1972.
"Anderson Sneaks in Phils' Back Door." *Philadelphia Inquirer*, March 8, 1972.
"Arm's Now Sound, Selma Tells Phillies." *Philadelphia Inquirer*, March 9, 1972.
"Astros Beat Phils on HR in 11th, 1–0." *Philadelphia Inquirer*, June 17, 1972.
"Astros Clobber Phillies." *Philadelphia Inquirer*, June 18, 1972.
"Baseball Accord Reached; Season Begins Saturday." *Philadelphia Inquirer*, April 14, 1972.
"Bateman Reports—with One Liners." *Philadelphia Inquirer*, June 16, 1972.
"Best in NL Since Koufax Had 27–9." *Philadelphia Inquirer*, October 4, 1972.
"Bonds' Home Run in Tenth Inning Beats Phillies, 8–6." *April 27, 1972*, April 27, 1972.
"Bottled in Bonds: Bobby Destroys Phils, 8–1." *Philadelphia Inquirer*, July 15, 1972.
"Bowa Breaks Up No-Hitter in 9th Inning as Astros Trample Phils, 10–0." *Philadelphia Inquirer*, June 19, 1972.

Bibliography 203

"Bowa Taken Out 'for Rest' in 6th, Lashes Owens After Phils Lose, 9–6." *Philadelphia Inquirer*, August 24, 1972.
"Bowa's 3 Hits, Luzinski Homer Helps Phils, Champion Top Cards." *Philadelphia Inquirer*, April 19, 1972.
"Bowa Trying to Demonstrate He's No. 1." *Philadelphia Inquirer*, March 3, 1972.
"Braves Blast Carlton's Bid for 16th in Row; 41,212 Watch Phils Fall in 11." *Philadelphia Inquirer*, August 22, 1972.
"Browne Does Job but Phils Lose, 3–1." *Philadelphia Inquirer*, March 25, 1972.
"Bucs, Orioles Picked." *Philadelphia Inquirer, 1972 Souvenir Baseball Guide*, April 9, 1972.
"Cardinals Drop Phils Twice; Quakers Lose 34th of 43." *Philadelphia Inquirer*, July 2, 1972.
"Cards Finish Off Phillies; Lucchesi Plans Changes." *Philadelphia Inquirer*, July 3, 1972.
"Cards Repel Phils, 5–4, on 2-Run Ninth." *Philadelphia Inquirer*, April 18, 1972.
"Carlton Blanks Cards as Phils Win 5 in Row." *Philadelphia Inquirer*, August 6, 1972.
"Carlton Blanks Cubs for 10th in Row." *Philadelphia Inquirer*, July 29, 1972.
"Carlton Blanks Pirates for 13th Straight Win." *Philadelphia Inquirer*, August 10, 1972.
"Carlton Captures 11 in Row After Phils Lose in 18th." *Philadelphia Inquirer*, August 2, 1972.
"Carlton Effective in 5-Inning Stint as Phillies Win, 7–4." *Philadelphia Inquirer*, March 15, 1972.
"Carlton Faces Juan Tough Pitcher Tonight." *Philadelphia Inquirer*, April 25, 1972.
"Carlton Faces Wise in the Big One." *Philadelphia Inquirer*, September 20, 1972.
"Carlton Fans 13 as Phils Beat Mets." *Philadelphia Inquirer*, June 30, 1972.
"Carlton Faster, Wilder." *Philadelphia Inquirer*, February 26, 1972.
"Carlton Gives One Hit, Fans 14, Wins, 3–0." *Philadelphia Inquirer*, April 26, 1972.
"Carlton Notches 5th Win as Phils Clout Giants, 8–3." *Philadelphia Inquirer*, May 8, 1972.
"Carlton Posts 23d Victory as Phillies Shade Cards, 2–1." *Philadelphia Inquirer*, September 8, 1972.
"Carlton Outpitches Wise, Notches 25th as Phils Win." *Philadelphia Inquirer*, September 21, 1972.
"Carlton Records 26th as Phils Nip Bucs, 2–1." *Philadelphia Inquirer*, September 29, 1972.
"Carlton Reports as Phillies Open Spring Training." *Philadelphia Inquirer*, February 27, 1972.
"Carlton 6-Hits Dodgers, 5–1; Phils Still Haven't Lost Series." *Philadelphia Inquirer*, May 4, 1972.
"Carlton Stingy with Old Mates as Phils Blast Cardinals, 7–1." *Philadelphia Inquirer*, March 20, 1972.
"Carlton Strong as Phils Win Opener, 4–2." *Philadelphia Inquirer*, April 16, 1972.
"Carlton Thanks Phils, Fans with 5–3 Victory Over Expos." *Philadelphia Inquirer*, September 16, 1972.
"Carlton Tops Braves, Fans 9 in 7th Victory." *Philadelphia Inquirer*, June 12, 1972.
"Carlton's Bid for 24th Comes to Dyer Ending." *Philadelphia Inquirer*, September 12, 1972.
"Colbert Hits 5 Runs Home as Phils Fall." *Philadelphia Inquirer*, July 9, 1972.
"Controversial Catch Helps Carlton Blank Ex-Mates." *Philadelphia Inquirer*, April 20, 1972.
"Cubs Break Tie in 9th, Beat Phils, Carlton, 3–2." *Philadelphia Inquirer*, May 18, 1972.
"Cubs Nip Phils in 8th as Jenkins Racks Up 6th 20-Win Campaign." *Philadelphia Inquirer*, September 9, 1972.
"Danny Ozarks Envisions Pennant for Phils; New Pilot to Name Aides — Subject to Owens' OK." *Philadelphia Inquirer*, November 2, 1972.

(Bruce Keidan, continued)
"Delay of Trade Has Johnson, Other Phils Upset." *Philadelphia Inquirer*, July 22, 1972.
"Deron Johnson — Master of Deadpan One-Liners." *Philadelphia Inquirer*, March 7, 1972.
"Did Rader Tally? Giants Nip Phils on Disputed Run." *Philadelphia Inquirer*, July 5, 1972.
"Dodgers Outslug Phils, 9–5." *Philadelphia Inquirer*, July 13, 1972.
"Don Money Guarantees Better Season After Hitting .223, Losing Position in '71." *Philadelphia Inquirer*, March 10, 1972.
"Doyle Ruins Arlin's No-Hitter in 9th." *Philadelphia Inquirer*, July 19, 1972.
"11,703 Defy Weather, See Phils Rip Orioles." *Philadelphia Inquirer*, May 9, 1972.
"Empty Bases Worry Greg." *Philadelphia Inquirer*, May 18, 1972.
"Expos Rally, Edge Phils; Error Leads to 2–1 Loss for Nash." *Philadelphia Inquirer*, June 24, 1972.
"Expos Win Nightcap; Champion Loses Job." *Philadelphia Inquirer*, August 14, 1972.
"Fans Pick Manager — 'Let Richie Do It.'" *Philadelphia Inquirer*, August 15, 1972.
"53,377 See Carlton Win 20th, 15 in Row." *Philadelphia Inquirer*, August 18, 1972.
"Flaws There, but Phils Are Moving." *Philadelphia Inquirer*, May 2, 1972.
"Flyers' Foley Wins Phils' HR Contest." *Philadelphia Inquirer*, July 28, 1972.
"For Mrs. Carlton, a Birthday Gift." *Philadelphia Inquirer*, August 18, 1972.
"For Sure, Bunning Not Going Back to Reading." *Philadelphia Inquirer*, November 2, 1972.
"Fryman Stops Jenkins, Cubs on Six-Hitter." *Philadelphia Inquirer*, May 16, 1972.
"Fryman Turns Back Pirates, 5–2, Before Phillies Lose, 3–2." *Philadelphia Inquirer*, July 30, 1972.
"Giants Offer Mays to Mets in Exchange for Pitcher." *Philadelphia Inquirer*, May 6, 1972.
"Giles Predicts a Record Attendance for Mets Series." *Philadelphia Inquirer*, May 9, 1972.
"Herniated Disc to Sideline Phils' Wilson — Probably for the Entire 1972 Campaign." *Philadelphia Inquire*, March 28, 1972.
"Honest Owens: Could He Pass Paul-ygraph?" *Philadelphia Inquirer*, July 12, 1972.
"How to Be on All-Star Team: Play in N.Y., L.A.." *Philadelphia Inquirer*, July 18, 1972.
"Hutton's Single, Luzinski's Power Halt Bucs." *Philadelphia Inquirer*, April 24, 1972.
"'Impulse Pitcher' Carlton 'Fantastic Competitor' — Tim." *Philadelphia Inquirer*, April 16, 1972.
"It Looks More Like Aug. 21 as Phils Win." *Philadelphia Inquirer*, March 22, 1972.
"Joe Hoerner Stands Firm in the Face of Swirling Trade Winds." *Philadelphia Inquirer*, March 6, 1972.
"Johnson at First When Phils Face Mets Tonight." *Philadelphia Inquirer*, May 19, 1972.
"Johnson Fails to Show at Phils' Camp, but Quinn Confident Accord Is Near." *Philadelphia Inquirer*, February 28, 1972.
"Johnson Is Headed for Tigers — Phillies Seek 'Top' Player." *Philadelphia Inquirer*, August 9, 1972.
"Johnson May Play Regularly in 10 Days." *Philadelphia Inquirer*, June 3, 1972.
"Johnson Signs for Reported $80,000." *Philadelphia Inquirer*, February 29, 1972.
"Johnson's Nerve Injury Puts Future in Jeopardy." *Philadelphia Inquirer*, May 31, 1972.
"Kaat, Twins Beat Phils, 3–1, Despite 3 Singles by Bowa." *Philadelphia Inquirer*, March 31, 1972.
"Larry Bowa May Worry Himself Right Off Ball Club." *Philadelphia Inquirer*, August 25, 1972.
"Lis and Robinson Recalled; Stone, Browne Demoted." *Philadelphia Inquirer*, June 23, 1972.
"Lucchesi Breathing Easier Now That Quinn's Gone." *Philadelphia Inquirer*, June 6, 1972.
"Lucchesi Status Report: Alive and Kicking." *Philadelphia Inquirer*, June 21, 1972.
"Lucchesi Will Stay, Owens Says." *Philadelphia Inquirer*, June 29, 1972.

"Luzinski's First Season: From Wonders of Spring to Heat of July." *Philadelphia Inquirer*, July 24, 1972.
"Luzinski's Hit in 12th Nips Padres." *Philadelphia Inquirer*, May 12, 1972.
"Luzinski's New Outfield Act: Bat, Helmet, Bushel Basket." *Philadelphia Inquirer*, February 28, 1972.
"Luzinski Wears Electric Blue After His HR Shocks Giants." *Philadelphia Inquirer*, April 28, 1972.
"Marvin Miller Raps Carlton-Wise Trade; Hints at Player Strike." *Philadelphia Inquirer*, March 8, 1972.
"Mauch's Strategy Beat Phillies, 4–1." *Philadelphia Inquirer*, August 12, 1972.
"McCarver's 9th-Inning Homer Wins for Phils, 5–4." *Philadelphia Inquirer*, March 11, 1972.
"Meanwhile, Phillies Fall Again, 6–5." *Philadelphia Inquirer*, June 4, 1972.
"Mets' 11–6 Win Over Phils Not Gaudy — but It Was Long." *Philadelphia Inquirer*, September 14, 1972.
"Mets Jar Phils into 3d Place." *Philadelphia Inquirer*, May 20, 1972.
"Mets Kill Phil Rally, Win, 4–3." *Philadelphia Inquirer*, September 13, 1972.
"Mets Thump Selma as Phils Lose, 6–1; Anderson Optioned." *Philadelphia Inquirer*, June 2, 1972.
"Mike Schmidt's First Homer Gives Phils Win Over Expos." *Philadelphia Inquirer*, September 17, 1972.
"Monday's 3 HRs 'Sicken' Phils." *Philadelphia Inquirer*, May 17, 1972.
"Money, Owens Feud Over Signals." *Philadelphia Inquirer*, July 30, 1972.
"Money's at Third So Vukovich Is Hustling at Second." *Philadelphia Inquirer*, February 29, 1972.
"Montanez a Holdout and His Lawyer Doesn't Know Why." *Philadelphia Inquirer*, March 2, 1972.
"Montanez Ends Holdout for $27,500 Pact." *Philadelphia Inquirer*, March 6, 1972.
"Montanez Has a Field Day, but Phils Fall to Expos, 3–2." *Philadelphia Inquirer*, August 13, 1972.
"Montanez, Phils Fail to Agree." *Philadelphia Inquirer*, March 4, 1972.
"Nash Bash Postponed by Agnes." *Philadelphia Inquirer*, June 20, 1972.
"Niekro Born April 1: Joke's on Steve." *Philadelphia Inquirer*, August 22, 1972.
"No Sign Yet of Rick Wise as Phils Play Cardinals in Third Series." *Philadelphia Inquirer*, August 5, 1972.
"Osteen Stymies Phillies, 3–1; 4-Base 'Bunt' Ruins Carlton." *Philadelphia Inquirer*, May 14, 1972.
"Owens Blows Debut to Dodgers, 6–4." *Philadelphia Inquirer*, July 11, 1972.
"Owens Chants Trade After Hapless Phils Fall." *Philadelphia Inquirer*, September 28, 1972.
"Owens Hopes to Name Phils' Manager by Late October." *Philadelphia Inquirer*, September 6, 1972.
"Owens Pressing for Deal — 'It's Trade or Perish' Now." *Philadelphia Inquirer*, July 24, 1972.
"Owens Yanks Montanez as Phils Bow to Pirates." *Philadelphia Inquirer*, August 1, 1972.
"Padres' Pilot Pays Phils' Carlton Supreme Compliment." *Philadelphia Inquirer*, July 19, 1972.
"Padres Pummel Fryman Early, Beat Phils on Kirby's 5-Hitter." *Philadelphia Inquirer*, May 11, 1972.
"Phantastic Phils End Best April Since — Remember — '64." *Philadelphia Inquirer*, May 1, 1972.
"Phew! Phils Fall in 17th, 6–3." *Philadelphia Inquirer*, June 3, 1972.
"Phillies Blank Padres." *Philadelphia Inquirer*, April 29, 1972.

(Bruce Keidan, continued)
"Phillies' Boss Numb, Dazed — Skid Hits 8." *Philadelphia Inquirer*, May 24, 1972.
"Phillies Chill Cards, 8–3, for Fourth Straight Win." *Philadelphia Inquirer*, August 5, 1972.
"Phillies, Cubs Split; Bloop Double Ruins Jenkins' No-Hitter." *Philadelphia Inquirer*, July 28, 1972.
"Phillies Drop 13th of Last 14." *Philadelphia Inquirer*, May 30, 1972.
"Phillies' Farm Director Sees Jon on Line." *Philadelphia Inquirer*, March 4, 1972.
"Phillies Get 4 in 1st, Top Giants; Carlton Notches 10th Win." *Philadelphia Inquirer*, July 4, 1972.
"Phillies' Infield Commits Five Errors as Seaver Pitches Mets to 7–4 Win." *Philadelphia Inquirer*, March 26, 1972.
"Phillies Put Bateman on Waiver List." *Philadelphia Inquirer*, January 18, 1973.
"Phillies' Short Is Hospitalized." *Philadelphia Inquirer*, June 30, 1972.
"Phillies Suffer 19th Setback in 20 Starts." *Philadelphia Inquirer*, June 7, 1972.
"Phillies Vote 28–0 to Support Strike." *Philadelphia Inquirer*, March 13, 1972.
"Phillies Win 2d for Split; Ryan (4 RBI) Hits Homer." *Philadelphia Inquirer*, June 28, 1972.
"Phils and Cards Solve Salary Problems — and Wise, Carlton Receive Increases." *Philadelphia Inquirer*, February 26, 1972.
"Phils' Attendance to Top One-Million Mark Today." *Philadelphia Inquirer*, August 13, 1972.
"Phils Back Strike but Stay in Camp." *Philadelphia Inquirer*, April 2, 1972.
"Phils Beat Mets on Johnson's HR in 9th, 5–3." *Philadelphia Inquirer*, August 3, 1972.
"Phils Blank Royals Behind Champion, 1–0." *Philadelphia Inquirer*, March 21, 1972.
"Phils Bow as Tigers Hit 2 HRs." *Philadelphia Inquirer*, March 27, 1972.
"Phils Can't Hit 'Knuckle-Curve Ball.'" *Philadelphia Inquirer*, April 17, 1972.
"Phils' Chris Short Reports at Svelte 207." *Philadelphia Inquirer*, February 25, 1972.
"Phillies Continue Their March to 100 Losses, Fall to Chicago." *Philadelphia Inquirer*, September 10, 1972.
"Phils' Deron Johnson Will be Put on Disabled List." *Philadelphia Inquirer*, June 13, 1972.
"Phils Didn't REALLY Plan to Strike." *Philadelphia Inquirer*, April 1, 1972.
"Phils Edge Twins on Pinch Home Run by Stone in 9th, 4–3." *Philadelphia Inquirer*, March 28, 1972.
"Phils Expected to Deal Off Deron Johnson." *Philadelphia Inquirer*, July 16, 1972.
"Phils Eye 1st — and Nobody's Laughing." *Philadelphia Inquirer*, May 5, 1972.
"Phillies Fall to Arlin, 4–0." *Philadelphia Inquirer*, April 30, 1972.
"Phils Fall to 7th Loss in Row; Expos Rally After 3-Run Deficit." *Philadelphia Inquirer*, May 23, 1972.
"Phils Fall, 2–1, to Red Machine's Spare Parts." *Philadelphia Inquirer*, March 13, 1972.
"Phils Find Lolich Tough After Snub." *Philadelphia Inquirer*, March 18, 1972.
"Phils Gain Virtual Tie for First." *Philadelphia Inquirer*, May 6, 1972.
"Phils Held to One Hit, Drop 9th in Row, 4–1." *Philadelphia Inquirer*, May 25, 1972.
"Phils Ignore 'New Look' of Cardinals." *Philadelphia Inquirer*, September 7, 1972.
"Phils Jar Chisox in 9th, 3–2, on Luzinski's 500-Foot Homer." *Philadelphia Inquirer*, March 29, 1972.
"Phils' Lack of Righties Is Showing." *Philadelphia Inquirer*, March 24, 1972.
"Phils Lose 8th in Row, 18th in 19 and Tumble into Last Place." *Philadelphia Inquirer*, June 5, 1972.
"Phils Lose Game, Trade; Anderson Hurt in Rout." *Philadelphia Inquirer*, March 30, 1972.
"Phils Lose in 9th and Owens Plans Some Winter Deals." *Philadelphia Inquirer*, August 23, 1972.

Bibliography

"Phils Lose in 10th, 2–1, to Gibson." *Philadelphia Inquirer*, September 20, 1972.
"Phils' Loss to Padres Proves Validity of the Peter Principle." *Philadelphia Inquirer*, July 10, 1972.
"Phillies' Losing Streak Hits 5 as Mets Take a Pair, 3–1, 2–1." *Philadelphia Inquirer*, May 21, 1972.
"Phils' Master Plan: Cut Down Mob of 1st Baseman." *Philadelphia Inquirer*, July 10, 1972.
"Phils, Montanez Are $5,000 Apart." *Philadelphia Inquirer*, March 5, 1972.
"Phils on Verge of Major Trade; Money or Bowa Likely to Go." *Philadelphia Inquirer*, October 24, 1972.
"Phils' 1–2 Punch? Carlton and Bateman! Battery KOs Expos, 1–0." *Philadelphia Inquirer*, June 26, 1972.
"Phils Outhit Giants, 13–8, but Are Defeated by 10–7." *Philadelphia Inquirer*, July 17, 1972.
"Phils Plan for Opener in Chicago." *Philadelphia Inquirer*, April 13, 1972.
"Phils Push Win Streak All the Way to 2." *Philadelphia Inquirer*, June 9, 1972.
"Phils' Roster for 1972." *Philadelphia Inquirer, 1972 Souvenir Baseball Guide*, April 9, 1972.
"Phils Score 11 (Count 'Em) Runs in One Inning, Beat Giants." *Philadelphia Inquirer*, July 16, 1972.
"Phils Sink Bucs in 12th, End Slump on Money's RBI with Borrowed Bat." *Philadelphia Inquirer*, May 28, 1972.
"Phils Snap Losing Streak at 6 as Ryan's Hit Beats Braves, 9–7." *Philadelphia Inquirer*, June 22, 1972.
"Phils' Steve Carlton Does It All: 5-Hit Shutout and 2-Run Triple." *Philadelphia Inquirer*, July 24, 1972.
"Phils' Streak Halted at 5 as Cardinals Win by 6–0." *Philadelphia Inquirer*, August 7, 1972.
"Phils Trade Hoerner to Braves for Nash." *Philadelphia Inquirer*, June 16, 1972.
"Phils Win, 8–7, as Stone Hits in Rare Start." *Philadelphia Inquirer*, March 23, 1972.
"Phils Win in 11th on Robinson Hit." *Philadelphia Inquirer*, July 20, 1972.
"Pirates and Briles Hand Phillies 10th Loss in Row." *Philadelphia Inquirer*, May 27, 1972.
"Pirates Score 2 in 9th to Defeat Phillies, 6–5." *Philadelphia Inquirer*, May 29, 1972.
"Pirates Turn Back Phils, 5–1." *Philadelphia Inquirer*, September 27, 1972.
"Pittsburgh in Future of Bowa?" *Philadelphia Inquirer*, June 9, 1972.
"Players, Club, City Paying for Strike." *Philadelphia Inquirer*, April 11, 1972.
"Quinn Finds Phils' Losses at Home Are Unsuitable." *Philadelphia Inquirer*, May 15, 1972.
"Quinn Fired as Phils' General Manager." *Philadelphia Inquirer*, June 4, 1972.
"Quinn Wanted Marichal, Kirby but Offered Only Straight Cash." *Philadelphia Inquirer*, April 30, 1972.
"Rain May Delay Phils' Opener Another Day." *Philadelphia Inquirer*, April 15, 1972.
"Reader Asks: Is Lucchesi Pro or Anti-Platooning?" *Philadelphia Inquirer*, July 2, 1972.
"Record Crowd Sees Mays Beat Phils." *Philadelphia Inquirer*, May 22, 1972.
"Red Sox Subdue Phils, 3–2." *Philadelphia Inquirer*, March 14, 1972.
"Reds Deal Reynolds 11th Loss in Row." *Philadelphia Inquirer*, August 26, 1972.
"Reds Down Phillies Behind Gullett, 3–0." *Philadelphia Inquirer*, August 16, 1972.
"Reds Rip Phils for 8th Time, 8–2, as Rose and Perez Lead Assault." *Philadelphia Inquirer*, August 17, 1972.
"Reynolds a Willing Worker in an Unneeded Bullpen." *Philadelphia Inquirer*, May 10, 1972.
"Richie Lauds Fans Who Picked Ashburn." *Philadelphia Inquirer*, August 15, 1972.
"Rip Makes 2 Trips Before Giants Take Phils on a Bad One." *Philadelphia Inquirer*, July 7, 1972.
"Robinson HR Helps Dodgers Edge Phils." *Philadelphia Inquirer*, July 23, 1972.
"Rookie Dazzles Phils as Tigers Win, 4–1." *Philadelphia Inquirer*, March 12, 1972.

(Bruce Keidan, continued)
"Rookie Rick Reuschel Shackles Phils as Cubs Score 11–1 Win." *Philadelphia Inquirer*, June 27, 1972.
"Rookie Hutton Impresses; Phils Turn Back White Sox, 8–6." *Philadelphia Inquirer*, March 16, 1972.
"Rudolph's Homer Helps Cubs Down Phillies, Nash, 5–3." *Philadelphia Inquirer*, September 11, 1972.
"Scarce Save Gives Phils 3d Straight Over Mets." *Philadelphia Inquirer*, August 4, 1972.
"Scarce Saves Carlton's 21st Win." *Philadelphia Inquirer*, August 27, 1972.
"Selma Too Strong for Own Good as Dodgers Rip 'Best Stuff,' 6–1." *Philadelphia Inquirer*, May 13, 1972.
"Series Action Is Secondary for Trade Minded Owens." *Philadelphia Inquirer*, October 17, 1972.
"Signs of Hope for Fans After Many Lean Years...." *Philadelphia Inquirer, 1972 Souvenir Baseball Guide*, April 9, 1972.
"Skipper's End: A Few Questions and Some Tears." *Philadelphia Inquirer*, July 11, 1972.
"Speier Foils Phillies Again." *Philadelphia Inquirer*, May 7, 1972.
"Stargell Swats Phils as Pirates Win, 4–2." *Philadelphia Inquirer*, August 9, 1972.
"Steve Carlton — How Good Is He?" *Philadelphia Inquirer*, August 16, 1972.
"Steve Carlton Ties for NL Lead, Wins 12th as Phils Top Dodgers." July 12, 1972.
"Stone's Handyman Role with Phils Never Changes." *Philadelphia Inquirer*, March 1, 1972.
"Strategy Backfires as Phils Fall in 10th." *Philadelphia Inquirer*, April 22, 1972.
"Strike Up the Band: Phillies Win One, 3–1." *Philadelphia Inquirer*, June 8, 1972.
"Surgery for Wilson." *Philadelphia Inquirer*, April 8, 1972.
"Sutton, L.A. Shut Out Phillies on 5 Hits, 3–0." *Philadelphia Inquirer*, July 22, 1972.
"The Great Game; This Could Be One That Everybody Loses — Including Bristol and the Phils Themselves." *Philadelphia Inquirer*, October 20, 1972.
"The Great Wallenda ... the Great Carlton; Steve Wins 14th in Row, Gives Expos 3 Hits." *Philadelphia Inquirer*, August 14, 1972.
"The Winnah: Roger, Joe, Jim, Pete, Don." *Philadelphia Inquirer*, June 26, 1972.
"...Then Shag Said to John: '%#$&!!.'" *Philadelphia Inquirer*, September 8, 1972.
"They All Call Luzinski Surefire Star." *Philadelphia Inquirer, 1972 Souvenir Baseball Guide*, April 9, 1972.
"Tick ... Tick ... Tick ... Boom!; Hebner's Blast Rips Phils." *Philadelphia Inquirer*, July 31, 1972.
"Tigers Buy Fryman from Phils." *Philadelphia Inquirer*, August 3, 1972.
"Tigers Fail to Make Deal; Johnson to Stay with Phils." *Philadelphia Inquirer*, August 11, 1972.
"Trade Is a Standoff, Says McCarver, Who Played with and Against Both." *Philadelphia Inquirer*, February 27, 1972.
"Twins Score 3 Runs in 9th to Beat Phils, 7–6." *Philadelphia Inquirer*, March 19, 1972.
"Twitchell Overpowers Houston, 4–0; Rookie Gives Up 5 Hits." *Philadelphia Inquirer*, August 20, 1972.
"Twitchell: The Itch to Pitch." *Philadelphia Inquirer*, March 9, 1972.
"Two-Run HR by Montanez Nips L.A., 2–1." *Philadelphia Inquirer*, May 2, 1972.
"Wallenda Tightropes Vet Today." *Philadelphia Inquirer*, August 13, 1972.
"West Chester's Matlack Throttles Phillies, 7–0, for 6th Straight Victory." *Philadelphia Inquirer*, May 31, 1972.
"What's Wrong with the Phillies? The Hitters Aren't Hitting and Pitchers Aren't Enough." *Philadelphia Inquirer*, May 26, 1972.
"Willie Montanez Drives in 5 Runs as Phils Top Dodgers, 9–1, for Split." *Philadelphia Inquirer*, July 11, 1972.

"Wilson Strikes Out 14, Coasts by Phillies, 3–1." *Philadelphia Inquirer*, August 21, 1972.
"Wise Remains Fan of Phillies Despite Trade to Cardinals." *Philadelphia Inquirer*, August 8, 1972.
"Wives Imitate Phils — Bow Before Mets." *Philadelphia Inquirer*, June 29, 1972.
"Woods' Vitamins 'Sicken' Phillies." *Philadelphia Inquirer*, June 25, 1972.
"Worth Noting: Luzinski Is Sick of Left Field; Was Ashburn Kidding?" *Philadelphia Inquirer*, July 14, 1972.
"Write-In Votes for New Phil Pilot Include Khayat, Raquel Welch." *Philadelphia Inquirer*, August 11, 1972.

Kendrick, Scott. "2009 Baseball Team Payrolls." December 23, 2009. http://baseball.about.com/od/newsrumors/a/09teamsalaries.htm?p=1 (accessed January 5, 2010).
Lewis, Allen. "Carlton Sets Sights on 30 Wins After Taking Cy Young Award." *Philadelphia Inquirer*, November 3, 1972.
_____. "Fans Support Phils' Shakeup." *Philadelphia Inquirer*, June 4, 1972, 3-D.
_____. "John Quinn: A Baseball Man, Past and Future." *Philadelphia Inquirer*, June 4, 1972.
_____. "John Quinn Looks Back; Phils' Collapse in '64 Biggest Disappointment." *Philadelphia Inquirer*, June 25, 1972.
_____. "Kiteman Crashes on the Vet's Slopes." *Philadelphia Inquirer*, April 18, 1972.
_____. "Lis Smashes Home Run but Cards Beat Phils, 4–1." *Philadelphia Inquirer*, July 1, 1972.
_____. "Phils Expect Boos to Disappear with Time." *Philadelphia Inquirer*, April 15, 1972.
_____. "Phils' New Manager Regarded by Dodgers as 'Another Alston.'" *Philadelphia Inquirer*, November 2, 1972.
_____. "Phils Split Twin Bill with Padres." *Philadelphia Inquirer*, July 8, 1972.
_____. "Steve Carlton." *Baseball Digest*, January 1973.
Luzinski, Greg. "Coaches Sign Only Look Complicated." *Philadelphia Inquirer*, March 12, 1972.
_____. "Father-in Law Arrives — and So Does My 1st Home Run." *Philadelphia Inquirer*, March 26, 1972.
_____. "'I'm Better Hitter Than Before.'" *Philadelphia Inquirer*, May 14, 1972.
_____. "Phils' Outfielder Hopes a Hit a Day Will Keep the Bench Away." *Philadelphia Inquirer*, March 19, 1972, 1, 2-D.
_____. "I Was Really Dragging and Gasping for Air." *Philadelphia Inquirer*, March 5, 1972.
Milwaukee Brewers 1973 Media Guide.
Morrow, Art. "...And in the Sixth Inning, Here Are All-Star Changes." *Philadelphia Inquirer*, August 19, 1972, 19.
_____. "McCarver Upset with Owens." *Lancaster New Era*, June 22, 1972.
_____. "Nationals Defeat Americans — Again, 5–1 or 8–3." *Philadelphia Inquirer*, August 20, 1972, 1-D, 14-D.
New Era Staff. "Gibson 4th in All-Time Strikeouts." *Lancaster New Era*, April 20, 1972.
_____. "Phillies Offering Carlton." *Lancaster New Era*, June 14, 1972.
Newman, Chuck. "Alas, Everything's Back to Normal; Phils Lose 2–0 Lead, Bow to Astros." *Philadelphia Inquirer*, August 19, 1972.
_____. "Three! Phillies Celebrate 'Trivia Night' by Turning Back the Braves, 4–3." *Philadelphia Inquirer*, June 10, 1972.
Newspaper Enterprise Association. "NEA All-Major League Team; National League Dominates." *Lancaster New Era*, September 27, 1972.
The Official Steve Carlton Website. http://www.carlton32.com.
Olsen, Eddie. "Phillies Trade Money for Lonborg In 7-Player Exchange with Brewers." *Philadelphia Inquirer*, November 1, 1972.
Pankin, Mark. "Retrosheet." http://retrosheet.org (accessed July 26, 2009 — July 31, 2011).

Philadelphia Inquirer Staff Articles

"Allen Draws Most Votes." *Philadelphia Inquirer*, July 18, 1972.
"Another Reason to Chew Out Phils." *Philadelphia Inquirer*, July 6, 1972.
"AP Reports Bristol in as Phil Pilot." *Philadelphia Inquirer*, October 19, 1972.
"Bateman's Fly Gives Phillies 3–2 Victory." *Philadelphia Inquirer*, September 18, 1972.
"Bean Ball Costs Carlton $50." *Philadelphia Inquirer*, June 28, 1972.
"Big Al Rumored to be Next Phillies Manager." *Philadelphia Inquirer*, June 1, 1972.
"Break Out Aspirin … and the Asterisks." *Philadelphia Inquirer*, April 14, 1972.
"Bunt Defense Misfires, Phils Fall to L.A. in 9th." *Philadelphia Inquirer*, May 3, 1972.
"But Phils Forgot to Reverse Score." *Philadelphia Inquirer*, June 7, 1972.
"Carlton to Buck Jinx Team." *Philadelphia Inquirer*, August 17, 1972.
"11 Runs? Here's How They Scored." *Philadelphia Inquirer*, July 16, 1972.
"Gamble, Lis Are Optioned." *Philadelphia Inquirer*, April 7, 1972.
"Greg's 1st Year: How It Compares." *Philadelphia Inquirer*, October 6, 1972.
"'Have No Choice but Go Along'—Lis." *Philadelphia Inquirer*, July 11, 1972.
"Here Today, Gone Today." *Philadelphia Inquirer*, July 11, 1972.
"Hey, Phils—Here Comes Hooton." *Philadelphia Inquirer*, May 16, 1972.
"How They Voted." *Philadelphia Inquirer*, July 18, 1972.
"Injured Harmon to Rejoin Phils Later in Week." *Philadelphia Inquirer*, May 22, 1972.
"Is Carlton Annual Phil Spectator?" *Philadelphia Inquirer*, July 25, 1972.
"League Orders Phils to Bar Field to Players." *Philadelphia Inquirer*, April 7, 1972.
"Luzinski's Diary Starts Sunday." *Philadelphia Inquirer*, March 4, 1972.
"Major Player Trades Made by John Quinn." *Philadelphia Inquirer*, June 4, 1972.
"Mrs. Carlton Gets Birthday Wish." *Philadelphia Inquirer*, August 18, 1972.
"New Auto for Carlton." *Philadelphia Inquirer*, September 15, 1972.
"Owens Rates High with Baseball Men." *Philadelphia Inquirer*, June 4, 1972.
"Phillies Carlton Atlanta-Bound?" *Philadelphia Inquirer*, June 14, 1972.
"Phillies Drill Today at Vet." *Philadelphia Inquirer*, April 14, 1972.
"Phillies' Opener—Who Knows?" *Philadelphia Inquirer*, April 6, 1972.
"Phillies Slip by Mets in 11." *Philadelphia Inquirer*, September 23, 1972.
"Phillies' Story at the All-Star Break." *Philadelphia Inquirer*, July 24, 1972.
"Phils Crush Reading, 10–2." *Philadelphia Inquirer*, June 6, 1972.
"Phils' Gate Soars When Steve Hurls." *Philadelphia Inquirer*, August 22, 1972.
"Phils Get Pinch-Flier for Kiteman." *Philadelphia Inquirer*, April 15, 1972.
"Phils Hire Bobby Wine as Coach." *Philadelphia Inquirer*, July 18, 1972.
"Phils' 20-Game Winners." *Philadelphia Inquirer*, August 18, 1972.
"Reynolds Ailing, Out a Week." *Philadelphia Inquirer*, March 5, 1972.
"Roberts Says Players Should Return." *Philadelphia Inquirer*, April 6, 1972.
"Sesame Street Gang." *Philadelphia Inquirer*, September 14, 1972.
"6–4 High School Hurler Phillies' No. 1 Draft Pick." *Philadelphia Inquirer*, June 7, 1972.
"6 More Starts for Steve." *Philadelphia Inquirer*, September 12, 1972.
"Steve's Streak." *Philadelphia Inquirer*, July 29, 1972.
"Through the Years with John Quinn." *Philadelphia Inquirer*, June 4, 1972.
"Twitchell Gets Chance as Starter." *Philadelphia Inquirer*, July 27, 1972.
"Who's Danny Ozark? He's Dodger Coach." *Philadelphia Inquirer*, November 1, 1972.
"Winning 20 in Cellar Is Tough." *Philadelphia Inquirer*, August 18, 1972.

Phillies 1973 Media Guide.
Phillies 2010 Media Guide.
Povich, Shirley. "Population Boom in $100,000 Players." *Philadelphia Inquirer*, March 14, 1972.
Sharkey, Joe. "And This One Has Fans Grumbling." *Philadelphia Inquirer*, April 2, 1972.

Bibliography

Sharkey, Joe. "Pennant Fever? The Bandwagon Is Rolling at Vet and Lots of Fans Have Climbed On." *Philadelphia Inquirer*, May 7, 1972.
Simmons, Bill. "Kiteman 2nd Is History — Long Live Kiteman 3d." *Philadelphia Inquirer*, April 17, 1972.
Special to the Inquirer. "Astros Beat Phils, 2–1, on May's HR." *Philadelphia Inquirer*, August 30, 1972.
———. "Carlton Breaks FAA Rules, Grounded." *Philadelphia Inquirer*, October 14, 1972.
———. "Fumbling Phils Help Astros Beat Carlton." *Philadelphia Inquirer*, August 31, 1972.
———. "Mets Spoil Carlton's Bid for 26th Triumph." *Philadelphia Inquirer*, September 25, 1972.
———. "Montanez and Bowa Benched, Phils Lose." *Philadelphia Inquirer*, September 1, 1972.
———. "Montanez Benched, Faces Fine as Phils Drop Pair to Pirates." *Philadelphia Inquirer*, September 5, 1972.
———. "N.Y. Mets Deal Phillies a 5–3 Defeat." *Philadelphia Inquirer*, September 24, 1972.
———. "Phils Beat Cards, 3–1, on Error." *Philadelphia Inquirer*, September 22, 1972.
———. "Phils Clinch Worst NL Record." *Philadelphia Inquirer*, October 3, 1972.
———. "Phils Nip Cubs in Finale." *Philadelphia Inquirer*, October 5, 1972.
———. "Phils Swap McCarver for Expo Bateman." *Philadelphia Inquirer*, June 15, 1972.
———. "Phils' Rookie Wins; Aaron Homers Twice." *Philadelphia Inquirer*, September 3, 1972.
———. "Phils Turn Tiger for Steve, Rap Six Homers in 11–1 Win." *Philadelphia Inquirer*, October 4, 1972.
———. "Reynolds Suffers 15th Loss as Expos Stage 8-Run Rally." *Philadelphia Inquirer*, October 2, 1972.
———. "Rose, Morgan Pace Reds to 7–2 Win Over Phils." *Philadelphia Inquirer*, August 28, 1972.
———. "Steve's Next Foe — Expos." *Philadelphia Inquirer*, August 10, 1972.
———. "Win Smirches Reynolds' Record." *Philadelphia Inquire*, September 2, 1972.
Sports Reference LLC. "Box Scores and Play by Play Accounts — Baseball-Reference.com." http://www.baseball-reference.com/boxes/ (accessed July 26, 2009–July 31, 2011).
———. "Steve Carlton Statistics and History — Baseball-Reference.com." http://www.baseball-reference.com/boxes/ (accessed July 26, 2009–July 31, 2011).
"Targets: Today's top players set their sights on the all-time leaders." *Sporting News Yearbooks 2011 Baseball*, February 2011.
"The Ballplayers — Steve Carlton/BaseballLibrary.com." http://www.baseballlibrary.com/ballplayers/player.php?name=Steve_Carlton_1944 (accessed July 26, 2009–July 31, 2011).
UPI. "Bench Tops NL Poll; Aaron, Torre Named." *Philadelphia Inquirer*, July 18, 1972.
———. "Doyle Sees Double When Brothers Play." *Philadelphia Inquirer*, June 14, 1972.
———. "4 AL Stars Were in NL in 1971; Clemente Happy to be in Game." *Philadelphia Inquirer*, July 25, 1972.
Vass, George. "The Biggest Surprises of the 1972 Season and What to Expect for 1973." *Baseball Digest*, January 1973.
Westcott, Rich. *The Fightin' Phils; Oddities, Insights, and Untold Stories*. Philadelphia: Camino Books, Inc., 2008.
Wikipedia. "Rick Wise." http://en.wikipedia.org/wiki/Rick_Wise (accessed July 26, 2009–July 31, 2011).
———. "Steve Carlton." http://en.wikipedia.org/wiki/Steve_Carlton (accessed July 26, 2009–July 31, 2011).

Wire Services. "Aaron Hits 648th Homer, Ties Mays for 2d Place." *Philadelphia Inquirer*, June 1, 1972.
_____. "Agreement Seen Today for End of Strike." *Philadelphia Inquirer*, April 13, 1972.
_____. "Carlton Notches 22d Win, Phillies Bomb Braves, 8–0." *Philadelphia Inquirer*, September 4, 1972.
_____. "Clemente's 300th Hit Sparks 3-Run Flare-Up as Pirates Win." *Philadelphia Inquirer*, October 1, 1972.
_____. "Elated Players Fly to Belated Openers." *Philadelphia Inquirer*, April 14, 1972.
_____. "Found! A No-Hit Pitcher Who Says, 'It Was a Fluke.'" *Philadelphia Inquirer*, April 17, 1972.
_____. "Fryman Beats Yanks, 6–0, but Tigers Bow in 2d, 2–1." *Philadelphia Inquirer*, August 10, 1972.
_____. "Mediation Service in Baseball Dispute." *Philadelphia Inquirer*, April 9, 1972.
_____. "Owners, Players Hit Hard in Pocketbook." *Philadelphia Inquirer*, April 6, 1972.
_____. "Owners Refuse to Budge on Ball Players' Demands." *Philadelphia Inquirer*, March 23, 1972.
_____. "Phils Split; Lersch Near No-Hit Game." *Philadelphia Inquirer*, October 1, 1972.
_____. "Players Told to Take Field, Talk Later." *Philadelphia Inquirer*, April 5, 1972.
_____. "Sparky Sets Save Mark; Yanks Win 2." *Philadelphia Inquirer*, September 25, 1972.
_____. "Talks Deadlocked in Baseball Strike." *Philadelphia Inquirer*, April 2, 1972.
_____. "Willie Mays, 10 Others Named to All-Star Squad." *Philadelphia Inquirer*, July 21, 1972.

Interviews Conducted by Author
(in Chronological Order)

Greg Luzinski. At Citizens Bank Park, Philadelphia, July 26, 2009.
Tommy Herr. At Clipper Magazine Stadium, Lancaster, PA, July 29, 2009.
Tim Raines. At Clipper Magazine Stadium, Lancaster, PA, July 29, 2009.
Sparky Lyle. At Clipper Magazine Stadium, Lancaster, PA, August 17, 2009.
Chris Wheeler. At Citizens Bank Park, Philadelphia, August 19, 2009.
Gary Matthews. At Citizens Bank Park, Philadelphia, August 19, 2009.
Rick Wise. Telephone interview, August 22, 2009.
Bill Conlin. Email interview, September 23, 2009.
Johnny Bench. At Valley Forge Convention Center, King of Prussia, PA, September 26, 2009.
Bob Boone. At Valley Forge Convention Center, King of Prussia, PA, September 27, 2009.
Bill Lyon. Telephone interview, October 11, 2009.
Bruce Keidan. Telephone interview, November 1, 2009.
Larry Shenk. At Citizens Bank Park, Philadelphia, January 7, 2010.
Marty Bystrom. At Reading Sheraton Hotel, Reading, PA, January 25, 2010.
Scott Palmer. At Reading Sheraton Hotel, Reading, PA, January 25, 2010.
Don Money. Telephone interview, January 27, 2010.
Larry Bowa. Telephone interview, February 3, 2010.
Rich Hebner. Telephone interview, March 6, 2010.
Willie Montanez. Telephone interview, March 25, 2010.
Ferguson Jenkins. At Ephrata Rec Center, Ephrata, PA, March 27, 2010.
Chris Wheeler. At Citizens Bank Park, Philadelphia, April 14, 2010.
Ross Grimsley. At FirstEnergy Stadium, Reading, PA, June 11, 2010.
Ruben Amaro, Jr. At FirstEnergy Stadium, Reading, PA, June 11, 2010.

Bill Lyon. Telephone interview, June 16, 2010.
Wayne Twitchell. Telephone interview, June 25, 2010.
Chris Speier. At Citizens Bank Park, Philadelphia, July 9, 2010.
Tommy Hutton. Email interview, July 15, 2010.
Greg Luzinski. At FirstEnergy Stadium, Reading, PA, August 4, 2010.
Joe Torre. At Citizens Bank Park, Philadelphia, August 11, 2010.
Larry Bowa. At Citizens Bank Park, Philadelphia, August 11, 2010.
Rick Monday. At Citizens Bank Park, Philadelphia, August 11, 2010.
Mike Krukow. At Citizens Bank Park, Philadelphia, August 18, 2010.
Tim Flannery. At Citizens Bank Park, Philadelphia, August 18, 2010.
Tito Fuentes. Telephone interview, September 18, 2010.
Chris Wheeler. At Citizens Bank Park, Philadelphia, September 25, 2010
Jayson Stark. At Citizens Bank Park, Philadelphia, September 25, 2010.
Dusty Baker. At Citizens Bank Park, Philadelphia, May 23, 2011.
Marty Brennaman. At Citizens Bank Park, Philadelphia, May 23, 2011.
Dan Baker. At Citizens Bank Park, Philadelphia, June 8, 2011.
Jerry Martin. At FirstEnergy Stadium, Reading, PA, June 20, 2011.
Ray Burris. At FirstEnergy Stadium, Reading, PA, June 20, 2011.
Jim Kaat. In Cooperstown, NY, July 23, 2011.
Steve Blass. At PNC Park in Pittsburgh, July 24, 2011.
Bob Walk. At PNC Park in Pittsburgh, July 24, 2011.
Mike Krukow. At Citizens Bank Park, Philadelphia, July 27, 2011.
Chris Wheeler. At Citizens Bank Park, Philadelphia, July 27, 2011.

INDEX

Aaron, Hank 74, 80, 107, 134, 154, 155, 161, 176
Adrecopoulos, Demosthenes 137
Agee, Tommie 172
Albright College 152
Alexander, Grover Cleveland 4, 8
all-burgundy uniform 57
All-Coast honors 137
All-Star 9, 58, 113, 120, 134, 149, 179; break 60, 124, 136, 152; Classic 96, 113, 119, 124, 134, 172
All-State honors 76
Allen, Richie 22, 75, 90, 163, 174
Alley, Gene 64
Alston, Walt 112, 115
Amaro, Ruben, Jr. 151, 175
Amaron, Ruben, Sr. 175
American League 29, 62, 109, 118, 120, 132, 134
American League Eastern Division 145
American League Most Valuable Player Award 5
American Legion 97
Anderson, Mike 21, 22, 25, 39, 46, 49, 53, 74–77, 105
Andujar, Joaquin 94
Arlin, Steve 46, 47
Arnold, Chris 39, 41
Ashburn, Richie 23, 98, 112–115
Associated Press 97, 114, 115
Astrodome 73, 120
Atlanta, Georgia 83, 84, 108, 124, 134, 154
Atlanta Braves 23, 39, 41, 55, 56, 60, 78–82, 84, 85, 106, 132, 154–156, 158, 160–162, 176, 180
Atlanta Constitution 85
Atlanta-Fulton County Stadium 120, 154

Bailey, Bob 146, 168
Baker, Dan 7, 32, 58, 151
Baker, Dusty 106, 154, 155, 161
Baltimore Orioles 46, 68, 148
Barnes, Lute 172
Barton, Bob 46, 47
baseball.about.com 28
Baseball Digest 4
Baseball Hall of Fame 3, 5–8, 12, 14, 15, 18, 19, 29, 31, 33, 37, 41, 42, 49, 59, 60, 64, 95, 96, 100, 116, 119, 122, 130, 132, 139, 140, 154, 156, 158–160, 166, 174, 177, 179, 180
Bastable, Jack 145
Bateman, John 8, 37, 38, 60, 81, 84, 86, 87, 107, 119, 121, 148, 156, 159, 163, 167, 172
Bayless, Pat 24
Beauchamp, Jim 165
Bednarik, Chuck 149
Belanger, Mark 68
Belinger, Harry 168
Bench, Johnny 5, 34, 64, 67, 68, 74, 140, 147, 148, 174
Benshoff, Al 84
Bernstein, Ralph 97, 115
Berra, Yogi 65, 74, 105
"The Big Red Machine" 53, 143, 147
Blass, Steve 4, 101, 104, 119, 125, 140–142, 179
Bob Carpenter Award 24
Bonds, Bobby 39, 41
Boone, Bob 8, 38, 52, 58, 60, 93, 96, 101, 118, 166, 167, 173
Boone, Rod 96
Boston Braves 69
Boston Red Sox 5, 15, 37, 76, 97, 145, 172, 178
Botello, Derek 92
Bottomley, Jim 68
Bowa, Larry 5, 19, 22, 23, 27, 28, 31, 33, 36, 39, 41, 48, 51, 53, 58–61, 63, 67, 68,

INDEX

Aaron, Hank 74, 80, 107, 134, 154, 155, 161, 176
Adrecopoulos, Demosthenes 137
Agee, Tommie 172
Albright College 152
Alexander, Grover Cleveland 4, 8
all-burgundy uniform 57
All-Coast honors 137
All-Star 9, 58, 113, 120, 134, 149, 179; break 60, 124, 136, 152; Classic 96, 113, 119, 124, 134, 172
All-State honors 76
Allen, Richie 22, 75, 90, 163, 174
Alley, Gene 64
Alston, Walt 112, 115
Amaro, Ruben, Jr. 151, 175
Amaron, Ruben, Sr. 175
American League 29, 62, 109, 118, 120, 132, 134
American League Eastern Division 145
American League Most Valuable Player Award 5
American Legion 97
Anderson, Mike 21, 22, 25, 39, 46, 49, 53, 74–77, 105
Andujar, Joaquin 94
Arlin, Steve 46, 47
Arnold, Chris 39, 41
Ashburn, Richie 23, 98, 112–115
Associated Press 97, 114, 115
Astrodome 73, 120
Atlanta, Georgia 83, 84, 108, 124, 134, 154
Atlanta Braves 23, 39, 41, 55, 56, 60, 78–82, 84, 85, 106, 132, 154–156, 158, 160–162, 176, 180
Atlanta Constitution 85
Atlanta-Fulton County Stadium 120, 154

Bailey, Bob 146, 168
Baker, Dan 7, 32, 58, 151

Baker, Dusty 106, 154, 155, 161
Baltimore Orioles 46, 68, 148
Barnes, Lute 172
Barton, Bob 46, 47
baseball.about.com 28
Baseball Digest 4
Baseball Hall of Fame 3, 5–8, 12, 14, 15, 18, 19, 29, 31, 33, 37, 41, 42, 49, 59, 60, 64, 95, 96, 100, 116, 119, 122, 130, 132, 139, 140, 154, 156, 158–160, 166, 174, 177, 179, 180
Bastable, Jack 145
Bateman, John 8, 37, 38, 60, 81, 84, 86, 87, 107, 119, 121, 148, 156, 159, 163, 167, 172
Bayless, Pat 24
Beauchamp, Jim 165
Bednarik, Chuck 149
Belanger, Mark 68
Belinger, Harry 168
Bench, Johnny 5, 34, 64, 67, 68, 74, 140, 147, 148, 174
Benshoff, Al 84
Bernstein, Ralph 97, 115
Berra, Yogi 65, 74, 105
"The Big Red Machine" 53, 143, 147
Blass, Steve 4, 101, 104, 119, 125, 140–142, 179
Bob Carpenter Award 24
Bonds, Bobby 39, 41
Boone, Bob 8, 38, 52, 58, 60, 93, 96, 101, 118, 166, 167, 173
Boone, Rod 96
Boston Braves 69
Boston Red Sox 5, 15, 37, 76, 97, 145, 172, 178
Botello, Derek 92
Bottomley, Jim 68
Bowa, Larry 5, 19, 22, 23, 27, 28, 31, 33, 36, 39, 41, 48, 51, 53, 58–61, 63, 67, 68,

215

Index

Downs, Dave 136, 166
Doyle, Denny 22, 33, 39, 53, 58, 61, 70, 74, 76, 106, 116, 119, 120, 156, 159, 160, 168, 171, 172
Drysdale, Don 32, 32, 107, 119, 177
Durango, Colorado 90, 99
Durocher, Leo 113
Dyer, Duffy 165
Dykstra, Lenny 57

Eastern League 113
Eckersley, Dennis 15
El Cortez Hotel 52
Ellis, Dock 138, 142, 143
Ennis, Del 23
Erving, Julius 152
ESPN 18, 109, 169
ESPN.com 6, 178
Eugene Emeralds 20–22, 76, 77, 105, 113, 114; Triple-A 73
Evans, Darrell 156
Everglades 96
expansion draft 47

Fairmount Park 114
Fanzone, Carmen 62
Fehr, Donald 28
Feller, Bob 33, 172, 177
Ferenz, Eddie 13, 16, 28, 84
Ferguson, Charley 4, 7, 135, 140
The Fightin' Phils — Oddities, Insights, and Untold Stories 15
Flannery, Tim 47, 99, 107, 130, 131
Flower, Joe 8, 91, 127
Flynn, John 96, 126
Foli, Tim 86–88
Foote, Barry 92
Fort Harrison Hotel 26
Foster, George 140, 147
Fox, Charlie 40
Foxx, Jimmie 74
Franklin Field 149
free agent draft 76, 136; signee 72
Freed, Roger 23, 52, 53, 74, 77, 105, 119, 121, 142, 167, 175
Fregosi, Jim 125
Fresno, California 25
Fryman, Woodie 23, 25, 45, 46, 49, 53, 56, 59, 136, 145, 159
Fuentes, Tito 39–41, 48, 99, 106
Fulgham, John 42
full-ride scholarship 55

Gagliano, Phil 116
Gaherin, John J. 27
Gamble, Oscar 23, 74, 105, 119, 175
Game Winner, Inc. 101
Garber, Gene 154

The Garden Seat 15
Garr, Ralph 79; "Gator" 80
Garvey, Steve 121
Gentry, Gary 24, 66, 73, 103, 105
Gibson, Bob 14, 29–33, 35, 89, 107, 118, 119, 122, 123, 132, 155, 161, 170, 175–179
Giles, Bill 32, 60, 71, 95, 97, 98, 115, 150
Gilliam, Junior 113
Giusti, Dave 101, 142, 143
Glassboro State College 32
Gooden, Dwight 178
"Goodnight Sweetheart" 72
Gossage, Goose 118
Grapefruit League 25, 76
Green, Dallas 60, 109, 111, 175
Greenberg, Hank 74
Griffin, Tom 24, 81
Grimsley, Ross 68, 146–148, 159, 162
Gross, Greg 92
Gross, Kevin 131
Grove, Lefty 122
Guidry, Ron 178

Hahn, Frank 3
Halladay, Roy 8, 131, 132, 151, 165, 169, 170
Haller, Tom 174
Hamels, Cole 166
Hamilton, Steve 24, 31
Hamner, Granny 23
Hardin, Jim 162
Harmon, Terry 22, 47, 48, 53, 74, 105, 106, 148, 156, 159, 160, 167, 174
Harrelson, Bud 72, 165
Hassler, Andy 42
Hebner, Rich 36, 56, 90, 123, 140, 142, 143, 163
Heintzelman, Ken 4
Helms, Tommy 159
Henderson, Ken 39–41
Hernandez, Felix 6
Hernandez, Ramon 143
Hernstein, John 19
Herr, Tommy 8, 12, 127, 132, 135, 168, 180
Hisle, Larry 23, 51
Hochman, Stan 91
Hodges, Gil 74, 80
Hoefling, Gus 40, 94, 95, 123, 126–130, 132, 139
Hoerner, Joe 24, 31, 37, 53, 54, 56, 60, 83–85, 100, 159
Hooton, Burt 32, 46, 50, 51
Hough, Charlie 156
Houston, Texas 83, 84, 108
Houston Astros 17, 24, 30, 39, 41, 60, 71, 72, 74, 79, 81, 83, 84, 106, 120, 132, 138, 159, 174
Howard, Ryan 50, 166
Hutton, Tommy 23, 31, 45, 47, 51–54, 61,

67, 74, 81, 90, 105, 120, 123, 148, 160, 166, 170, 171

Jack and Jill 5
Jack Russell Stadium 16, 26, 79
Jack Tar Hotel 16, 17
Jackson, Harold 152
Jackson, Larry 19
James, Po 152
Japan 57
Jarry Park 87, 88
Javier, Julian 67
Jenkins, Fergie 3, 19, 29, 31, 49, 59, 77, 82, 119, 122, 132, 136, 174
Jobe, Jeff 32
John, Tommy 121
Johnson, Deron 23, 33, 39, 45, 46, 51, 74–76, 105, 108, 145, 148, 162
Johnson, Jerry 119
Johnson, Randy 179, 180
Johnson, Richard 32
Johnson, Walter 33, 122, 133, 177–179
Jones, Cleon 136

Kaat, Jim 100, 130, 152, 161
Kalas, Harry 94, 98
Kaline, Al 74
Kansas City Athletics 52, 84, 97
Kansas City Royals 25
Keidan, Bruce 18, 23–26, 28, 31, 42, 43, 45, 46, 52, 54–56, 58, 69, 78, 85, 92, 93, 108, 109, 113–115, 117, 123, 156, 158, 170, 178
Kelley, Ray 109, 114
Kendall, Fred 15
Kennedy, Ron 76
Kershaw, Clayton 124
Kessinger, Don 174
Kingman, Dave 39, 41, 106
Kirby, Clay 44, 120
Kiteman 32
Koegel, Pete 52, 74, 87
Koegel, Warren 52
Koosman, Jerry 53, 65, 66, 73, 123, 135, 136, 165, 166
Kosco, Andy 124
Koufax, Sandy 5, 7, 32, 48, 119, 122, 123, 133, 143, 172, 174, 177–179
Kruk, John 57, 59
Krukow, Mike 30, 94, 95, 98, 127–131, 134
Kuhn, Bowie 134
Laboy, Coco 168

Lancaster Intelligencer Journal 84
Landreth Elementary School 151
Larson, Dan 132
Las Vegas, Nevada 52, 101
Laxton, Bill 24, 56

Lee, Cliff 67, 119, 161, 169
Leonard, Jeff 41
Lersch, Barry 22, 25, 44–46, 59, 60, 79, 114, 136
Leshnock, Don 174
Lewis, Allen 4, 109, 114
Liberty Bell 50
Lidge, Brad 103
Lieber, Jon 8
Lincecum, Tim 135
Lis, Joe 23, 52, 53, 86–88, 105, 120, 160, 162, 167, 174
Liske, Pete 152
Little League 72, 96, 97
Lolich, Mickey 48, 172
Lonborg, Jim 97, 118, 174
Lopez, Javy 37
Los Angeles, California 44, 94, 124
Los Angeles Dodgers 5, 6, 23, 39, 46, 47, 49, 51, 52, 54, 62, 66, 84, 94, 112, 113, 115, 116, 119, 121–124, 135, 155, 177
Lucchesi, Frank 20, 26, 54, 69, 70, 74, 76, 88, 108–111, 115, 131
Lum, Mike 154–156
Luzinski, Greg 3, 6, 7, 21, 25, 27, 28, 30, 32, 33, 39, 49, 51, 53, 58–60, 66, 70, 72, 73, 75–77, 81, 83, 105, 119, 121, 138, 141, 146, 148, 156, 160, 162, 163, 167, 168, 170, 171, 174, 175
Lyle, Sparky 62, 89, 103, 122, 129, 152, 174
Lyon, Bill 12, 34, 49, 52, 58, 77, 85, 105, 110, 115, 121, 122, 132, 133, 138, 145, 148, 152, 160, 163, 164, 166, 172, 173, 175, 179, 181

Mack, Henry 92
Maddox, Elliott 42
Maddox, Gary 40, 41, 61, 79
Maddux, Greg 37, 178
Major League Baseball All-Star Tour 57
Major League Baseball annual draft 71
Major League Baseball Network 18, 178
Major League Baseball Players Association 26, 27, 114
Maloney, Jim 32
Mantle, Mickey 74
Manuel, Charlie 115
Manuel, Jerry 158
Marichal, Juan 29–32, 38, 39, 41, 42, 44, 85, 119, 132
Marquard, Rube 146
Marshall, Dave 104
Martin, Jerry 11, 12, 79, 92, 100, 103, 128
Martinez, Ted 103
Marysville High School (Wash.) 71
Mathewson, Christy 122, 178
Matlack, Jon 53, 65, 73, 166

Index

Matthews, Gary 80, 81, 88, 89, 99, 106, 118, 129
Matula, Rick 41
Mauch, Gene 56, 86–88, 108, 110, 113
Maxvill, Dal 33
May, Lee 81
May, Milt 143
Mays, Willie 39, 42, 63, 64, 80, 89, 136
Mazeroski, Bill 140
Mazzilli, Lee 42
McAnally, Ernie 86–88, 146
McAndrew, Jim 65, 166
McCarver, Tim 3, 23, 31, 36–39, 41, 46, 47, 60, 74, 78, 84, 85, 91–93, 100, 101, 111, 138, 140
McCovey, Willie 39, 74, 106
McDowell, Sam 172
McGlothlin, Jim 159
McGraw, Tug 36, 61, 92, 94, 119
McGwire, Mark 52
McKay, John 77
McLain, Denny 165, 170, 177
McMahon, Don 119
McRae, Hal 140
Memorial Hall 114
Mendoza Line 46, 117
Mexico 32
Miami-Dade Junior College 97
Mike Douglas Television Show 168
Millan, Felix 41, 154, 156
Miller, Marvin 16, 28, 114
Miller, Russ 160
Milner, John 165
Milwaukee Braves 69, 110
Milwaukee Brewers 21, 56, 108, 113, 118, 138, 174, 176
Minnesota Twins 3, 11, 12, 105, 130, 135, 175
Moffitt, Randy 119
Monday, Rick 31, 62, 82, 134
Money, Don 21, 22, 23, 25, 35, 39, 41, 46, 47, 54–57, 59, 60, 72, 74, 83, 86, 105, 116–118, 123, 135, 148, 165, 168, 172, 174, 176
Montanez, Willie 21, 29, 33, 34, 39, 41, 47–49, 53, 61, 74–76, 78, 79, 83, 85, 116, 119–121, 134, 141, 146, 148, 162, 163, 167, 168, 171, 172
Montreal, Canada 58, 84, 88, 108, 132
Montreal Expos 8, 9, 25, 36, 39, 44, 45, 53, 57, 58, 60, 68, 82, 84, 86–88, 113, 119, 132, 135, 145, 146, 158, 167, 168, 179, 180
Moose, Bob 140, 142, 172
Morgan, Joe 134, 147, 148, 174
Morton, Carl 53, 84
Most Valuable Player Award 113
Mota, Manny 121

Moyer, Jamie 55
Mulcahy, Hugh 160
Mulholland, Terry 131
Munson, Thurman 145
Murcer, Bobby 145
Murphy, Dale 132, 155
Murtaugh, Danny 119
Musial, Stan 74
Myatt, George 20, 109

Nahorodny, Bill 41
Nash, Jim 84, 85, 87, 136
Nashville Sounds 118
National Anthem 72
National Football League 52
National League 3, 5, 6, 9, 18, 29, 39, 41, 45–48, 56, 58, 60, 64, 65, 78, 82, 84, 85, 107, 113, 116, 119, 120, 132, 143, 159, 165, 174
National League Championship Series 140, 148
National League Eastern Division 4, 20, 21, 25, 28, 39, 44, 49, 58, 60, 65, 66, 76, 83, 86, 95, 116, 122, 124, 139, 140
National League Gold Glove Award 72
National League pennant 23, 57, 66, 69, 95, 112, 147
National League Western Division 57, 108, 146
Neibauer, Gary 84, 85, 136
New York, New York 58, 73, 95, 136, 152
New York Americans 4, 35
New York Giants 146
New York Mets 3, 14, 18, 24–26, 38, 39, 41, 42, 48, 49, 54, 55, 58, 63–66, 68, 72, 73, 80, 103, 104, 108, 119, 120, 123, 135, 136, 155, 165–167, 172, 174, 177
New York Yankees 7, 58, 62, 119, 123, 130, 145, 148, 174
Newark Bears 180
Newhouser, Hal 5
Newspaper Enterprise Association All-Major League Team 174
Niekro, Phil 81, 82, 156
Nixon, Pres. Richard 27
Nolan, Gary 119
Notre Dame High School 76

Oakland Athletics 66, 145, 148
Oakland Raiders 52
Oliver, Al 140, 142
Opening Day 32
Oregon State University 137
Osteen, Claude 46, 49, 62, 78
Oswalt, Roy 30
Ott, Mel 74
Owens, Paul 15, 18, 20, 21, 23, 25, 59, 60, 69, 70, 75, 77, 81, 83, 85, 105, 108–110,

112–114, 116, 118, 143, 145, 160, 162, 164, 174–176; "Pope" 84
Ozark, Danny 110, 115, 116, 129, 133

Pacific Coast League 22, 51, 76, 130
Pagan, Jose 143
Palm Beach, Florida 9
Palmer, Lowell 24
Palmer, Scott 19, 93
Palumbo's 111
Pan American Airlines 97
Pappas, Milt 24, 134
Parker, Dave 34, 143, 144
Parker, Wes 123
Paxton, Mike 15
Peninsula Phillies 22
Penn, Billy 46
Penn State All-American 52
Penn State University 137
Perez, Eddie 37
Perry, Gaylord 119, 134
Peters, Ray 52
Phanavision 71, 151
Philadelphia, Pennsylvania 3, 4, 5, 7, 11–13, 16, 20, 22, 29, 32, 33, 36, 42, 49, 56, 63, 69, 73, 74, 75, 81, 93, 98, 103, 118, 125, 146, 150, 151, 154, 164, 166, 172, 173
Philadelphia Daily News 5, 42, 91
Philadelphia Eagles 149, 152
Philadelphia Flyers 152
Philadelphia Inquirer 12, 18, 25, 26, 28, 33, 34, 42, 44, 45, 49, 56, 69, 74, 83, 85, 86, 95, 96, 108, 113, 114, 126, 166, 178
Philadelphia Phillies 3–8, 12–14, 16, 18–28, 30, 32, 33, 35, 36, 38, 39, 44–64, 66–81, 83–87, 91, 92, 95–99, 100, 103–122, 124, 125, 127, 131, 132, 134–136, 138, 139–146, 148, 150–152, 155, 156, 159–162, 164–170, 172–180
Philadelphia 76'ers 85, 145, 152
Phillips, Adolpho 19
Phoenix, Arizona 69
Pittsburgh, Pennsylvania 58, 83, 90
Pittsburgh Pirates 4, 20, 25, 26, 39, 53, 55, 56, 58, 61, 64–66, 84, 95, 97, 99, 101, 116, 119, 124, 125, 138, 140–144, 148, 159, 172, 174
Plaster of Paris 101
Playboy Magazine 128
players strike 26, 33
Plummer, Bill 148
Pope Paul VI 112
Portland, Oregon 67, 138
powder blue uniforms 56, 57
Powell, Frank 109
"Prime Nine" 178
Puerto Rico 29, 78
Pujols, Albert 3

Pulaski Phillies 22
Pulitzer Prize 5

Quinn, John 14–16, 20, 24, 44, 45, 59, 60, 68, 78, 81, 84, 108, 109

Rader, Dave 92
Rader, Doug 159
Raines, Tim 8, 9, 11, 83, 139, 144, 158, 179, 180
Rauch, Bob 105
Rawley, Shane 8, 131
Reading Phillies 21, 22, 81, 113
Reaves, John 152
Reberger, Frank 119
Reed, Ron 61, 79, 160
Reitz, Ken 163, 171
Reuss, Jerry 17, 71–73, 106, 159, 161
Reynolds, Ken 25, 46, 54, 59, 67, 79, 105, 133, 136, 160, 174
RFK Memorial Stadium 120
Richards, J.R. 118
Richardson, H. B. 83
Richmond Braves 85
Rippelmeyer, Ray 46, 66, 104, 114
Rivera, Mariano 181
Rixey, Eppa 7
Rizzo, Frank 110
Roberts, Robin 4, 113, 114, 122, 132, 135, 168
Robertson, Bob 83, 172
Robinson, Bill 105, 120, 121, 136, 138, 148, 156, 170–172, 174
Robinson, Brooks 23
Robinson, Craig 167
Robinson, Frank 113, 123
Rock Hill Cardinals 97
Rogers, Steve 83
Rollins, Jimmy 166
Roman god/goddesses 101
Rookie of the Year Award 21, 22, 78
Roque, Jorge 171
Rose, Pete 61, 80, 91, 147, 148, 154
Ruth, Babe 74, 178
Ruthven, Dick 67
Ryan, Mike 36, 74
Ryan, Nolan 18, 63, 118, 127, 133, 135, 158, 172, 181

Sabathia, C.C. 119, 132, 175
Sadecki, Ray 105
Saint Louis, Missouri 29, 37, 48, 63, 84, 88, 94, 95, 126, 150, 164, 170
Saint Louis Cardinals 3, 7, 9, 12–20, 23, 25, 28, 29, 31–34, 36, 37, 42, 58, 63, 68, 70, 85, 88, 97, 100, 101, 116, 119, 120, 122–124, 126, 130, 138, 139, 147, 148, 161, 163, 165, 167, 170–172, 174, 175, 177, 180

Index

Saint Petersburg, Florida 15
Sandberg, Ryne 19
Sanders, Ken 105, 118, 174
San Diego, California 44, 45, 120
San Diego Padres 39, 44, 46, 47, 49, 54, 57, 58, 60, 81, 107, 108, 120, 138
San Francisco, California 41, 44, 51, 96
San Francisco Giants 3, 11, 12, 14, 29, 38, 39, 41, 42, 44, 45, 47–49, 58, 61, 63, 79, 85, 94, 106, 118, 119, 135, 148
Sanguillen, Manny 140, 142, 172
Santa Claus 74
Santorini, Al 138, 161, 163, 164, 170
"Saturday Night Specials" 57
Scarce, Mac 60, 136, 159
Schilling, Curt 8, 57, 131, 133, 151
Schmidt, Joe 96
Schmidt, Mike 36, 52, 57, 58, 60, 61, 75, 92, 144, 156, 163, 166, 167
Schoendist, Red 124
Schuylkill Expressway 151
Scientologist Headquarters 16
Scully, Vin 68
Seattle Mariners 6, 67, 169
Seattle Pilots 138
Seaver, Tom 3, 6, 33, 63–66, 73, 107, 108, 119, 120, 152, 155, 172
Selma, Dick 25, 32, 45, 46, 54, 56, 59, 60, 81, 136, 159
Seminick, Andy 23, 113, 114
"Sesame Street Gang" 166
Shea Stadium 172
Shenk, Larry 9, 15–19, 23, 36, 41, 54, 57, 66–69, 75, 76, 80, 85, 91, 93–98, 108, 110, 111, 116, 123–125, 128, 138, 142, 143, 151, 155, 158, 161, 166
Sheppard, Bob 7
Shodokan Karate 126
Short, Chris 7, 23–25, 38, 55, 56, 60, 79, 146, 159
Simmons, Al 74
Simmons, Curt 7
Simmons, Ted 33, 42, 124, 178
Sinatra, Frank 111
Singer, Bill 47
Sizemore, Ted 34, 92, 171
Skinner, Bob 20, 73, 110
Smith, Reggie 76
Spahn, Warren 33, 122
Spartanburg Phillies 22, 92
Speier, Chris 39–42, 45, 48
Spinks, Scipio 17
Spokane Indians 51
SPORT magazine 8, 91, 127
Sports Illustrated 100
spring training 9, 13–16, 21, 23, 24, 26, 27, 72, 73, 76–79, 117, 122, 156, 167, 178
Stanford University 137

Stanley Cup 152
Stargell, Willie 52, 74, 140, 143, 172, 174
Stark, Jayson 6, 178, 179
Staub, Rusty 65, 88
Stearns, John 118
Stein, Bill 164
Stello, Dick 88
Stengel, Casey 113, 130
Stennett, Rennie 84, 140, 142, 172
Stephenson, Earl 118, 174
Stewart, Jimmy 71
Stone, Ron 23, 24, 31, 69, 77
Stoneman, Bill 119
Sutter, Bruce 180
Sutton, Don 6, 49, 84, 116, 119, 121
Swoboda, Ron 17
Syracuse University 178

Tate, Randy 41
Tebbetts, Birdie 110
Texas Rangers 118
Thornton, Andre 84
Three-I League 24
Three Rivers Stadium 64
Tiger Stadium 120
Tolan, Bobby 148
Topps All-Rookie Team 52
Torre, Joe 17, 31, 122, 124, 125, 139, 171, 163, 164, 170, 171, 174
Torrez, Mike 161, 167, 168
Tovar, Cesar 105, 174
Trillo, Manny 92
Triple Crown 4, 177
Tucson, Arizona 126, 137
Tulsa Oilers 97, 130
Turn Around Night 71
Twitchell, Ralph 137
Twitchell, Wayne 25, 39, 40, 42, 46, 54, 55, 59, 60, 67, 81, 89, 90, 99, 132, 136–138, 155, 156, 159, 160

United States Marine Corps 116
University of Arizona 137
University of California, Los Angeles 137
University of Notre Dame 137
University of Oregon 137
University of Southern California 76, 137
University of Texas 50
University of Washington 137
Unser, Del 61, 175
USA Today 28
Utley, Chase 77, 166

Valentine, Bobby 123
Valenzuela, Fernando 180
Veale, Bob 32
Veterans Stadium 7, 32, 36, 45, 47, 56, 58, 62, 68–71, 78, 80, 90, 94, 95, 97–99,

109, 112, 113, 116, 134, 145, 146, 150, 151, 158, 167, 172, 173
Virdon, Bill 140
Vukovich, John 23, 57, 116, 118, 173, 174

Waddell, Rube 172
Wade, Ed 133
Wagner, Honus 159
Wakefield, Tim 158
Walk, Bob 81, 99, 104, 132
Wallenda, Karl 145, 146
Walt Whitman Bridge 150
Washington, D.C. 27, 120
Washington State University 137
Watson, Bob 81
Wedgewood, Terry 175
Werth, Jayson 166
West Chester, Pennsylvania 53
Westcott, Rich 15
Wheeler, Chris 15, 16, 18, 27, 28, 32, 33, 37, 38, 44, 52, 55, 56, 59, 61, 66, 80, 82, 87, 88, 90, 91, 98, 100, 101, 103, 106, 107, 109, 112–115, 126–128, 130, 135–137, 146, 149, 156, 158, 164, 167, 169, 173, 179
Williams, Billy 63, 174
Williams, Earl 78, 155
Williams, Mitch 59

Williams, Rick 41
Williams, Ted 67, 130
Williamson, John 32
Wilmington, New Jersey 28
Wilson, Bill 24, 60
Wilson, Don 81
Wilson, Hack 74
Winnipeg, Canada 97, 99
winter meetings 109
Wise, Rick 3, 12–19, 23, 48, 63, 121, 137, 169, 170, 171
Wood, Wilbur 82, 174
World Championship 99, 119, 147, 152
World Series 9, 13, 21, 35, 37, 38, 56, 60, 61, 66, 69, 79, 85, 93, 95, 97, 113, 122, 134, 139, 140, 142, 161, 166; Fall Classic 69, 97, 140, 143, 148, 179
Wrigley Field 30, 32, 46, 77, 82, 128, 174; bleacher bums 82
Wynn, Jim 81, 83, 84, 159

Yastrzemski, Carl 74
Young, Cy 33, 133
Youngblood, Joel 42

Zachary, Chris 161

www.ingramcontent.com/pod-product-compliance
Lightning Source LLC
Chambersburg PA
CBHW030107170426
43198CB00009B/526